D0000234

CRITICAL ISSUES IN EARLY LITERACY

Research and Pedagogy

CRITICAL ISSUES IN EARLY LITERACY

Research and Pedagogy

Yetta Goodman
Prisca Martens

LEA
LAWRENCE ERLBAUM ASSOCIATES, PUBLISHERS
2007 Mahwah, NJ London

Copyright © 2007 by Lawrence Erlbaum Associates, Inc.
All rights reserved. No part of this book may be reproduced in any form, by photostat, microform, retrieval system, or any other means, without prior written permission of the publisher.

Lawrence Erlbaum Associates, Inc., Publishers
10 Industrial Avenue
Mahwah, New Jersey 07430
www.erlbaum.com

Cover design by Tomai Maridou

Library of Congress Cataloging-in-Publication Data

Critical issues in early literacy : research and pedagogy / edited by Yetta M. Goodman, Prisca Martens

p. cm.

Includes bibliographical references and index.
ISBN-13 978-0-8085-5899-0 (c : alk. paper)
ISBN-10 0-8058-5899-7 (c : alk. paper)
ISBN-13 978-0-8058-5900-3 (p : alk. paper)
ISBN-10 0-8058-5900-4 (p : alk. paper)
1. Language arts (Preschool) 2. Reading (Preschool) 3. Literacy. 4. Children—Language. I. Goodman, Yetta M., 1931– II. Martens, Prisca.

LB1139.5.L35C75 2006
372.21—dc22 2006033266
CIP

Books published by Lawrence Erlbaum Associates are printed on acid-free paper, and their bindings are chosen for strength and durability.

Printed in the United States of America
10 9 8 7 6 5 4 3 2 1

Contents

Preface

Yetta Goodman and Prisca Martens

Three year old Harold brings a book to his father and says: "I read a story," and turning the pages, following the text with his eyes, he improvises...a tale which is a compound of what he has heard and his own imaginings. Harold is learning to read.... Harold takes up a letter that has been received, read and discussed by... family members.... [T]urning up the blank side of the sheet, he says: "I want to write."...[He is]occupied for five minutes. He takes the scrawled-over sheet to his grandmother.... She promptly reads from it,...greatly to his joy and satisfaction. Harold is learning to write. (Iredell, 1898 p. 235)

Engaging with young children as they work with the literacy artifacts in their world is an exciting process of discovery. Children's responses reveal their thinking about literacy and, as a result, the professionals who work with young children become aware of the complexity of the human mind as it seeks to understand the role literacy serves in the world in which we live. As we illuminate children's literacy learning, we not only answer our questions about their development, but we reconsider our understandings about the history of the human invention of literacy and ask new questions—many addressed by the authors in this volume.

For more than 100 years, research in early literacy (see the opening quotation) has enriched our understandings of young children's literacy learning. We have become aware that children learn about literacy long before they come to school as they engage and participate in literacy experiences with the people in their homes and communities. As they observe the functions and purposes that literacy serves in their culture, as they actively participate in literacy practices with other children and adults in their communities, and when they play at literacy practices with siblings and peers, they build their concepts and their perceptions about literacy. Within these social cultural contexts children construct concepts about what literacy is, what it does, and how it positively or negatively impacts their lives. They develop attitudes and beliefs about what counts as literacy, who is considered literate, and the degree to which they are literate.

As they enter school, what they already know about literacy influences the ways in which they respond to their opportunities and experiences with literacy. As we learn about children's literacy learning, at home or at school, we understand that personal engagement in reading and writing results in literacy learning but becoming literate is also the result of social literacy experiences surrounded by talk and attitudes about literacy and the literate.

The voices of researchers, teacher researchers, teacher educators, and teachers in this volume add to our understandings about the power and complexity of the forces in the lives of young children that impact their literacy learning. Their descriptions of successful teaching, understandings about cultural literacy practices at home, and consideration of the political nature of schooling for young children provide new insights for those who work most closely with children. This knowledge influences the development of curricula that support children's curiosity about the printed world and impacts children's literacy development at home and at school.

We are well aware that learning experiences are not always positive. In the same literate environment, children's perceptions of who is literate and what counts as literacy are vastly different. These perceptions influence their literacy learning. Therefore, understanding how children come to know literacy, and the spaces in which literacy learning occurs is critical to the individual history of literacy learning in each young reader and writer.

With this understanding, we use the term *critical*. The critical issues presented in this book emerge from interpretative research and teaching practices that address the complexity of literacy learning. We borrow the term *critical* from Whitmore and Crowell (1994), who use the term *critical events* to"shed light on the power structures of a classroom from a political perspective, a perspective that intentionally situates the event in the broader context of a triadic relationship between literacy, schooling, and the sociocultural complexities of our real world" (p. 6). The issues we address in this book are critical because they emerge from in-depth understandings of young children reading and writing in purposeful, everyday events at home, at school, and in their sociocultural communities. They are critical because they include the literacy histories of children who are often not privileged in our societies.

Much of the research is interpretive in nature. As Erickson (1986) states,"Interpretive fieldwork research involves being unusually thorough and reflective in noticing and describing everyday events in the field setting, and in attempting to identify the significance of actions in the events from the various points of view of the actors themselves" (p. 121). Interpretive research in early literacy builds sensitivity to the range of literacy experiences in which children engage. As children respond to specific literacy tasks and as we observe their literacy interactions with parents and teachers, we learn about individual children's perceptions of literacy: how they come to know literacy as a cultural object within their social communities.

The teaching that is the focus of many of the chapters here dramatically shows the knowledge and experience of teachers and their influences on children's literacy learning. Many of the teachers are researchers in their own right, who know how to document the literacy experiences of children in classroom settings. They are able to articulate how curriculum, materials and instructional practices impact children's perceptions of literacy and literacy learning as they examine their own teaching. They are thoughtful "kidwatchers" capable of building insights into their children's knowledge about literacy and of making use of that knowledge to build curricular experiences that highlight literacy learning. The authors view children's literacy learning from different lenses. The knowledge from each expands the knowledge of all. Through the conversations that result from the reading of these chapters, researchers and teachers come together to learn with and from each other.

The research, inquiry, and teaching in the chapters that the authors provide have a respected and theoretical tradition in the field of learning and curriculum. These chapters are antidotes to the harmful present political context, in which political agendas are being used to define literacy, literacy teaching and learning, and literacy research in narrow ways. These chapters are written by professionals who embed their work in interpreting and understanding the sociocultural settings in which young children with diverse backgrounds learn literacy and the constructive nature of their learning. The more we understand children's literacy learning in their micro- and macroenvironments, the more we are able to provide the rationale for a pedagogy that supports a safe and enriched curriculum for children from a wide range of cultural communities.

A VISION

The chapters in this book were originally part of a conference: Critical Issues in Early Literacy Development, held at the University of Arizona in Tucson. The conference coincided with Yetta Goodman's retirement. She wanted to bring together outstanding researchers, teacher educators, teacher researchers, and classroom teachers to share their knowledge and to sustain a discussion of literacy development that has for years provided profiles of young children as meaning makers and inventors of their own literacy. She wanted to provide a forum for those with this perspective of young children's literacy development to grapple with the critical issues we are currently facing in a time of governmental mandates, controlled agendas, regulations, and narrowing definitions of reading, research, and curriculum. The issues address ways to establish rich literacy environments that respect all children as learners.

It is our vision that the critical issues that resulted from the conference and are explicated in this volume will generate discussions and raise to conscious awareness the rights of teachers and researchers to continue their search for knowledge about literacy learning and teaching and to establish forums for talking, thinking, and inquiring together about literacy learning and teaching. These chapters have been organized around critical issues that provide opportunities for discussions and knowledge dissemination with a wide group of voices, nationally and internationally.

Overview of the Volume

The book is organized in four parts. Part I, What Children Know about Literacy, documents how individual children actively construct their knowledge of literacy and contribute to their own literacy learning. Part II, Literacy Learning in the Classroom, includes chapters that explore the critical issues involved in literacy learning in the social contexts of classrooms, and in Part III, Literacy Learning through Home and School Collaborations, the authors focus on the sociocultural aspects of literacy learning and explore home and school collaborations that foster such learning. In Part IV, Cultural and Political Perspectives on Early Literacy, the authors relate ideological issues that are relevant to literacy learning.

We organized the chapters into the most relevant parts. The issues related to literacy learning are complex and interrelated so understandably, the issues in the sections overlap. We list all of the critical issues here and we introduce each part with those most relevant to it.

What Children Know About Literacy: Theory and Research:

- Children contribute to their own literacy development.
- Literacy learning is a constructive and inventive process.
- All children become literate as they actively engage with the literacy practices of their culture and community.
- Interpretive research and the analysis of children's literacy artifacts provide evidence of young children's knowledge about literacy.

Literacy Learning in the Classroom:

- Knowledgeable professionals use kidwatching in classrooms to document children's learning through insightful observation, interaction, and evaluation.
- Teacher research is an ongoing process of kidwatching, self-reflection, and curriculum development.
- Researchers and teachers develop knowledge and understanding about literacy and literacy learning that provide them with evidence that children are learning literacy all the time.
- Children learn literacy in their classrooms as they learn about their world through a variety of subject areas.
- Children develop their views about literacy from the classroom environment that may expand or narrow their concepts about literacy.

Literacy Learning Through Home and School Collaborations:

- Families and communities are rich in funds of knowledge that influence and affect literacy learning.
- Parents and caregivers are children's earliest teachers.
- Home languages and cultures are rich resources for children's literacy learning.
- The curriculum and all members of the school community benefit from true collaborations between home and school.
- Literacy learning is a social process.

Cultural and Political Perspectives on Early Literacy:

- Understanding children's early literacy learning with an international perspective supports organizing classrooms that honor social justice and democracy.
- Teachers need to reframe the language of schooling in response to governmental mandates and controls.
- A diversity of research methodology is necessary to develop the richest insights and understandings of literacy learning.
- The power of literature and instructional material written for children impacts their views of themselves as learners, as readers and as members of the human community.
- Literacy learning in social contexts establishes the social conventions for literacy learning.

ACKNOWLEDGMENTS

We want to acknowledge the importance of the contributions that the authors have made to our thinking and to the enrichment of the early literacy field. We also thank those who have been instrumental in supporting the publication of this book through reviewing and editing: Bess Altwerger, Gretchen Owocki, Michael McManus, and Naomi Silverman.

REFERENCES

Erickson, F. (1986). Qualitative methods in research on teaching. In M. C. Wittrock (Ed.), *Handbook of research on teaching* (Vol. 3, pp. 119–161). New York: Macmillan.
Iredell, H. (1898, December). Eleanor learns to read. *Education,* pp. 233–238.
Whitmore, K. F., and Crowell, C. G. (1994). *Inventing a classroom: Life in a bilingual whole language learning community*. York, ME: Stenhouse.

DEDICATION

To young children around the world who continue to teach and amaze us.

About the Contributors

Poonam Arya is an associate professor of reading, language, and literature at Wayne State University. Her research and teaching interests include reading process and theory, assessment, and studying children's reading and retellings using miscue analysis.

Joel Brown (PhD, University of Arizona) is the technical advisor for the Eye Movement and Miscues Analysis (EMMA) lab at the University of Arizona. He is also interested in using photography to document children in various literacy events.

Barbara Cohen is an assistant professor of literacy studies at Hofstra University, New York. She teaches courses in children's literature and early language and literacy development and is interested in pedagogical practices that reflect students' personal interests and experiences.

M. Ruth Davenport (PhD, University of Missouri, Columbia) is at Eastern Oregon University, where she leads a cohort in the teacher preparation program and teaches online courses in the graduate literacy program. Her research interests focus on miscue analysis and its classroom applications. She is the author of *Miscues, Not Mistakes: Reading Assessment in the Classroom.*

Anne Haas Dyson is a professor in the language and literacy/early childhood divisions at University of Illinois at Champaign/Urbana. She studies the social lives and literacy learning of schoolchildren. Among her publications are *Multiple Worlds of Child Writers: Friends Learning to Write*, *Social Worlds of Children Learning to Write in an Urban Primary School*, which was awarded the National Council of Teacher Education (NCTE) David Russell Award for Distinguished Research, *Writing Superheroes: Contemporary Childhood, Popular Culture, and Classroom Literacy*, and *The Brothers and Sisters Learn to Write: Popular Literacies in Childhood and School Cultures*.

Janet Evans is a senior lecturer in education at Liverpool Hope University, where she teaches post-graduate teacher education courses. She has written eight books on language, literacy and mathematics education for early years and elementary educators, her latest being *Literacy Moves On: Using Popular Culture, New Technologies and Critical Literacy in the Elementary Classroom* (2005). Janet's ongoing research interests include children's literature, critical literacy, reader response and interactive writing linked to popular culture.

Emilia Ferreiro is a full professor at the Center for Research and Advanced Studies (CINVESTAV), Mexico City. She received her PhD in psychology under the direction of Jean Piaget (University of Geneva, 1970). Since then she has also received six *honoris causa* doctorates and several international distinctions (among them the International Citation of Merit of IRA, 1994) due to the impact of her research on the psychogenesis of written language.

Barbara Flores is a professor in the Department of Language, Literacy, and Culture in the College of Education at California State University, San Bernardino. She is a mother, teacher educator, and scholar-activist. Her teaching and research interests are in collaborative action research and teaching with children, teachers and administrators in the areas of literacy and biliteracy development, teaching/learning contexts across the curriculum, and the development of pedagogy, curriculum, and materials in bilingual, multicultural, and English contexts.

Alan Flurkey is an associate professor of Literacy Studies at Hofstra University, where he teaches courses on reading and assessment. As a researcher, he studies retrospective miscue analysis and uses miscue analysis to investigate oral reading rate. Dr. Flurkey has authored several journal articles and book chapters. His books include coediting *Many Cultures, Many Voices: Proceedings of the Whole Language Umbrella Conference* and *On the Revolution of Reading: The Selected Writings of Kenneth S. Goodman*.

Dana Fox is an associate professor in the English Education and Reading, Language and Literacy programs in the Department of Middle/Secondary Education and Instructional Technology at Georgia State University, where she also coordinates the TEEMS English education alternative MEd degree program. Her research interests include teacher preparation and professional development in secondary English, teacher beliefs and knowledge, academic writing in graduate education, gender and literacy, and the critical examination of children's and adolescent literature and how this literature is used in classrooms.

Debra Goodman is an associate professor in the Literacy Studies Department at Hofstra University. She taught in the Detroit Public School for 15 years. She received her PhD from Michigan State University, where she explored the social nature of literacy learning in whole language classrooms in inner city Detroit. She has worked with teachers and teacher educators across the United States, speaking and writing on topics such as theme cycles, community study, literature study, evaluation, and revaluing struggling readers and writers. She is author of the book *The Reading Detective Club* (Heinemann, 1999).

Yetta Goodman is Regents Professor Emerita at the University of Arizona, College of Education, Department of Language, Reading, and Culture. Her research focus includes miscue analysis, retrospective miscue analysis, and early literacy development. She travels extensively to consult and present about whole-language curriculum, literacy learning and teaching, kidwatching and the reading process.

Heather Sample Gosse has a master's degree in communication disorders and a certificate of clinical competence from the American Speech–Language–Hearing Association. She is a speech-language pathologist and doctoral candidate in elementary education at the University of Alberta. Her research interests include language and literacy connections and school speech–language pathology.

Eve Gregory is a professor of language and culture in education at Goldsmiths, University of London, where she teaches and researches young children's home and school literacy practices and multilingualism. She also directs a research project promoting Bangladeshi British children's bilingual learning strategies in school.

Yueh-Nu Hung received her PhD from the University of Arizona and is an assistant professor in the Department of English Teaching at National Taichung University, Taiwan. She teaches and researches in the areas of children's literacy development, reading processes, reading instruction, and bilingual education.

Bobbie Kabuto is an assistant professor of literacy education at Queens College, CUNY, where she teaches courses in the areas of early language and literacy, language and literacy in the elementary years, and assessment and instruction. In addition to early bi/literacy, her research interests include identity and language ideologies in bilingual/biliteracy contexts, using retrospective miscue analysis to revalue readers and writers, and working with the families of struggling readers and writers.

Koomi Kim is an assistant professor at State University of New York, Geneseo, in the School of Education. She teaches reading and literacy to preservice and in-service teachers. Her research interests include miscue analysis, eye movement and miscue analysis, and social justice issues.

Marge Knox (PhD, University of Arizona) is an adjunct assistant professor in the Language, Reading, and Culture Department at the University of Arizona. Her primary professional interests include miscue analysis and music as necessary components of understanding and facilitating the learning process of students.

Carol Lauritzen (PhD, University of Missouri, Kansas City) is a professor of education and the Director of Teacher Education for Eastern Oregon University. She has served as a literacy project leader in Croatia, Serbia, Bosnia, and the United States. Her research interests include early literacy, the role of story in learning, inquiry, and integrated curriculum. She is the coauthor of *Integrating Learning Through Story: The Narrative Curriculum* and coeditor of *Memoirs of Thaddeus S. C. Lowe: My Balloons in Peace and War.*

Wen-Yun Lin (PhD, University of Arizona) is an assistant professor at the National Taipei University of Education, Taiwan, ROC. She is also Chair of the Taiwanese Teachers Apply Whole Language (TTAWL). Her research and teaching interests include applying whole language in Taiwan, early literacy development, and miscue analysis in Chinese language. She has been working closely with elementary school teachers in developing whole-language curriculum and instruction.

Susi Long is an associate professor at the University of South Carolina, where she teaches courses in language, literacy, and culture. Her research interests include the early years of teaching, and home and community literacies as they relate to culturally relevant classroom pedagogy.

Prisca Martens is an associate professor in the Department of Elementary Education at Towson University, where she teaches courses on reading, assessment, and children's literature. Her research interests include early literacy, miscue analysis and retrospective miscue analysis.

Rick Meyer taught young children for almost 20 years before earning a PhD at the University of Arizona. He is presently a professor at the University of New Mexico, where he teaches and researches on young children's literacy development, new teachers of reading, and the influences of political forces on the lives of children and teachers in schools and communities.

Linda M. Phillips is a professor and Director of the Canadian Centre for Research on Literacy at the University of Alberta. Her current research projects focus on family literacy, commercial reading programs, biomedical applications to reading, and scientific literacy.

Mary Eunice Romero-Little (Cochiti Pueblo) is an associate professor in the Curriculum and Instruction Division at Arizona State University, Tempe. She earned her PhD in education from the University of California at Berkeley, and has copublished several articles on American Indian education, indigenous language renewal, and the socialization of Native children.

David Schwarzer (PhD, University of Arizona) is an associate professor at the University of Alabama at Birmingham School of Education. His research interests include innovative methodologies in teaching and researching emergent literacy development in multilingual settings.

Kathy G. Short is a professor in the Department of Language, Reading, and Culture at the University of Arizona and has worked extensively with teachers to develop curricula that actively involve students as readers and inquirers. She has coauthored many books, including *Creating Classrooms for Authors and Inquirers, Learning Together through Inquiry, Literature as a Way of Knowing, Talking About Books, Teacher Study Groups,* and *Stories Matter: The Complexity of Cultural Authenticity in Children's Literature.*

Denny Taylor is a professor and Doctoral Director of Literacy Studies at Hofstra University. She has been engaged in ethnographic literacy research since 1977 and was inducted into the Reading Hall of Fame in 2004. For the past six years her ethnographic research has focused on the impact of catastrophic events on the lives of children and the social response of the educational community to mass trauma. Her most recent publication *The Kate Middleton Elementary School: Portraits of Hope and Courage*, published by Scholastic, provides support for teachers who are first responders following a catastrophic event.

Dinah Volk is Professor of Early Childhood Education at Cleveland State University, Cleveland, Ohio. She is coauthor (with DeGaetano and Williams) of *Kaleidoscope: A Multicultural Approach for the Primary School Classroom* and coeditor (with Gregory and Long) of *Many Pathways to Literacy: Young Children Learning With Siblings, Grandparents, Peers, and Communities.* Her research interests include the literacy practices of young bilingual children and their families.

Danielle Welner is an elementary school teacher in Oceanside, NY. She has taught second and fourth grades and especially enjoys teaching writing, as well as writing for her own personal pleasure.

Kathryn F. Whitmore (PhD, University of Arizona) is a researcher and associate professor in language, literacy and culture at the University of Iowa. She studies how communities of learners are invented in schools and classrooms with diverse populations and is especially interested in how language, literacy, and culture play roles in that process. In addition to numerous chapters and articles, her publications include *Literacy and Advocacy in Adolescent Family, Gang, School, and Juvenile Count Communities: CRIP 4 LIFE* (with Debbie Smith); *Inventing a Classroom: Life in a Bilingual, Whole Language Learning Community* (with Caryl Crowell); and *Whole Language Voices in Teacher Education* (with Yetta Goodman).

Pat Wilson is an assistant professor of childhood education at the University of South Florida, Sarasota/Manatee, where she teaches courses related to literacy and assessment. Her research includes analysis of the reading of children and the study of children's use of arts-based mediums as tools of thinking.

Part I

WHAT CHILDREN KNOW ABOUT LITERACY

A cognitive system is an open system in a social context, in permanent interaction with other persons and objects socially situated. However, these external influences cannot act by themselves. In order to act inside the cognitive system they always need to be incorporated, that is, interpreted by the psychological subject. (Emilia Ferriero, this volume, p. 60)

Long before they come to school or are involved in reading and writing instruction, children from a wide range of cultural, socio economic and language communities are able to talk about and participate in the literacy events that exist in *their* world. The chapters in Part I, *What Children Know about Literacy,* show how children actively and personally contribute to their *coming to know* literacy—the continuous expansion and reorganization of concepts that children construct as they engage and transact with literacy practices and the users of literacy in their lives. Learning is always both personal and social. As a result of the literacy opportunities in their homes and communities and with the people in these various environments, children apply their unique understandings as they differentiate drawing from conventional systems of writing and other symbol systems. They come to know how written language serves their own specific literacy functions. They use play acting, illustration, numeracy and talk to support their literacy development and to develop their own understandings about the characteristic differences in these systems and how each relates to reading and writing.

To develop insights into what children know about language, the authors in this part carefully analyze children's engagements with the artifacts in their environment: their writing and reading, their use of numbers, their responses to musical notation, to illustrations and to the wide ranges of types of print in different environments. As a result, they interpret and provide evidence of young children's expanding knowledge about literacy and its relation to the communities in which they live. Such microanalysis of children's literacy practices reveal how children actively and continuously develop their literacy concepts in transaction with the uses of literacy and the users of literacy in their lives. They show that literacy development is a profoundly constructive and inventive process.

Children from rich and poor communities, growing up with different ethnic, linguistic, and racial backgrounds from different countries show similarities in the ways in which they respond to and learn from literacy opportunities and experiences. At the same time, their literacy development is influenced by the attitudes that society has about how literacy is learned, who is considered literate and what is considered to be literacy.

CRITICAL ISSUES RELATED TO WHAT CHILDREN KNOW ABOUT LITERACY

- Children contribute to their own literacy development.
- Literacy learning is a constructive and inventive process.
- All children become literate as they actively engage with the literacy practices of their culture and community.
- Interpretive research and the analysis of children's literacy artifacts provide evidence of young children's knowledge about literacy.

Chapter 1

Effective Young Beginning Readers

Debra Goodman, Alan Flurkey, and Yetta Goodman

In an interview with the school librarian, 5-year-old Lauren[1] is asked if she is a good reader. Lauren says, "I don't know how to read. But I know how to read my Barney book."

When asked, "How can you read that [Barney book]?" Lauren replies, "I like to read." She goes on to say, "And sometime I be making up stories. And books."

"You mean like look at a book and make up a story? Is that how you do it?"

Lauren agrees, "If I don't know how to read then I'll do that." She adds, "Sometimes I look at the pictures to figure out. I practice and I use the *alfulbet* to learn it."

"How does the alphabet help you to read?"

Lauren explains, "Like if...like...I take a book and I open this book and I make the story up and I read it. And sometimes I don't know how to read, or it's bedtime—my mommy reads a story to me and then we'll watch TV and then go to bed."

Lauren says she doesn't know how to read. Yet her comments reveal that she has had a lot of experiences with texts, and has already developed strategies for making sense of books. Her talk reflects how reading is a part of the everyday family routines that shape her life.

[1] All children's names are pseudonyms.

Our studies of young children's reading have shown that the majority of kids in every classroom are reading connected texts in books related to their own background knowledge and language within a year or two after kindergarten. And a growing number of children are coming to school already reading. Many of these students are eager and enthusiastic about reading. They have been read to for years. They have been encouraged to read along with their teachers and parents. They sit for a long time examining the illustrations and exploring the printed text, sometimes reading aloud to friends, dolls, or imaginary audiences.

At this point in their development, most young readers are using all the language cueing systems and available resources with their major focus on making sense of the text, making effective use of reading strategies. We use the phrase *effective young beginning readers* to describe children from the age of 4 to 8 who are intelligently sorting out how reading works, but who are still inexperienced in selecting and integrating the language cueing systems (graphophonic, syntactic, semantic, and pragmatic) and their reading strategies (i.e., sampling, selecting, predicting, inferring, and confirming).

Parents and caretakers enjoy watching their preschooler's playful responses to books and development of early reading strategies. But once children reach school age, parents and teachers worry when young children's reading does not conform to adult conventions. They become concerned when young readers make up parts or reread portions of a written text, use clues in the illustrations to complete the story, or substitute words that look different from the text. The response of concerned adults is to ask readers to pay attention to the accurate reproduction of the text. Instead, we encourage parents and teachers to kidwatch (Owocki & Goodman, 2002) and appreciate the reading development taking place before their eyes.

Effective young beginning readers already know a lot about reading. Like Lauren, they are aware of the function print serves in their daily lives. They read and write their names and the names of people they love. They know that the letters in their names relate to the sounds of oral language. They know that the language of birthday cards is different from the language of their favorite stories. They know stories and books are organized differently from grocery lists. They know how to open books and are aware of the directionality of the print.

Like all learners exploring new areas, young readers are tentative as they become more independent in their response to print in books. They are using language cueing systems and reading strategies but not always with the confidence that comes with greater experience. They are not always sure about what features of text to pay most attention to. They are influenced by their own problem-solving strategies to construct meaning with the printed text as they become aware of the relationship between the written and oral language systems. At the same time, they are influenced by social interactions and instructional practices of parents and teachers.

Young readers are coming to know reading in the same way that all of us are always developing our reading abilities—through working with new and unfamiliar texts. But in their short literacy histories, they are still exploring the complexity of making meaning with written texts. In the United States these readers are most commonly in first grade. But we have worked with effective young readers in preschools and kindergartens, and some second and third graders are still working through the process of becoming effective readers. Our observations that reading involves working hard[2] with a text helps us to view struggling readers in a different light. We consider struggling to make sense an important and integral part of reading development. This language-learning-as-problem-solving (Taylor, 1993) continues and expands throughout readers' lives.

In this chapter, we describe the strategies and qualities of effective beginning readers based on research observations and miscue analysis (Y. Goodman, Watson, & Burke, 2005). We document children learning to read through experiences with texts and the process of working at making sense. We discuss influences of instruction at home and in school and make suggestions for supporting meaning making in beginning readers. We begin with Mike.

MIKE READS *WE PLAY ON A RAINY DAY*

Mike was in the second half of first grade when his parents brought him to the Reading/Writing Learning Clinic at Hofstra University because of concerns about his reading. Mike was asked to read the book *We Play on a Rainy Day* (Medearis, 1995) as part of an evaluation. In order to demonstrate making sense as a "text construction process," Figure 1.1 compares the printed story text to Mike's oral reading (Mike's Text). We've numbered the sentences for reference sake.

When compared to the printed text, Mike's oral reading appears substantially different. For example, in sentences 17–19, he substitutes *put* for *wear* and in sentence (S) 22 he substitutes *played* for *pies*. He omits words (S3. *We have fun in sun./ We have fun in the sun.*), and even entire sentences (S14, S15, S16). He inserts words (S4. *We took rides./ We ride*) He even inserts a sentence (S23b. *We ran in the ocean.*). He also constructs sentences that are quite different in wording from the author's text (i.e., S22. *We played in dirt.* for *Mud pies bake.*).

However, if we read Mike's response as a separate text—a "reader's text" constructed during the reading process (K. Goodman, 1996)—Mike has constructed a comprehensible story that parallels the author's text in overall meaning and tone. Mike's text varies from the printed text in wording and phrasing, but both texts are about children playing in the sun, running inside when it starts to rain, and making the best of a rainy day. In this re-

[2] The notion of reading as "*working hard with a text*" evolved during a discussion with Peter Duckett at the 5th Miscue Conference, Hofstra, New York, July 2005.

Printed Text	**Mike's Text**
1 We skate.	1 We skate.
2 We run.	2 We run.
3 We have fun in the sun.	3 We have fun in sun.
4 We ride.	4 We took rides.
5 We slide.	5 We slide.
6 We swing.	6 We swing.
7 We sing.	7 We swing.
8 The clouds come one by one.	8 We were cold one by one.
9 Good-bye, sun.	9 Good-bye, sun.
10 It rains. 11 It pours.	10/11 It was raining.
12 We run indoors.	12 We ran into the house.
13 We pout. 14 We shout.	13/14 We were bored.
15 We want to go out!	15/16
16 We want to go out!	
17 We wear hats.	17 We put hats.
18 We wear coats.	18 We put coats.
19 We wear boots, too.	19 We put boots too.
20 Purple, red, blue.	20 Zippered right, coats.
21 Boats float.	21 We sailed.
22 Mud pies bake.	22 We played with dirt.
23 We play in puddles the rain makes.	23 We played in puddles.
	23b We ran in the ocean.
24 We splash.	24 We drank water.
25 We play.	25 We played.
26 We have fun on a rainy day.	26 We had fun in the rain.

Figure 1.1. Mike's reading of *We Play on a Rainy Day* (Medearis, 1995). (Roseanna Lanzilotta collected these RMI data.)

gard, Mike's reading is emblematic of other effective beginning readers that we have studied.

Mike's retelling also reflects his understanding of what he has read:

"They had fun in the sun, but it rained and they had nothing to do so they put on their coats, jackets, hats and their boots. And they zippered their coats up so they wouldn't get cold. They were playing in puddles and drinking the rain."

We define an effective reader as a reader who is successful at constructing meaning with a text. Mike's reading is effective because he consistently focuses on making sense as he reads, is able to construct a meaningful text that parallels the author's text, and retells the story with understanding. A close inspection of Mike's reading demonstrates effective strategies and sophisticated understandings of linguistic and textual cueing systems.

Mike's Effective Reading Strategies

Mike uses the illustrations to support his text construction process. The book typically has one illustration for each sentence and children are seen skating, sliding, swinging, and so on. When Mike reads *We drank water.* for *We splash* (S24), he is looking at an illustration showing children catching rain in their open mouths. It might appear that Mike is constructing much of the text through picture cues. However, in S1 (*We skate.*) and S2 (*We run.*) the illustrations only show *one* child skating and another running. The sun does not appear in the illustrations when Mike reads *We have fun in sun.* (S3) and *Good-bye, sun.* (S9). And it would be difficult to predict abstract concepts such as "fun" and "good-bye" from pictures. These examples show that Mike uses illustration to support, but not drive, his meaning construction process. A recent study of the eye movements of first grade readers shows, counterintuitively, that young readers sample text cues much more frequently than illustrations (Duckett, 2003).

A picture showing sandy terrain provides one explanation for Mike adding S23b (*We ran in the ocean.*). However, when Mike is asked during the retelling if he ever has fun in the rain, he reports that he doesn't play in rain because his mom won't let him. When asked if he ever plays in puddles, he says, "Sometimes I just jump in or I jump in the waves." These responses illustrate that Mike is drawing on own experiences as he reads. He doesn't play in water when it rains, but he does play in water at the beach.

In addition to bringing life experiences to reading, Mike brings experiences with language and texts. When Mike substitutes *We were bored.* for *We pout* (S13), he uses intuitive understanding of English syntax when he substitutes one verb for another (*bored/pout*) and inserts *were* to maintain conventional grammar. Mike's construction seems close to the author's intended meaning because *pouting* might suggest boredom; however, his wording is quite different. And it would seem that Mike omits S14–15 because his experiences with this text lead him to predict one sentence on each page, while this page in the text breaks that pattern by including four sentences.

Here Mike demonstrates Meek's (1988) concept that readers learn from their transactions with text. The sentences where Mike's text varies most from the author's text provide further illustrations of how Mike is constructing a story rather than reading words on a page. Mike's substitutions are indicated above the text.

```
   We   sailed
21 Boats float.
```

We played with dirt.
22 Mud pies bake.

In these sentences, Mike appears to have abandoned the printed text and made up a text. Drawing on his experiences with the language and patterns of picture book stories, he uses the illustration to make up a text. This is a common strategy for beginning readers, as Lauren mentioned earlier. It is an effective strategy because it allows Mike to continue to construct a meaningful text when the graphic cues do not provide enough support for meaningful predictions. However, Mike's predictions also follow the syntactic pattern of this text, where most sentences start with *We*. It is only when the author breaks this pattern that Mike constructs a sentence that varies widely from the printed text.

We were cold
8 The clouds come one by one.

Although Mike's text varies from the printed text, he has not abandoned the printed cues entirely. Mike is likely sampling the graphic cues *(come* or perhaps *clouds)* as he predicts *cold*. Use of graphic cues is also evident in sentence 22 above (*played/pies*). Using the resources and understandings available to him, Mike is doing what more experienced proficient readers do: using the graphophonic cues selectively with a focus on making sense of the text. In this reading, 20 of the 23 sentences (87%) that Mike produces are semantically acceptable or meaningful. The only sentences he produces that are not syntactically or semantically acceptable are sentences 17 through 20:

put
17 We wear hats.

put
18 We wear coats.

put
19 We wear boots, too.

Zippered right, coats.
20 Purple, red, blue.

In this case, it is likely that Mike is confused by the author's wording and syntax. *We put on our hats.* is a more familiar structure than *We wear hats.*, especially because the illustrations show the children are not *wearing* their hats but *putting them on*. In the retelling, Mike says, "So they *put on* their coats, jackets, hats and their boots. And they *zippered their coats up* so they wouldn't get cold." This response shows Mike's comprehension, but it also indicates that *We put hats* is not syntactically acceptable (grammatical) in

Mike's oral language. When he reads these sentences, Mike attends closely to the graphic cues and structural pattern (i.e., three-word sentences), but abandons his intuitive understanding of syntax, and as a result he does not insert the word *on* in order to make the syntax acceptable.

One reason that the author's language includes less predictable wordings and syntactic structures is because the text is actually a poem and the author is making use of rhythm and rhyme. This explains unusual sentence structures such as *Boats float. Mud pies bake. We play in puddles the rain makes.* Poems tend to be challenging for young readers because their syntax is unfamiliar and less predictable. In addition, because this book is formatted with one or two lines on each page, even experienced readers must read several pages before realizing the text is a poem. In his reading, Mike shifts the entire text from the unfamiliar genre of a poem to the more familiar genre of a past tense narrative. This shift starts with sentence 4.

```
    took rides
4 We ∧ ride.
```

After sentence 8 (see Figure 1.1), Mike consistently constructs—or reads—a past tense narrative. We are using the terms *construct* and *read* as synonyms to emphasize that reading is a process of ongoing constructing and interpreting the linguistic and textual cues.

```
     was raining
10 It ∧ rains.  11 (It pours.)

         ran into the house
12 We run indoors.

    were bored
13 We ∧ pout.  14 (We shout.)
```

Note: Circled text indicates an omission.

Mike's shift from poem to past-tense narrative shows the intuitive understanding of syntax that he brings to reading. He consistently shifts verb forms from present to past tense, or progressive past tense, inserting words in order to construct grammatically acceptable sentences. At this point, Mike is well into the text and actively involved in constructing the story. The teacher who conducted the miscue session notes that he adds sentence 23b (*We ran in the ocean.*) as he quickly turns the page to see what happens next. Mike's story ending shows his use of textual as well as linguistic cues as he parallels the opening line, *We have fun in the sun*.

```
   had     in the rain.
26 We have fun on a rainy (day.)
```

Mike provides a strong example of an effective beginning reader, because he is using all of the resources available to him to make sense of this text. He uses illustrations to support text construction. He makes connections between his own experiences and the text. He samples graphic cues with a focus on meaning construction. He uses intuitive understandings of syntax, particularly sentence structure within picture books. He uses knowledge about the language of stories, and the language of this text. And he uses holistic meaning making strategies when faced with unfamiliar graphic cues or unexpected syntactic structures. Observations of Mike and other young readers have led us to the following qualities of young effective beginning readers.

- Effective young beginning readers may construct text meanings that vary widely from more experienced readers.
- Miscues of effective young beginning readers reflect their current knowledge and beliefs about texts, reading, and the reading process
- Effective young beginning readers draw on earlier holistic strategies when they are struggling to make sense.
- Effective young beginning readers allow "texts to teach" (Meek, 1988).
- Young readers are tentative as they work hard or struggle with text.
- Miscues of beginning readers show influences from reading experiences and reading instruction.

YOUNG MEANING MAKERS

Like Mike, all readers construct a "reader's text" that varies from the printed text or author's text (K. Goodman, 1996). While there are many possible interpretations of a story or poem, interpretations of experienced readers tend to overlap because of shared assumptions, common cultural perspectives and similar experiences with texts. Young readers have a shorter history with texts, with the literacy events and social activities around texts, and with the topics and cultural experiences represented by text authors. For these reasons young readers' responses to texts in reading and retellings may vary widely from the interpretations of mature readers.

As reported earlier, Mike was referred to the Reading/Writing Learning Clinic because of concerns about his reading development. Teachers' and parents' concerns about readers like Mike may stem from common assumptions about reading: (a) that reading involves accurately producing the words of the text; or (b) that meaning resides within a text and reading involves getting the meaning of the printed text. We, however, assume readers bring meaning to a text, and that reading involves meaning construction and interpretation. Mike's interpretations are reflected through inferences in his retelling, "And they zippered their coats up so they wouldn't get cold."

A transactional theory of reading recognizes that all readers experience and interpret texts differently (Rosenblatt, 1994). This is reflected in miscue analysis findings that all readers make miscues. High school and college students are encouraged to express their own interpretations of a piece of literature. We want to encourage young children to construct and express personal meanings, rather than being concerned when they don't produce accurate renditions of a text. We expect that young children will have text interpretations that are different from our interpretations as experienced readers, particularly when children have different cultural backgrounds and experiences than their teachers.

Would Phonics or "Word Attack" Strategies Be Helpful for Young Readers?

Some may argue that phonics instruction or sight-word drills might help Mike produce a more accurate rendition of the text. However, the examples already given show that Mike uses phonics cues efficiently, while keeping his focus on meaning construction. Calling Mike's attention to phonics cues or accurately producing "author's words" takes his attention away from using all available resources (i.e., illustrations, background experiences) and cueing systems (i.e., meaning, grammar, and phonics) with a focus on making sense. Take the example of Timothy, another first grader, who is reading Mercer Mayer's *I Was So Mad* (1999). Timothy's substitution miscues are written above the author's text. The $ indicates a nonword.

```
        went                                      bathroom
S1: I wanted to keep some frogs in the bathtub but

    what
 Mom wouldn't let me.

S2:I was so mad.

    want                      sister
S3:I wanted to play with my little sister's

2. dollars
1. doll-         $wunt    $leet
dollhouse but Dad wouldn't let me.
```

Timothy's meaningful substitutions of *went* and *want* for *wanted* and *bathroom* for *bathtub* show that he uses semantic cues and pictures as resources for making sense of the story. Timothy also uses syntactic cues to make grammatically acceptable substitutions such as *dollars* for *dollhouse*. Mercer Mayer's illustrations and repetitive text support children through these "little critter" stories, and Timothy's retelling indicates that he understands the gist of the story. He says, "Every time he wants to do something he gets so mad." When asked why the character was mad, Timothy provides examples of things the character's mom wouldn't let him do.

However, while Timothy uses meaning making strategies, he does not use them consistently. Many of Timothy's substitution miscues are nonwords (S3. *but dad wunt leet me*.) or words that are graphically similar to the text but don't make sense (S1. *but Mom what let me*). In S3, he misses an opportunity to use the picture to predict the concept carrier *dollhouse*. In S8, as shown next, Timothy uses a picture of the character painting the house to predict the structure *I painted*. However, as he proceeds through the sentence, Timothy seems to use a strategy of pronouncing the words rather than confirming or revising his prediction.

```
         painted    $becant     homes
S8: So I decided to decorate the house

                              can not     $erie
but Grandpa said, "No you can't do that either."

          © angry
S9: Was I ever mad.
```

In S9, Timothy substitutes *angry* for *mad*, demonstrating that he is constructing a meaningful story. His unnecessary correction of this meaningful miscue again reveals a concern for accuracy. Reading Miscue Inventory statistics show that 76% of Timothy's word substitutions have high graphic similarity, or look like the printed text, and an additional 20% have some graphic similarity. However, only 10 of 28 sentences Timothy reads (36%) are semantically acceptable or meaningful. In this reading, Timothy is able to use many of the meaning-making strategies that Mike uses, but Timothy's focus on accuracy and "sounding it out" interferes with his ability to construct a meaningful text.

It's important to notice that all of Timothy's miscues reflect his use of reading strategies. Miscues do not occur randomly because readers are careless or sloppy. However, Timothy's strategies do not always help him to make sense. Proficient readers use graphophonic cues selectively with a focus on meaning making (K. Goodman, 1996). These points lead us to believe that some of the instructional "reading strategies" teachers recommend to young readers do not support the development of the meaning focused reading strategies proficient readers actually use while reading.

These instructional strategies may actually divert young readers' attention away from making sense. Word-oriented reading strategies such as "stretch it out," or "look for the little word in the big word," or "chunk it" seem useful to teachers within a particular context (such as a compound word). However, these instructional strategies can be confusing to beginning readers when they attempt to apply them across a text. In the following example, Emily, a first grader, is asked to read Mayer's *I Just Forgot* (1988) during an evaluation. Again, substitutions are typed above the text and omissions are circled.

```
             (uc)
               \  me me               ©
   So           \ me me       so       \it      forgot.
1 Sometimes I \remember and sometimes\I just forget.

   Is  in
2 This morning I (remember) to (brush) my (teeth)

       f---                b-
(but) I (forgot) to make my bed.

          breakfast
3I put my dishes in the sink (after)(breakfast)

 but I forgot to put the milk away.
```

As she reads, Emily initially tries the strategy "look for the little word in the big word." However, substitutions using this strategy (*so/ sometimes, me/ remember, is/ this, in/ morning*) are not helpful in meaning making. When this instructional strategy fails her, she begins to skip words rather than making any attempt to predict unfamiliar text. In S3, Emily predicts *breakfast* for *dishes* and constructs a meaningful sentence, illustrating that she does have intuitive strategies for making sense. However, word oriented strategies appear to take precedence over Emily's meaning-making strategies and her developing concepts about how reading works. The evaluator reports that Emily receives pull-out support four times per week, and her reading teacher says she is progressing "very slowly." The strategy of skipping words indicates Emily is accustomed to receiving assistance from the teacher and has little confidence in her own strategies for constructing meaning.

Children like Emily develop "instruction-dependent personalities" (Board, 1984). In reading interviews, these children report that their main reading strategy when they "come to something you don't know" is to ask an adult for the word. When asked to read a text without adult assistance, these young readers become so tentative or uncertain of their ability to successfully make use of graphophonic cues that they simply refuse to respond to the text. We sometimes describe readers like Emily as "Swiss cheese" readers, because their oral readings are marked by omissions, indicated on typescripts by circling the omitted text. Readers like Timothy, on the other hand, overuse the graphophonic cueing system at the expense of making sense. In both cases, these young readers have given up on their own effective strategies.

Mike's reading, marked by a consistent focus on making sense, appears more impressive in light of these examples. Mike illustrates how effective young readers bring their world knowledge, experiences, and linguistic understandings to their reading. Effective beginning readers use illustrations selectively and know that the print plays an important role in the story telling (Duckett, 2002). They predict events or concepts, as well as text language, based on their previous experiences with texts and genres (i.e., stories), their experiences with oral and written language, and their experiences with the text they are reading. If graphic cues don't provide enough information to make sense of the text, effective beginning readers draw on illustrations, text language, and world experiences to predict a meaningful sentence. What we believe these young readers are doing is making use of an earlier repertoire of beginning reading strategies that Lauren describes at the beginning of this chapter. ("I take a book and I open this book and I make the story up and I read it.")

Supporting Young Meaning Makers

The examples of Mike, Timothy, and Emily show that drawing on earlier meaning-making strategies is a hallmark of literacy development rather than demonstrating regression. Perceptive teachers support young readers in using all of their meaning-making strategies as resources for making sense of text. For example, many teachers encourage young children to take a "picture walk" before they read an unfamiliar text. Rather than suggesting instructional strategies, they create opportunities for readers to practice making sense and discuss with young readers the effective reading strategies they use intuitively. After Emily's reading of *I Just Forgot*, she was asked to read the nonfiction book *Cats & Kittens* (1976), a text with predictable, repetitive language that is well supported with illustrations. Emily examined the book and then asked the teacher if she could "make up her own story" as she looked through the pictures (see Figure 1.2).

SENTENCE	Printed Text	Emily's Text
1	Cats play.	Cats play.
2	Kittens play too.	Kittens play too.
3	Cats like milk.	Cats drink milk.
4	Kittens like milk too.	Kittens drink milk too.
5	Cats keep clean	Cats can run.
6	They lick their fur.	They can sit down.

Figure 1.2. Emily reads *Cats & Kittens* (1976).

In this reading Emily no longer looks like a swiss cheese reader. Encouraged to use effective strategies, and provided with a supportive text, Emily shows she is able to construct a meaningful text. She makes meaningful substitutions such as "drink" for "like." When the text is less supportive (S6), she uses an earlier strategy of "making up a story." In our experience, these examples where the reader's text varies widely from the printed text represent a brief but important developmental moment.

OBSERVING AND CELEBRATING YOUNG READERS

These case studies have shown that close observation and documentation of beginning readers is essential to informed teaching. The goal is for children to become thoughtful readers as they make sense of texts in ways that are personally meaningful. We want to encourage readers to work through their own strategies for making sense of text, rather than focusing on "getting the words," or deriving *the* meaning of a particular text. We ask them what they are thinking and to revisit the text to talk about their reading strategies. Through observing children as they read, we come to appreciate the knowledge and effective strategies that young beginners bring to reading, and the opportunities for language learning that meaningful reading experiences and texts provide. We have come to trust that young readers' responses are tentative and their proficient strategies are developing.

It's important to celebrate young readers' focus on making sense and their willingness to work at the puzzles and struggles of becoming a reader. Duckworth (1996) says that what supports children's further cognitive development are the environments in which "accepting surprise, puzzlement, excitement, patience, caution, honest attempts and wrong outcomes [are] legitimate and important elements of learning" (p. 69). Teachers who are informed "kidwatchers," knowledgeable about young readers and the reading process, provide opportunities for young readers in these accepting and safe environments.

ACKNOWLEDGMENT

The authors thank Roseanna Lanzilotta and Bonnie Granat for providing some of the reading samples discussed in this chapter.

CHILDREN'S LITERATURE REFERENCES

Cats & Kittens. (1976). Glenview, IL: Scott, Foresman.
Mayer, M. (1988) *I just forgot*. New York: Golden Books.
Mayer, M. (1999) *I was so mad.* New York: Golden Books.
Medearis, A. S. (1995) *We play on a rainy day.* New York: Scholastic.

REFERENCES

Board, P. (1984). *Toward a theory of instructional influence: Aspects of the instructional environment and their influences on children's acquisition of reading.* Unpublished dissertation, University of Toronto.
Duckett, P. (2002). New insights: Eye fixations and the reading process. *Talking Points, 13*(2), 16–21.
Duckett, P. (2003). Envisioning story: The eye movements of beginning readers. *Literacy Teaching and Learning: An International Journal of Early Reading and Writing,* 7(1&2), 77–89.
Duckworth, E. (1996) *The having of wonderful ideas* (2nd ed.) New York: Teachers College Press.
Goodman, K. (1996) *On reading.* Portsmouth, NH: Heinemann.
Goodman, Y. M., Watson, D. J., & Burke, C. L. (2005). *Reading miscue inventory: From evaluation to instruction.* New York: R. C. Owen.
Meek, M. (1988). How texts teach what readers learn. In M. Martin (Ed.), *The word for teaching is learning: Essays for James Britton* (pp. 82–106). Portsmouth, NH: Heinemann.
Owocki, G., & Goodman, Y. (2002). *Kidwatching: Documenting children's literacy development.* Portsmouth, NH: Heinemann.
Rosenblatt, L. M. (1994). The transactional theory of reading and writing. In R. B. Ruddell, M. R. Ruddell, & H. Singer (Eds.), *Theoretical models and processes of reading* (4th ed., pp. 1093–1130). Newark, DE: International Reading Association.
Taylor, D. (1993) *From the child's point of view.* Portsmouth, NH: Heinemann.

Chapter 2

The Literacy Stories of Tang-Tang and Tien-Tien

Wen-Yun Lin

In this chapter I interpret the language stories (Harste, Woodward, & Burke, 1984) of two native Chinese children in Taiwan, Tang-Tang and Tien-Tien, to explore how they develop in their understanding of written language. I also compare these findings to the research about emergent literacy in English-speaking children. My purpose is to provide knowledge about emergent literacy in Chinese by sharing two children's journeys in constructing their literacy.

EARLY LITERACY DEVELOPMENT

Ken Goodman (1986) suggests that the use of language is meaningful, purposeful, contextualized, and social. He especially stresses that written language is not secondary to oral language but is language in its own right. His research and the studies of Harste et al. (1984) and Dyson (1990) find that the process of acquiring written language is similar to oral language.

Ferreiro and Teberosky (1982) studied Spanish-speaking children aged 4 to 6 and explored children's hypotheses about language. Instead of looking at children as passively waiting for external reinforcement, their research shows that "children actively attempt to understand the nature of the language spoken around them, and in trying to understand it, formulate hypotheses, search for regularities, and test their prediction.... Children reconstruct language for themselves, selectively using information provided by the environment" (p. 8).

Language is always used for a purpose. Halliday (1982) stresses that children learn language and develop knowledge about language as they use it. Frank Smith (1988a) supports Halliday's idea of the strong relationship between language and its functions and argues that this idea could be applied to both spoken and written language.

A handful of Chinese studies explore early literacy development from an emergent perspective. Lee (1990) applied Yetta Goodman's (Goodman, Altwerger, & Marek, 1989) research design in Taiwan and found that young readers are developing various concepts about literacy in Chinese and they are able to produce written forms close to the conventions of written Chinese. Lee also found environmental print to be influential in early literacy development.

Wu and Huang (1994) explored preschool children's concepts about Chinese print by using a Chinese version of Clay's (1973) Concepts about Print test and analyzing miscues in beginning reading in Taiwan. They found that by the time children attend first grade, they already possess much knowledge about conventions in Chinese orthography and the functions of print in everyday life. They also found that the miscues of first-grade children reflected the children's use of their linguistic knowledge to construct meaning while they read.

Ko (1994) analyzed reading and writing miscues in elementary school children and discovered regularities and strategies related to their linguistic knowledge of Chinese that is not taught by their teachers. Anderson and his colleagues (Shu, Anderson, & Zhang, 1995) and Chang and Watson (1988) have made similar statements about Chinese literacy learning in their works. Thus, there is a slowly growing body of literature on Chinese literacy development that is consistent with the findings of research with English- and Spanish-speaking children.

ANALYSIS OF TANG-TANG AND TIEN-TIEN'S LITERACY

Ken Goodman (1965) states that he uses authentic, rather than controlled, situations in his reading research to observe "real readers" reading "real text." Similarly, to develop a rich picture of literacy development, I observed and interacted with my participants in different authentic situations to explore how they conceptualize the language in their environment.

The participants are my two nieces Tang-Tang and Tien-Tien born 4 years apart. Their mother read to them from birth, first Tang-Tang, and later Tien-Tien. Family members were always available to read to Tang-Tang before she was 4. Tien-Tien also brought books and asked adults to read to her but she had fewer experiences. Both children, though, grew up in a supportive, language-rich environment.

Tang-Tang's data were collected from age 1 to half a year after she started elementary school, at age 7. Tien-Tien's data were collected from the age of 1 to 4. All the stories given in this chapter have been chosen from this pool of data.

LANGUAGE STORIES ON CHILDREN'S CONCEPTS OF PRINT

Story 1: Recognizing Written Chinese Among Other Symbols

Tang-Tang (2;6; 2 years and 6 months) was shown a card with "Thank you" written in many different languages. I asked her which was our (Chinese) word (symbol). She pointed to the Chinese characters although she was unable to read or to understand them. Tien-Tien was shown the same thank-you card and responded in the same way.

Interpretation. Both children recognized the writing system in their society at an early age even though they had not learned to read. This is in keeping with the findings in emergent literacy research, which show that children develop an understanding of what their language looks like without direct adult instruction.

Story 2: It Is the Characters and Not the Pictures

Tang-Tang, before 3 years, was eating cookies from a package.

Wen: What are you eating?
Tang: *Man-Tien-Xing.*
Wen: (pointing to the package) Where does it tell you *Man-Tien-Xing*?
Tang: (pointing to the characters on the package) *ManàTien…Xing.*
(Her fingers pointed to the three characters one by one from right to left, but the characters were printed from left to right. What she pointed to was *XingàTien…Man.*)
Wen: (directing attention to the picture logo, *Man-Tien-Xing*)
Tang: No. You do not read there.
Wen: (pointing to the English words) *Man-Tien-Xing.*
Tang: No. It is not there either.

When Tien-Tien was young (2;6) and eating the same kind of cookies, I talked to her as I had to Tang-Tang:

Wen: What are you eating?
Tien: *Man-Tien-Xing.*

Wen: Show me where it tells you it is *Man-Tien-Xing*.
Tien: (pointing to the characters from left to right, the correct direction) *Man-Tien-Xing*.
Wen: (pointing to the pictures) Does this read *Man-Tien-Xing*?
Tien: No.
Wen: (pointing to the English) Does this read *Man-Tien-Xing*?
Tien: Yes.

Interpretation. Both children showed confidence in their knowledge of print and demonstrated their knowledge of reading. They did not really decode the individual symbols, but knew the meaning from the context. As Yetta Goodman (1984) states, children read the world before they read the print.

Both children had experiences in listening to English on TV and in seeing written English in picture books. Tang-Tang knew that English and Chinese sounded different. Perhaps she said that the English words did not say *Man-Tien-Xing* because she thought that it should sound differently from Chinese. Tien-Tien's answer may have been different from Tang-Tang's because she focused on the meaning and not the sound.

Story 3: Chinese Is Straight and English Is Curved

Tang-Tang (3;5) showed me her writing both in Chinese and in English, which she had written on the same day. She told me, "I know how to write Chinese and I also know how to write English." She pointed to her script and said, "This is Chinese. It is straight. This is English. It is curved." Two months later, Tang-Tang (3;7) wanted to write to her aunties in New York.

Tang: Do people who live in America use English?
Wen: Yes.
Tang: Since my aunties live in America, I should write to them in English. (She wrote a letter in invented English)

Interpretation. Tang-Tang discovered differences in Chinese and English orthography. She had not been taught to write either Chinese or English, nor had we discussed the appearance of the two languages. She discovered the differences through her interactions with the two languages in her daily life. This is a form of meta-linguistic awareness that comes from language contact. Tang-Tang hypothesized that people in different geographic areas use different languages. She also knew that the writer has to sign a letter, showing a concept of author and audience as well as letter writing format.

LANGUAGE STORIES ON LEARNING TO READ

Story 4: It Means What You Want It to Mean

Tang-Tang at about 3 years old:

Wen:	What are you drinking?
Tang:	Xian-Cao-Mi. (A kind of jelly drink)
Wen:	How do you know that it is Xian-Cao-Mi?
Tang:	(pointing to the characters on the can one by one, reading conventionally) Xian—Cao —Mi (Turning the can around to read the fine print that lists the ingredients, she continued to read) Grandpa bought it. Not for Auntie.

Interpretation. Tang-Tang was really confident that the print could be made to serve her purpose, even if it was something that she had not written.

Story 5: We Can Get the Meaning by Reading the Pictures

Tang-Tang's father brought home a new kind of coffee. Grandma had some difficulty reading the name of the coffee.

Grandma:	(to herself) What is the name of this coffee?
Tang:	(went over and pointed to the picture) It is Red–Black Coffee.

Interpretation. The package only had abstract patches of red and black. Obviously Tang-Tang connected the design to the meaning of the words. Tang-Tang showed that a reader brings many cues to her reading. She knew a good deal about what the print ought to say on a package label and she knew that print had a communicative function on the basis of contextual information. So she assigned it an appropriate meaning. At this time, Tang-Tang already knew many Chinese characters and she knew that we read words and not pictures. But in this instance, she read the picture. At a time when adults were confused by the print, Tang-Tang helped them disambiguate by using another symbol system. She demonstrated her strength as a reader by applying an alternative reading strategy.

This story supports Ferreiro and Teberosky's (1982) observation that "children suppose initially that pictures and print are close in meaning but different in form" and that "they do not suppose that print represents language" (p. 85).

Story 6: Children Read Before They Read Actual Characters

My family likes to read newspapers. When we read, Tang-Tang always wanted to read too. We taught her to read the title of the paper *Min-Sheng-Bao*. The first few times we showed her where those three characters were: the top left of the front page and on the top of each inner page. After she knew how to read *Min-Sheng-Bao*, Tang-Tang began to read newspapers very often. She would look for the three characters in the entire copy and read those characters aloud.

Once, Tang-Tang picked up another newspaper and read *Min-Sheng-Bao,* but it was really *Lian-He-Bao*. She seemed confident about her reading. Another time, Tang-Tang picked up *Zhong-Guo-Shi-Bao* and started to read aloud, pointing to the red characters one at a time. After she read the third character, there was still one red character left. From her facial expression, it seemed that she noticed that there was something wrong, but she did not know what.

Months later, *Min-Sheng-Bao* sent us a package, with the three characters written in green ink and in a different font from the newspaper. Tang-Tang told us that *Min-Sheng-Bao* sent us something. Tang-Tang knew the single characters *Min* and *Bao* in different contexts.

Interpretation. From reading environmental print, Tang-Tang gradually accumulated orthographic information that allowed her to recognize characters in different contexts, and she applied what she learned from environmental print to reading texts. She read the meaning before she could read the actual characters. She learned to read from whole to part, from complete meaningful units to each individual logographic symbol. In the beginning, she read with the help of the color and the location. At this stage, reading Chinese characters may be like reading pictures or logos. Then, gradually she knew to read characters themselves. As Smith (1988b) suggests, how we recognize a word is comparable to how we recognize a face: we recognize it all at once instead of one part at a time.

Story 7: Use Prior Knowledge to Interpret Text

When Tang-Tang was about five, she saw some regulations posted in the library: *Qing-Bao-Chi-An-Jing* (Please be quiet). Tang-Tang read: *Qing-Bao-Chi-An-Quan* (Please be safe). Then she said: "Because the floor is so smooth, it is easy to slip. The librarian is afraid of people falling, so they made this sign to remind people to watch their step."

Interpretation. We often reminded Tang-Tang to be safe, but seldom asked her to be quiet (Tang-Tang is a quiet child). So the word "safe" is more common than the word "quiet" in her daily life. Tang-Tang used her linguistic knowledge to read the characters and her experience and knowledge about the world to interpret what she read, making a miscue. Again we see Tang-Tang bringing her experience to her reading comprehension. She was not satisfied with reading just words. She had to make what she reads meaningful and rational.

Story 8: Make Predictions and Test Them Out

Tang-Tang (6;3) was reading an advertisement to herself, "I thought I would win a Ji-Che (motorcycle), but then I see it is a Ji-Huei (chance)." The advertisement had Ji-Huei written on it. Apparently Tang-Tang saw the first character Ji and predicted that the next character would be the word Ji-Che to make up the sentence: "You will have a motorcycle." When she found out that the next character was Huei, she corrected herself.

Interpretation. Ken Goodman (1996) believes that all good readers bring their expectations to bear on their reading. Rarely, though, will we find a child who is so conscious and expressive of her own cognitive monitoring. These stories from Tang-Tang show that her reading is driven by very much the same motivations and strategies that American children demonstrated in Goodman's research.

LANGUAGE STORIES ON LEARNING TO WRITE CHARACTERS

Story 9: Invented Characters

Tang-Tang (2;2) made symbols and then told us that she was writing. She had marks to represent different members of the family. Tien-Tien (1;8) had a similar writing system. She also used different symbols to represent family members, but instead of cursive writing like Tang-Tang's, Tien-Tien used strokes to compose her characters.

Tang-Tang (4;8) knew how to write her last name "Lin" and the character for "little." In a letter that she wrote to her Little Auntie, Tang-Tang used three kinds of symbols: two Chinese characters, many made-up characters, and a mixture of straight and curved lines that represented strokes. She read the entire letter to Grandma, pointing to one symbol at a time while she read aloud.

Interpretation. This finding is consistent with that of Ferreiro and Teberosky (1982) who discovered that young children have a "name hypothesis"; that is, they see print as a way of representing objects or people. This kind of hypothesis is especially suited to learning Chinese, for in

Chinese, each character does indeed have a name and an associated concept, and many of the graphemes that make up characters are really able to stand alone as characters. Here we see Tang-Tang using a mixture of symbols that are all part of the symbol system in her culture to express her personal meaning. That is the way writing should be, with the focus on the message rather than the formation of characters, words. and sentences.

Story 10: Alternate Symbols for Names

Tang-Tang (3;5) was showing me her drawing and writing:

Tang:	See, I draw a picture to Little Auntie and I write *Xiao* (little).
Wen:	The little dot in X*iao* should be on the bottom instead of on top.

A couple of days later, Tang-Tang was writing to her Little Auntie again. She showed me a drawing with the character *San* (three or third) written next to it.

Tang:	Is Little Auntie also Third Auntie?
Wen:	Yes.
Tang:	I don't know how to write *Xiao*," but I know how to write *San*.

After a while *Xiao* began to show up in her writing again as she regained confidence with the character. Some weeks later, she not only wanted to write to represent Little Auntie, but also wanted to write *Yi* (auntie), but the character was difficult to write.

Tang:	(after a while) English seems easier to write. What is her name in English?
Wen:	Annie. Her English name is Annie.

Tang-Tang sounded out the name with me and she wrote down Annie in invented English without hesitation and without asking me to write for her. Tang-Tang (4;7) wrote a postcard to Little Auntie. She did not ask adults to help, but everyone knew to whom she was writing. Her auntie's name is "林欣怡" and she wrote " 林*一."

She wrote the first character "林" conventionally, added a star for the second character, and substituted "—" for the third character. She knew how to read the names of every family member long before this age, because she always sorted our mail. Now she was writing her Chinese invention of her auntie's name.

Interpretation. These vignettes show that Tang-Tang is familiar with many symbolic systems—Chinese, English, both in invented and conventional forms. She was able to integrate her different systems for her personal needs. As in Dyson's (1990) observations, she used the symbols to represent personal meaning and then used the personal meaning to establish meaning socially. She showed us her linguistic strength, her knowledge about the family structure, and her strategies in making language function for her purpose.

Story 11: Development of Chinese Characters

This is the story of Tien-Tien's Chinese calligraphy from 1 to 4 years. At 1, she was making marks but we do not know whether she was trying to express anything.

At age 1;9 she imitated letter writing by making a mark on a sheet of paper and putting it into an envelope.

At age 2;1, she used circles to represent family members.

At age 2;2, she imitated character writing by making small round marks that looked like Chinese characters (see Figure 2.1). Her characters were composed of many individual marks.

At 2;6, she used strokes to compose her character (see Figure 2.2).

Figure 2.1. Tien-Tien (2;2) imitates Chinese character writing.

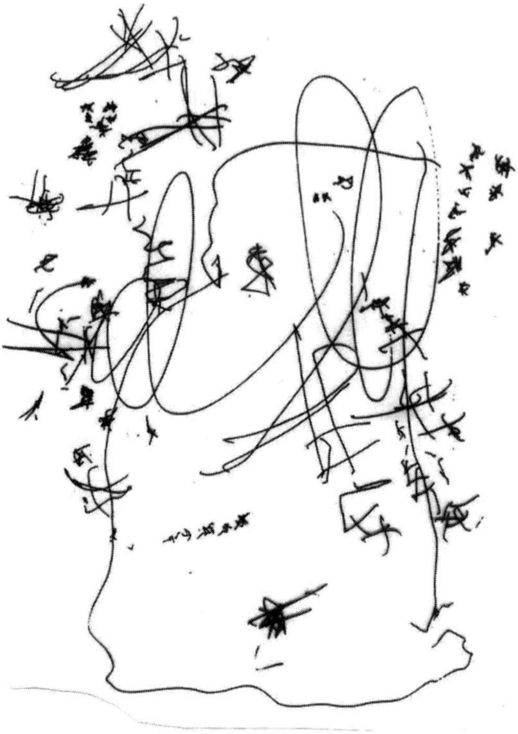

Figure 2.2. Tien-Tien (2;6) uses strokes to compose Chinese characters.

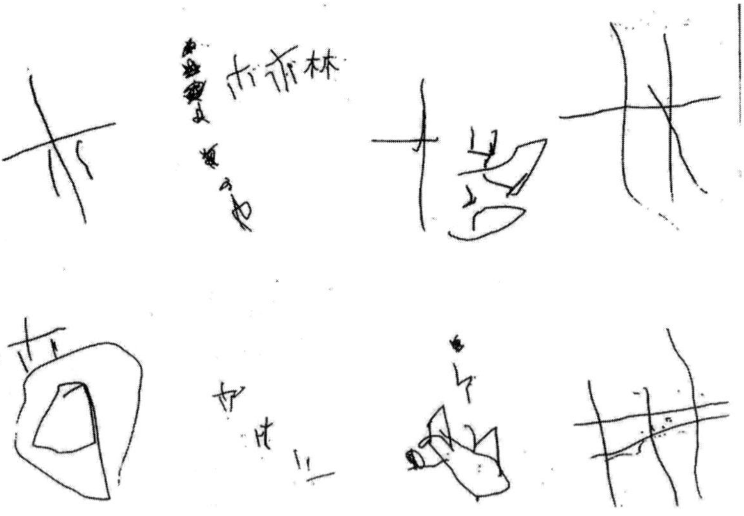

Figure 2.3. Tien-Tien (3;1) explores writing her last name.

Compared to those made at age 2;2 (see Figure 2.1), they looked more and more like Chinese. Not only did she have the general outline of the character, she also had details.

At age 3;1, she explored writing her last name (see Figure 2.3). At this point she could write actual characters.

Interpretation. Doake (1981) found that learning one's own name is enormously interesting for children, and this has been evident in the stories described earlier. The family name was among the few characters that Tang-Tang and Tien-Tien tried to read and write when they began to learn to read and write actual characters. They learned to read the family name by reading all the mail and later each family member's name by assigning mail to each of them. Learning to read and write their names shows that there is a need for authorship from a very young age.

LEARNING FROM TANG-TANG AND TIEN-TIEN

Concepts of Print

Although many young readers of alphabetic languages gradually discover the relationship between letter and sound (Ferreiro & Teberosky, 1982), the young Chinese readers that I observed did not make this hypothesis. That is because most written Chinese symbols do not represent sounds. Children do, however, quickly connect syllable and symbol both in reading and writing. There are, of course, sound components and sound cues in the characters, but because they are indirect and because their use is discouraged by teachers, the partial-sound hypothesis comes later in literacy development.

Ferreiro and Teberosky's (1982) children discovered a "variation hypothesis," that "the grapheme must be varied for a text to be readable" (pp. 31–33). Lee's (1990) study also showed this hypothesis in Chinese when she asked children to write. When Tang-Tang was 2 years old, she imitated a friend's homework writing by composing a text with similar marks in straight lines.

Tien-Tien, at age 3, had the experience of seeing her older sister writing "homework characters." Once, she created a text composed of small circles. Although these marks looked similar to me, they may have been different for her. I do not see such writing often because most of the writing the girls do is in response to real-life situations and is composed of different invented characters.

Learning to Read

Research data indicate that young children transfer the knowledge of environmental language to reading and learning how to read (Doake, 1981; Y.

Goodman, 1978). Tang-Tang and Tien-Tien demonstrated an understanding of the purpose of environmental print. Their experiences with various forms of environmental print clearly contributed to their understandings of the functions of written language and the acquisition of written language itself. Tang-Tang's miscues also provided evidence of her reading comprehension. Many of her miscues show how much effort she exerted to understand the language, and how creative but reasonable her miscues were.

Learning to Write

Tang-Tang and Tien-Tien were active creators of the writing system and understood the communicative functions of language. As the "babbling child talks," so the "scribbling child writes." Tang-Tang and Tien-Tien learn to read and write in the same way and for the same reasons that they learn to speak and listen.

The two children made the journey from personal invention to social convention. Much of my research shows how the children contribute to their own personal inventions, but their inventions were also constrained by the shared meanings or conventions of their society. This constant tension between invention and convention forced them to move toward a mutually understandable symbol system in order to achieve the task of communication, and helped them shape their language according to social convention.

Vygotsky (1983) views children's drawing as a preliminary stage in the development of written language called "graphic speech," a way of telling a story. He also found that children gradually shift from "drawings of things to drawing of words" (p. 289). I found that most of Tang-Tang and Tien-Tien's pictures tell stories. The pictures they drew did not represent their oral language, but their meaning. When Tang-Tang first tried to write, she acted like she was drawing characters instead of writing characters.

LEARNING THROUGH JOINING THE LITERACY CLUB

In my explorations with Tang-Tang and Tien-Tien, I learned to become a kidwatcher (Y. Goodman, 1978). I learned that children's nonconventional ways of speaking and writing were not only "cute," but showed their logic. Once I followed the children's thought and logic, I saw their strengths. Through Tang-Tang's and Tien-Tien's language and literacy stories, I learned to appreciate the effort they put into learning the language. The family also learned to value their literacy.

The acceptance of the children's literacy attempts by the adults around the child is crucial. The entire family was involved in nurturing Tang-Tang and Tien-Tien's literacy development. We created opportunities to encourage the immersion in literacy practices, not only by making the literacy materials accessible to them, but also in our attitudes and behaviors. We participated in their literacy activities and allowed them to participate in ours so that they might understand firsthand how and why we wrote letters, completed homework, took notes, and read labels and other environmental print. Although there was no formal literacy instruction, the adults served as facilitators and mediators, and they invited the children to join their literacy club (Smith, 1988a).

REFERENCES

Chang, Y. L., & Watson, D. J. (1988). Adaptation of prediction strategies and materials in a Chinese English bilingual classroom. *The Reading Teacher, 42*(1), 36–45.

Clay, M. M. (1973). *Concepts about print.* Aukland: Heinemann.

Doake, D. B. (1981). *Book experience and emergent reading behavior in preschool children.* Unpublished doctoral dissertation, University of Alberta, Edmonton, Alberta, Canada.

Dyson, A. H. (1990). Weaving possibilities: Rethinking metaphors for early literacy development. *The Reading Teacher, 44*(3), 202–213.

Ferreiro, E., & Teberosky, A. (1982). *Literacy before schooling.* Exeter, NH: Heinemann.

Goodman, K. (1996). On whole language. Speech at the Conference of Whole Language Education. Tapai: Taiwan Provincial Institute for Elementary School Teachers Insenile Education.

Goodman, K. S. (1965). A linguistic study of cues and miscues in reading. *Elementary English, 42*(6), 639–645.

Goodman, K. S. (1986). *What's whole in whole language? A parent/teacher guide to children's learning.* Portsmouth, NH: Heinemann.

Goodman, Y. M. (1978). Kidwatching: An alternative to testing. *National Elementary Principal, 57*(4), 41–45.

Goodman, Y. M. (1984). The development of initial literacy. In H. Goelman, A. A. Oberg, & F. Smith (Eds.), *Awakening to literacy: Literacy before schooling* (pp. 102–109). Exeter, NH: Heinemann.

Goodman, Y. M., Altwerger, B., & Marek, A. (1989). *Print awareness in pre-school children: The development of literacy in preschool children.* Occasional Paper: Program in Language and Literacy. Tucson: University of Arizona.

Halliday, M. A. K. (1982). Three aspects of children's language development: Learning language, learning through language, and learning about language. In Y. M. Goodman, M. M. Haussler, & D. S. Strickland (Eds.), *Oral and written language development research: Impact on the school* (pp. 7–19). Newark, DE/Urbana, IL: IRA/NCTE.

Harste, J. C., Woodward, V. A., & Burke, C. L. (1984). *Language stories and literacy lessons.* Portsmouth, NH: Heinemann.

Ko, H. W. (1994). Tou Er Tueng Hwuei Cuo Yi Er Zi Tang tao er Tueng Xie Zi Fan Fa [Explore children's writing through their writing errors]. In *Chinese instructional method and material for elementary school III* (pp.). Taipei, Taiwan: Taiwan Provincial Institute of Inservice Teachers Education.

Lee, L. J. (1990). *Developing control of reading and writing in Chinese.* Occasional Paper: Program in Language and Literacy. Tucson: University of Arizona.

Shu, H., Anderson, R. C., & Zhang, H. (1995). Incidental learning of word meanings while reading: A Chinese and American cross-cultural study. *Reading Research Quarterly, 30*(1), 76–95.

Smith, F. (1988a). *Joining the literacy club: Further essays into education.* Portsmouth, NH: Heinemann.

Smith, F. (1988b). *Understanding reading: A psycholinguistic analysis of reading and learning to read* (4th ed.). Hillsdale, NJ: Lawrence Erlbaum Associates.

Vygotsky, L. S. (1983). The prehistory of written language. In M. Martlew (Ed.), *The psychology of written language: Developmental and educational perspectives* (pp. 279–291). New York: John Wiley & Sons.

Wu, R., & Huang, C. -F. (1994). You Er Duei Wen Zi Yueng Tu De Ren Shi [Young children's concept of Function of print]. In *Chinese instructional method and material for elementary school III* (pp. 37–46). Taipei, Taiwan: Taiwan Provincial Institute of Inservice Teachers Education.

Chapter **3**

Biliteracy As Social Practice in Schooling: A Bilingual First Grader's Journey in Learning to Read and Write in L1 and L2

Barbara M. Flores

Throughout the world, biliteracy is a common social practice in and out of schooling; in fact, multiliteracy and multilingualism are common social practices. In the United States there are many Native Americans and immigrants speaking many languages other than English, including native Spanish speakers who are descendents of the Spanish and Mexican rulers who once occupied what is now the southwestern United States as their nation. Today, we experience biliteracy on television, the news, the radio, packages for purchased commodities, and medicine labels, and in subtitles for movies, airports and airplanes, songs, books, stores, and so on. We are living in a global society that is not only biliterate but multiliterate. If this is so, how do we in the United States promote everyday biliteracy in schooling as a social practice?

Michael Halliday (1978) posits that languages (oral or written, first and/or second) are learned based on need, purpose, and function. He claims that the need to communicate is learned within the context of its use. Given this tenet and the challenge to organize and teach biliteracy as a social practice, this chapter traces the biliteracy journey of a first grader, Nancy, who represents a prototype of many children who are Spanish speakers in the United States. She is from a poor socioeconomic family and is visually impaired without glasses.

CREATING A SOCIAL USE FOR LITERACY AND BILITERACY

Guided by Halliday's premise, Nancy's teacher, Ms. Mendoza, and I decided that the interactive journal writing in her classroom is an ideal social practice to observe. The children and Ms. Mendoza engage in authentic communication by using a variety of sign systems, such as drawing and oral and written language, to construct and communicate meaning. This literacy event is one of many that Nancy engages in throughout the day. She is in a bilingual whole language classroom where both oral and written languages, are used authentically. (Edelsky, Draper, & Smith, 1983; Freire, 1970; Freire & Macedo, 1987; Goodman, K., 1994). The children engage in instructional practices in Spanish, the majority of time, in a 90/10 model, which means that 90% of the classroom instruction is in Spanish and 10% is in English. The teacher engages the children in many holistic instructional strategies, such as daily read alouds, guided reading, shared reading, literature response logs, literature studies, theme cycles, and so on. Within all of these social practices, knowledge of the cueing systems such as graphophonics is made visible and taught by metalinguistically talking about their function and purpose.

In this chapter, I analyze Nancy's bilingual first-grade writing development in Spanish and English during 1 year. I chose her from the many hundreds of bilingual students I have observed to show that she not only epitomizes the norm, but also represents a prototype of the socioeconomic, health, and immigrant challenges facing teachers today. By using monthly samples of her daily journal entries, I not only trace the evolution of her conceptual interpretation of written language (Ferreiro & Gomez Palacios, 1982; Ferreiro & Teberosky, 1979, 1982) across time in one literacy event in the classroom, but also illuminate the significant role that the teacher's pedagogical knowledge, attitudes about language teaching/learning, culture, and class play in the social practice of the children's biliteracy development.

During interactive journal writing (Edelsky, 1986; Milz, 1980), the children choose a topic on which to write. Ms. Mendoza initially guides them in selecting topics by asking the children to name three. Each child then chooses one or something else of interest. The children draw about their topics and then write about them. When they are finished, Ms. Mendoza listens to each child read his or her written language because she cannot read the child's writing yet. By doing this, she values and respects the children's prior and growing knowledge about written language. She understands that the children are still developing their alphabetic knowledge. When the child finishes reading the entry, Ms. Mendoza writes an authentic response, perhaps relating a similar experience, stating a genuine interest, or asking a question. As Ms. Mendoza writes her response, the child watches and listens. In effect, Ms. Mendoza and the child are engaged within a zone of proximal development (Vygotsky, 1978); that is, the child writes at her developmental level and mediates her written language by reading it aloud for Ms. Mendoza, and likewise Ms. Mendoza writes at the potential (the goal is for the child to eventually write at the alphabetic level) and mediates her written response with oral language. Thus, they both are on equal footing, mediating each other's written language with a common oral language. This social practice is the essence of sharing knowledge about written language and how it works within the context of its authentic use. Mediation within and during the zone is key to how the children "come to know" how written language functions in the adult's cultural everyday world.

PEDAGOGICAL KNOWLEDGE GOVERNING THE PRAXIS (TEACHING/LEARNING)

As a result of years of working with teachers and children in the classroom, I have discovered that it is the "why," the theoretical understanding, that provides the guidance for the practice. The pedagogical practice of interactive journal writing and the interpretive analysis of Nancy's writing development is guided by sociopsycholinguistics, psychogenesis, and sociocultural traditions. Halliday provides theoretical guidance in understanding how language is learned within the context of its authentic use (Halliday, 1975, 1978). K. Goodman and Y. Goodman (1979) report that learning to read is "natural" across contexts and genres. By using reading and writing in real meaningful ways, children engage in their own processes of figuring out how the parts work and function in the whole by seeing it used (K. Goodman, 1996), by observing adults (experts) demonstrate how it's used, (Harste, Woodard, & Burke, 1984), by talking about language (Y. Goodman, 1980, 1990; Halliday, 1978), and by socially constructing the knowledge (Vygotsky, 1978) through social interactions based on their present conceptual interpretation (Ferreiro & Teberosky, 1979, 1982) of the alphabetic languages. Thus, these theoretical frameworks about language use, language development, and language learning are the essential guideposts governing teaching/learning in this context.

BACKGROUND

Ms. Mendoza reports discovering Nancy's vision problems early in the school year. As Ms. Mendoza scans the classroom, she observes Nancy trying to read something she has just written in her journal. At first she doesn't realize that Nancy is trying to read because Nancy is holding her journal to the right of her head which is turned to the left. Ms. Mendoza observes more closely and notices Nancy's right eye sporadically moving about as Nancy moves the paper up and down. Throughout the day, Ms. Mendoza continues to observe Nancy's behavior and decides to ask the school nurse to examine Nancy's vision. The nurse finds a definite severe problem with Nancy's vision and recommends that Nancy be examined by a physician. Nancy's examination reveals that Nancy not only has limited peripheral vision without the glasses, but that she is legally blind.

Ms. Mendoza then contacts Nancy's grandmother and legal guardian, who tells Ms. Mendoza that she cannot afford an exam nor the necessary prescription glasses. Mr. Rojas, the school principal, and Ms. Mendoza contact the local Lions Club, which generously pays for the prescription glasses. It takes about a month to get the prescription glasses, but Nancy continues to attend school.

Ms. Mendoza is caring and organizes teaching/learning environments supportive of children. The children know that every child is a valued person in the classroom and that children's knowledge, abilities, and experimentations are valued, too. The teacher establishes the social expectations in the classroom:

1. Asking questions.
2. Sharing knowledge.
3. Solving problems collectively.
4. Talking and sharing with neighbors.
5. Respecting each other.

Given this facilitative social environment and Ms. Mendoza's growing pedagogical knowledge and attitudes about children's learning and living together, it is evident why Nancy's progress in using written language developed just like any other "normal" child. Ms. Mendoza is very key not only in organizing the social uses and practices of language(s), both oral and written across social contexts, but also in the type of social interactions, sociocultural rituals, expectations, and *respeto*/respect that become the ways of knowing, the ways of being, the ways of acting, the ways of doing, and the ways of socially interacting in the classroom.

NANCY IN THE SOCIAL CONTEXT OF INTERACTIVE DIALOGUE JOURNALS

In order to trace Nancy's writing development across a school year, I developed a matrix to explain the written social interaction between Nancy and Ms. Mendoza. Figure 3.1 shows a monthly representative sample from

Nancy's First Grade Writing Development in L1 (Spanish) and L2 (English) Using Interactive Journal Writing		
Date	**Child's Written Entry Only**	**Teacher's Response**
09/09/85	NIOCH CAPrCO UFNTC [Something about a ghost scarying her.]	¿Y le tuviste miedo al fantasma? [And, were you afraid of the ghost?]
10/25/85	Yo geko AlaPELOta Qon M hr mo (Yo juego a la pelota con mi hermano.) [I play ball with my brother.]	¿Que clase de juegos juegan tu y tu hermano con la pelota? [What kind of ball games do you and your brother play?]
11/06/85	A Ora es ElQM PLEanos de mi MaMa. (Ahora es el cumpleanos de mi mama.) [Today is my Mother's birthday.]	¿Le van hacer una fiesta? Ojala que la pase muy bien. [Are you going to give her a party? I hope that she has a great time.]

Figure 3.1. Nancy's first-grade writing development in L1 (Spanish) and L2 (English) using interactive journal writing. (*continued on next page*)

01/10/86	Mi Abuelita juega Con Mi Perra y juega Con Mi Perro Muerrde. Muy Resio [My Grandmother plays with my female dog and she plays with my male dog. He bites really hard.]	¿Quién muerde recio? ¿Tu perrito o tu abuelita? Who bites really hard? Your little dog or your Grandma?
02/04/86	Yo en mi casa tengo muchas plaantas con flore s y mi abuelita las Riega mucho [In my house I have a lot of plants with flowers and my grandmother waters them a lot.]	Yo tambien tengo muchas plantas pero no dan flores. Me gustan mucho. I, too, have many plants but they do not give flowers. I like them a lot.
03/07/86	Yo vi a la "chibra" y me gusto mucho y tambien salieron los enemigos de "chibra" y los enemigos de "Hi man" y "Hi man" y me compraron muchos chuchulucos mu ama les dice asi. [I saw "Shera" and I like it alot and "Shera's" enemies also appeared and so did the enemies of "He Man" and "He Man" and they bought me a lot of trinkets. My Mom calls them that.]	La "Shera" esta muy bonita ¿Verdad? Yo a veces miro el programa porque mi niño lo mira mucho. "Shera" is very pretty. Isn't she? I sometimes watch the program because my son watches it a lot.

Figure 3.1. Continued. (*continued on next page*)

04/04/86	A mime gustan mucho los arcoiris Porque tienen muy bonitos colores. [I really like rainbows because they have such beautiful colors.]	¿Has visto un arcoiris? Yo he visto muchos y tambien se me hacen muy bonitos por sus colores. Did you see a rainbow? I have seen many and I, too, think that they are very beautiful because of their beautiful colors.
05/01/86	Me and Tracy mace a plante fore Mistr Rojas but whea frogaret I put a flawer. [Me and Tracy make a plant for Mr. Rojas but we forgot it. I put a flower.]	When are you going to bring the plant to school? I bet Mr. Rojas will like it.

Figure 3.3. Continued.

Nancy's daily journal entries. The first column notes the month, the second, Nancy's written entry with an English translation below it, and the third column includes Ms. Mendoza's written response also with an English translation. Following the figure, I analyze each sample to show the progress Nancy makes during her first grade experience.

September

In September, in spite of not having glasses, Nancy demonstrates her knowledge of written language. Her conceptual interpretations of the Spanish alphabetic writing system are characterized by the use of the presyllabic and syllabic hypotheses (Ferreiro & Teberosky, 1979). One of the characteristics evidenced in the presyllabic interpretation is Nancy's use of strings of letters to represent meaning, such as NIOCH CAPrCO UFNTC. During the syllabic interpretation, she begins to relate phonetic aspects of oral language with written language. In other words, one symbol is used to represent one syllable—in this case, for example, *un fantasma* has four syllables, which Nancy represents with five letters: "U" stands for "un and "FNTC" stands for "fantasma". Prior to Ferreiro and Teberosky's (1982) psychogenesis contributions, some researchers would have said that Nancy had knowledge of different letters. But now, based on Ferreiro and Teberosky's work, we know that she not only assumes that her writing is representing meaning (the semantic system), but also that she is using a letter to represent a syllable. Nancy is also willing to take risks, knowing that her "writing" does not look exactly like the writing of the adults in her life (Edelsky & Draper, 1986). Nancy has accepted that children learn to write by doing it "their way" first. By watching others, by figuring it out, by asking questions, and by interpreting, she learns how the adult culture uses the writing system. Meanwhile, she accepts that her symbols represent meaning and that she is going to mediate their meaning by reading them aloud to the teacher. In turn, Ms. Mendoza knows that Nancy does not yet understand the teacher's symbolic representation of meaning. Knowing this, Ms. Mendoza also mediates with oral reading as she writes her response with Nancy watching in the act of interpreting. The expert (Ms. Mendoza, in this case) provides the novice (Nancy) with a deliberate daily demonstration of shared knowledge and mediates the process (Diaz, Moll, & Mehan, 1986), even though the novice is not yet able to totally grasp the complexity of the written exchange without deliberate mediation. In this zone of proximal development (Vygotsky, 1978), each participant is in the act of communicating a message using the sign systems available and simultaneously demonstrating the knowledge that each has at that moment about written language. Ms. Mendoza is not apprehensive about Nancy's present conceptual interpretations because she knows that Nancy will eventually evolve to the alphabetic conceptual interpretation that governs alphabetic languages such as Spanish and English. Clearly the pragmatic rules governing this social context do not discourage exploration in learning; nor does Ms. Mendoza treat Nancy as a passive receptor of knowledge. Instead, Ms. Mendoza allows Nancy to be an active participant engaged in interpreting this social semiotic, the writing system.

October

In October Nancy's conceptual interpretation evolves to a syllabic/alphabetic one (Ferreiro & Teberosky, 1979). At this conceptual interpretation two forms of corresponding relations between letter and sound coexist: the syllabic and the alphabetic hypothesis. During the use of the syllabic hypothesis the child may use single graphemes (letters) to represent a syllable and at other times to represent a phoneme (sound). The use of the syllabic/alphabetic hypothesis represents the passage between the syllabic and the alphabetic writing systems. Ferreiro and Gomez Palacios (1982) note that at this point in time children begin to see that to some degree sound/letter correspondence patterns exist in the orthographic system. Thus, the myth of the phonetic hypothesis emerges, that is, one letter per sound, which we know is not consistently true in Spanish or English orthography. For example, *through, said, have,* and *of* in English are not phonetic; nor are *hermano, quiero,* and *cielo* in Spanish.

In her October entry, Nancy demonstrates her knowledge of the graphophonic, syntactic, and orthographic systems. Her word segmentation is notably more conventional than in her September sample except for the noun phrase "alaPELOTa," which she represents as a single linguistic unit. Ferreiro and Teberosky (1979, 1982) report that such syntactic segmentation is evident among 4-, 5-, and 6-year-olds, and Edelsky and Gilbert (1985) affirm this phenomenon among bilingual first graders. Graphophonically, Nancy is experimenting with the phonetic hypotheses. Her substitution of /k/, a voiceless velar stop, for a voiced velar stop, /g/, demonstrates her tacit knowledge of this particular phoneme's point of articulation with the phoneme's voiceless and voiced qualities.

Hudelson (1981–1982) reports that Spanish-speaking children's orthographic knowledge is developmentally consistent. Nancy's use of "Qon" for "Con" also demonstrates her use of letter name knowledge for the phoneme "c." The letter name in Spanish for the letter "Q" is "cu" so Nancy uses this for the initial letter in "con." Nancy's use of "M" for "Mi," Hrmo" for "Hermano," "Hr" for "Her," "M" for "Ma," and "O" for "No"demonstrates her syllabic hypothesis. In addition, Nancy uses her visual memory knowledge of the orthographic system because she includes the "H" in *hermano*, which is silent in the initial position in Spanish.

November

In November Nancy is still generalizing the "Q" for "C" in her use of "QMPLEanos," but it is now more refined. The letter name "Cu," substitutes nicely for the actual "CU" in *cumpleaños*. Her word segmentation is approaching written convention except for "El QMPLEanos." Her experimentation with mixing upper and lower case letters is also interesting. Ms. Mendoza does not teach the letters of the alphabet in isolation nor does she teach handwriting by rote practice; however, she does teach about the form and how to make the letters in a variety of other contexts, such as during morning message, ABC time, collaborative text, and language experience. In other words, "letters" are demonstrated and talked about across many of the daily literacy events and social practices in the context of their use.

January

In January Nancy's journal entry approximates the cultural expectations of conventional Spanish writing. Nancy now uses the alphabetic hypothesis that governs the Spanish writing system. Collaboratively, she, her peers, and Ms. Mendoza have engaged in using written language authentically. Class members share knowledge about the writing system in actual use and can actively construct their evolving knowledge of this cultural object: written language in Spanish. At this point, Nancy no longer needs to use oral reading to mediate her written responses to the teacher, as she reads the teacher's written message without any oral mediation.

Every time Ms. Mendoza responds to Nancy's journal entry in front of her and the other students, she demonstrates and mediates how all the parts work and function in the whole. By reading the written language aloud, Ms. Mendoza is making visible how meaning (the semantic system), the structure (syntax—word order), the letter/sound correspondences (the graphophonic system) and the conventions of language (the orthographic system) are used to communicate. K. Goodman's (1994) miscue research and sociopsycholinguistic theory show that proficient readers use all the linguistic cueing systems plus the universal reading strategies (predicting, self correcting, comprehending, inferring, terminating) to construct meaning. At this point in Nancy's literacy development in L1 (Spanish), she integrates the use of all the cueing systems and the universal reading strategies. In January, in this social context, she is a proficient reader and writer of Spanish.

February

By February Nancy's sample provides evidence of more experimentation, but still, consistent and conventional use of Spanish orthography. She doesn't represent punctuation yet, but she uses space logically. When she comes to the end of a line and runs out of space, she finishes the word on the next line—"con flore"... (on the next line is the final letter "s" in the word *flores*). She invents the spelling of *Plantas* by adding an additional "a"—"Plaantas." Also notable is that she is using upper and lower case conventionally with only one exception, "Riega." This is an amazing accomplishment for any first grader in the month of February. Ms. Mendoza's authentic written responses are vital to Nancy's evolution and development. She does not write down what Nancy says, but dialogues authentically with her. Ms. Mendoza also demonstrates conventional uses of written and oral language authentically and on a daily basis. As a result, Nancy is socially engaged in using written and oral language to make and receive meaning in a genuine and caring social context. Besides knowledge being shared through social interaction, caring is also mutually exchanged to the benefit of all participants. In fact, when the children in this class were asked what they liked best about interactive journals, they repeatedly said that they liked that the teacher touched each one of them daily, if only for a few minutes.

March

In March Nancy's entry relates to her experiences watching cartoons. She knows that "Chibra" and "Himan" are in English so she puts them in quotation marks! Her invented spellings in English show that she is applying her Spanish orthographic knowledge. She introduces a new word, "Chuchulucos," and intuitively knows that the teacher may not know its meaning because she adds, "Mi ama les dice asi." In each response, Ms. Mendoza centers on the message and relates her experiences to Nancy's message, genuinely sustaining the communication. It is now a dance of synchronicity. For the first time Nancy uses punctuation at the end of her piece. This is a beginning and throughout the rest of the year she continues to experiment and use punctuation appropriately.

April

By April Nancy's development toward conventional writing still has remnants of stylistic choices. Although she does not segment the two words [mi me], "Mime," she definitely has figured out the conventional uses of the graphophonic, syntactic, semantic, and orthographic systems. She uses punctuation and spellings conventionally. Again, Ms. Mendoza responds authentically to Nancy's declaration of liking rainbows by agreeing and adding that many colors make rainbows beautiful. Ms. Mendoza asks a question, "Did you see a rainbow?" and follows it with "I have seen many and I, too, think that they are very beautiful because of their beautiful colors." This extended response values Nancy as a partner in communication.

May

In May Nancy attempts to write in English. She has not been formally taught English, but she has heard it, seen it written, and uses it to communicate with her English speaking classmates. Nancy is in a dual immersion bilingual classroom. where both dominant English speakers and dominant

Spanish speakers are learning each other's languages. However, in this 90/10 model, the majority of instructional time is in Spanish.

By choosing to write in English, Nancy demonstrates that she is now comfortable in making this choice. Remember, she is in a whole-language bilingual classroom where the teacher values experimentation and risk taking. She knows how to read and write in Spanish. Ms. Mendoza also knows how children "come to know" and learn reading and writing in meaningful contexts with the teacher as a deliberate sociocultural mediator (Diaz & Flores, 2001). Thus, it is no surprise that Nancy applies her knowledge of the alphabetic concept in the Spanish language to the alphabetic language of English. She appropriates and applies her L1 (Spanish) schema to her L2 (English).

Nancy's invented spellings in English, are "Mace" for "Make," "Plante" for "Plant," "Fore" for "For," "Mistr" for "Mister," "Whea" for "We," "Forgaret" for "forgot it," and "Flawer" for "Flower." She is using not only the phonetic hypothesis but also visual memory strategies; for example, she uses the silent "e" in "mace" for "make." She overgeneralizes the silent "e" in "plante" and in "fore." Yet for "mister" she leaves out the "e" but in "flawer" she includes it. Also, her word segmentation of "forgaret" is logical. More than half of the words in this English entry are conventional whereas the other words are invented.

From this day forward, Nancy writes in English and in Spanish whenever she chooses. Ms. Mendoza is surprised because she did not formally teach English writing!!! Usually the 10% of English is spent on oral language development.

Based on this evidence, Nancy shows that written language may be used to mediate oral language acquisition in both L1 and L2. Teachers do not need to wait for children to have productive oral control of L2 before using written language in L2 as long as they deliberately mediate. Deliberate mediation means that the teacher knows how and when to support children within their zone of proximal development as Ms. Mendoza did with Nancy.

An important clarification is that Nancy's ability to write in English (L2) does not mean that she must be transitioned into an English-only class. Her growing proficiency in Spanish across different genres must continue to be developed so she can use her knowledge of Spanish and apply it to her use of English. The more proficient she is in Spanish, the better her English will be. Y. Goodman, K. Goodman, and Flores (1979) posit that it is only necessary to learn how to read once and preferably in the mother tongue. As a result, readers use their knowledge about reading in their first language and apply it to their second, third, or fourth language.

IMPLICATIONS

Nancy's writing accomplishments offer opportunities to learn from her and Ms. Mendoza. Throughout the year, Ms. Mendoza meets regularly with her teacher support group. The group members and I mentor and guide each other and continue to develop our pedagogical knowledge from the theoretical frameworks (sociocultural, sociopsycholinguistics, psychogenesis, and sociopolitical) as well as the praxis of theory-in-practice. This collaborative effort enables Ms. Mendoza to organize facilitate, mediate, and evaluate not only Nancy's literacy and biliteracy development, but also the development of all of her classmates.

Nancy's success epitomizes the success of her first grade peers. By the end of April and beginning of May all of Ms. Mendoza's first graders are using the alphabetic concepts that govern both Spanish and English language (Diaz & Flores, 2001; Flores, 1990). They are not afraid to use their Spanish and English biliteracy and bilingualism as a social practice everyday in school (Moll, Saez, & Dorwin, 2001). They are engaging in authentic uses of biliteracy to communicate across time and space.

What does this in-depth study mean for teachers, parents, and administrators? It demonstrates the importance of the teacher's pedagogical knowledge. The implications are profound and show the significance of the praxis of theoretical and pedagogical knowledge in action. They also show that:

1. Bilingual teachers need to know how children learn oral and written language in meaningful classroom contexts so that they may organize the teaching/learning of biliteracy as social practice.
2. Bilingual teachers need to acquire the knowledge from the theoretical frameworks of sociopsycholinguistic, sociopsychogenesis, and sociocultural traditions to teach to children's potential.
3. Bilingual teacher educators need to collaborate with bilingual teachers and district administrators to effectively implement this pedagogical knowledge into practice through long-term professional development.
4. Bilingual teachers need to collaboratively organize social contexts and practices so that children and teachers engage in meaningful oral and written dialogue (Diaz & Flores, 2001; Flores, 1990; Flores & Garcia, 1984; Stanton, 1984).
5. Biliteracy as social practice in school is possible and essential in a multilingual and multicultural world.
6. It is possible for all bilingual children in first grade who are economically poor, who may have physical impairments, or who do not know English, to learn to read and write proficiently in their first and second languages.

The challenge is ours, their teachers, their parents, their administrators, and their school board members. We have the knowledge. *Sí Se Puede!*

REFERENCES

Diaz, E., & Flores, B. (2001). Teacher as sociohistorical, sociocultural mediator: Teaching to the potential. In M. de la Luz Reyes & J. Halcon (Eds.), *The best for our children* (pp. 29–47). New York: Teachers College Press.

Diaz, E., Moll, L., & Mehan, B. (1986). Sociocultural resources in instruction: A context specific approach. In California Department of Education (Ed.), *Beyond language: Social and cultural factors in schooling language minority students* (pp. 186–230). Sacramento: California Department of Education.

Edelsky, C. (1986). *Writing in a bilingual classroom: Habia una vez.* Norwood, NJ: Ablex.

Edelsky, C. & Draper, K. (1986). Reading/"reading;" writing/"writing;" text/"text/". *Reading-Canada-Lecture,* 7, 201–216.

Edelsky, C., Draper, K., & Smith, K. (1983). Hookin' 'em at the start of school in a whole language classroom. *Anthropology and Education Quarterly, 14*(4), 135–156.

Edelsky, C., & Gilbert, K. (1985). Writing of bilingual children: Lessons for all of us. *Volta Review, 84*(5), 57–74.

Ferreiro, E., & Gomez Palacios, M. (1982). *Nuevas perspectives sobre los procesos de lectura y escritura.* Mexico: Siglo XXI (1982).

Ferreiro, E., & Teberosky, A. (1979). *Los sistemas de escritura en el desarrollo de los ninos.* Mexico: Siglo XXI.

Ferreiro, E., & Teberosky, A. (1982). *Literacy before schooling.* Portsmouth, NH: Heinemann.

Flores, B. (1990). The sociopsychogenesis of literacy and biliteracy. In *Proceedings of the First Research Symposium of the Office of Bilingual Education and Minority Language Affairs* (pp. 281–320). Washington, DC: U.S. Department of Education.

Flores, B., & Garcia, E. (1984). A collaborative learning and teaching experience using journal writing. *National Association of Bilingual Education Journal, 8*(3), 67–83.

Freire, P. (1970). *Pedagogy of the oppressed.* New York: Herder and Herder.

Freire, P., & Macedo, D. (1987). *Literacy: Reading the word & the world.* South Hadley, MA: Bergin & Garvey.

Goodman, K. (1994). Reading, writing, and written texts; A transactional sociopsycholinguistic view. In R. B. Ruddell, M.R. Ruddell, & H. Singer (Eds.), *Theoretical models and processes of reading* (pp. 1093–1130). Newark, DE: International Reading Association.

Goodman, K. (1996). *On Reading.* Portsmouth, NH: Heinemann.

Goodman, K. & Goodman, Y. (1979). Learning to read is natural. In L. B. Resnick & P. A. Weaver (Eds.), *Theory and practice of early reading* (pp. 137–155). Hillsdale, NJ: Lawrence Erlbaum Associates.

Goodman, Y. (1980). The roots of literacy. In M. P. Douglass (Ed.), *Claremont Reading Conference forty-fourth yearbook* (pp. 1–32). Claremont, CA: Claremont Reading Conference.

Goodman, Y. (Ed.). (1990). *How children construct literacy: Piagetian perspectives.* Newark, NJ: International Reading Association.

Goodman, K., Goodman, Y., & Flores, B. (1979). *Reading in a bilingual classroom: Literacy and biliteracy.* Rosslyn, VA: National Clearinghouse for Bilingual Education.

Halliday, M. A. K., (1975). *Learning how to mean: Explorations in the development of language.* London: Edward Arnold.

Halliday, M. A. K., (1978). *Language as social semiotic.* Baltimore, MD: University Park Press.

Harste, J., Woodard, V., & Burke, C. (1984). *Language stories and literacy lessons.* Portsmouth, NH: Heinemann.

Hudelson, S. (1981–1982). An investigation of children's invented spelling in Spanish. *National Association of Bilingual Education Journal, 9*, 53–68.
Milz, V. (1980, Summer). First graders can write: Focus on communication. *Theory into Practice*, pp. 179–185.
Moll, L., Saez, R., & Dorwin, J. (2001). Exploring biliteracy: Two students case examples of writing as a social practice. *The Elementary School Journal*, *101*, 435–449.
Stanton, J. (1984). Thinking together: Language interaction in children's reasoning. In C. Thaiss & C. Suhor (Eds.), *Speaking and writing, K–12: classroom strategies and new research* (pp. 144–187). Urbana, IL: National Council of Teachers of English.
Vygotsky, L. (1978). *Mind in society: The development of higher psychological process.* Cambridge, MA: Harvard University Press.

Chapter 4

Eye Movement and Strategic Reading

Koomi Kim, Marge Knox, and Joel Brown

As we visit in primary classrooms, we occasionally hear teachers say to their students, "Just read more carefully"; "Look at the word"; "Sound it out"; or "What letter does the word begin with?" Recently researchers engaging in eye movement and miscue analysis studies found that instruction that focuses children on looking at letters and words and sounding out is contrary to what is being discovered (Duckett, 2001; Paulson & Freeman, 2003). Documenting what readers' eyes actually look at while they are reading orally provides information that has previously been unavailable to the teacher.

Consider this example from a second grader reading the following text: *One evening when he came home from work, he said to his wife, "What do you do all day while I am away cutting wood?"* Her miscues show that she makes several attempts at *One evening*. She reads: *on every, one every, when ev-, one everythi-, $eve(r)y-ing, $every-hing*... She spends time on ***One evening*** and then goes silent, her eyes proceeding forward across the sentence, then returning to the beginning of the sentence, she reads confidently: "One evening when he came home from work..." (see Figure 4.1).

The reader shows her concern for making sense. Her problem solving as shown by her miscues and her eye movements requires strategic thinking, knowing where to search for additional information.

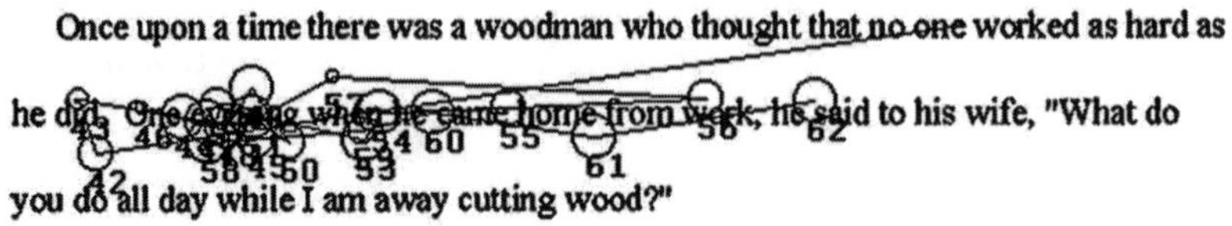

Figure 4.1. Eye movements of a second grader reading *The Man Who Kept House*.

In this article, we report on eye movement and miscue analysis (EMMA) research that documents young children's reading strategies and their construction of meaning to provide answers to the following questions:

- Do readers look ahead as they read?
- Do readers sample text as they read?
- What information do readers use to self-correct?
- Is it okay to skip words and to orally repeat or look back over a text?
- Does the meaning a reader brings to a text relate to the ease with which the text is read?

EYE MOVEMENT AND MISCUE ANALYSIS RESEARCH

To provide answers to the preceding questions, we focus on data from two 8-year-old English language learners. The first reader shows strategy use in reading a short passage called *The Boat in the Basement* (K. Goodman, 1996); the second reader transacts simultaneously with two interwoven semiotic systems, music and a text. We show the relationships between reading strategies, such as sampling, inferring, predicting, integrating and confirming or disconfirming, and eye movements. We explore how EMMA research contributes to understanding the strategies readers apply in their meaning construction.

Eye Movement Data Collection

We collect and record eye movement data using an eye tracking camera, a processing computer, and a computer that displays the texts being read. The camera is calibrated to a reader's left eye to record eye movement. These data are processed to display *fixation points* and *saccades*. A fixation point is a point at which the eye stops, and is the only time during which there is information available to the reader, including information in the reader's peripheral vision. Only four to six letters are in focus to the reader at a fixation point. A saccade is when the eye moves between fixations. During saccades no information is available to the reader; the text is simply a blur. An audio record is made of each reading.

Research Texts

We use three texts: *The Boat in the Basement* (K. Goodman, 1996), *The Little Overcoat* (Y. Goodman, 1998), and *I'm the King of the Mountain* (Cowley, 1993).

To familiarize readers with EMMA and our procedure, we use the short passage, *The Boat in the Basement.* This text was created by K. Goodman with embedded errors to give teachers and student teachers experience in critically examining the perceptual nature of the reading process as well as how readers make use of their language and reading strategies (Gollasch 1980; Kim, Goodman, Xu, & Gollasch, in press; Xu, 1998). In eye movement research we discovered that this passage uniquely underscores the significance of the findings of over 40 years of miscue analysis research (Brown, Goodman, & Marek, 1996).

For readers both reading written text and sight-singing musical notations we used *I'm the King of the Mountain* (Cowley, 1993) and *The Little Overcoat* (Y. Goodman, 1998) for musical eye movement miscue analysis (MEMMA). The melody of *I'm the King of the Mountain* is structured on what is referred to by Bernstein (1976) as the universal melody. According to Bernstein, singing games around the world use the same two notes (E and G) extended to a pattern of three notes (E, G, and A).

The Little Overcoat (Y. Goodman, 1998) is a traditional folk tale. The story involves a predictable text that begins with an overcoat that slowly is rendered into smaller and smaller pieces of clothing until nothing is left but a song.

Readers and Singers

Julie and Janna studied music in their school for 2 years with the Opening Minds through the Arts (OMA) program in Tucson, AZ (Rinehart, 2004). For this study they each read *The Boat in the Basement* before reading and singing *I'm the King of the Mountain* and *The Little Overcoat.* We show how Julie transacted with *The Boat in the Basement* and then how Janna transacted with the other two texts.

Julie

Julie is proficient in both Portuguese and English and her family is conscientious about providing her with a broad range of educational experiences. Julie's mother brought her to the EMMA lab, observed our work, and discussed her view of reading with us.

We asked Julie to read *The Boat in the Basement* and as soon as she finished, we took the text off the screen. Then we asked her to retell the story.

Her retelling was comprehensive and detailed. "The woman was building a boat, and she found out the boat was too big to go through the door. So, she should have planned it ahead." We asked Julie: "How did the woman solve the problem?" Julie replied, "She had to take it apart." Figure 4.2 shows Julie's eye movements while she was reading the text.

What does Julie's reading show? First, it is important to keep in mind that the reader does not see any written text information during saccades, only the fixations points provide print information to the reader. Each fixation point (shown by a dot) indicates where Julie's eyes were fixated. Julie made 56 fixations (#3-#58) and they are not of equal duration. The varied size of each dot indicates how long her eyes fixated at that particular place - the larger the dot, the longer the duration of the fixation. Her average fixation was .56 seconds, her shortest fixation was .15 and her longest was 1.22. She does not fixate on every word. She skips function words, *in, when*, *the*, *it*, *to*, and *so*.

Julie fixated on 22 content words (e.g., woman, boat, she, boot) and 11 function words (e.g., a, the, to, etc.). Julie does not fixate on every letter nor on every word, and she knows that content words provide more information than function words.

Discussion of Text Errors

When we asked Julie if she remembered any "errors" in the story, she told us that she remembered two. She said "he for she, and the other one is a comma." She was able to name only one of the six errors embedded in the text: *he* for *she*.

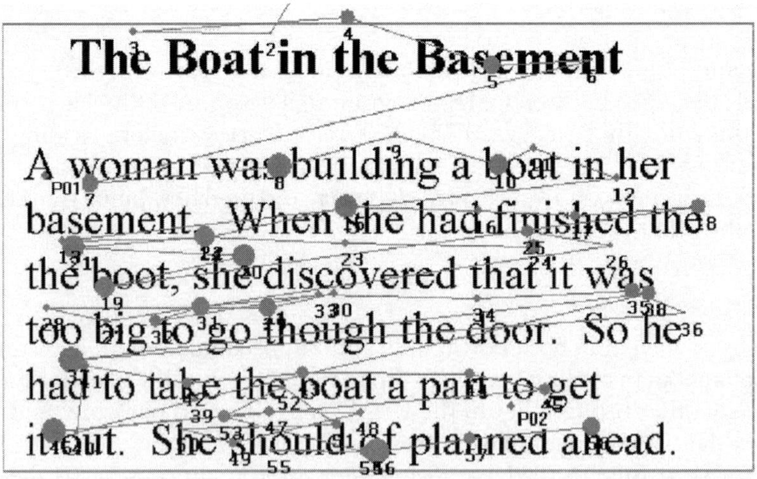

Figure 4.2. Julie's first reading of *The Boat in the Basement* with fixation points.

Although Julie fixated on *boot*, she only fixated on one *the*. She made repeated fixations on *should,* and spent long duration times on *of* and *though*, but she did not report these as errors. Rather, she read *boat* for b-o-o-t and *through* for t-h-o-u-g-h. In her retelling, we found that she reported many of the words as if the text were written conventionally. "The woman was building a *boat*, and she found out the boat was too big to go *through* the door." When we asked Julie how the woman had solved the problem, she said, "She had to take it *apart*." Her retelling shows that she was reading five out of the six text discrepancies "correctly." She demonstrated her knowledge by "perceiving" the embedded errors conventionally in her attempt to transact with text and efficiently construct meaning.

We encouraged Julie to read *The Boat in the Basement* a second time. We invited her to look for "errors." The fixation points for the second reading are presented in Figure 4.3. Julie made 48 fixations, 8 fewer than the 56 she made for the first reading. Also, the average fixation point duration time for the second reading was shorter (0.462 seconds) than for the first reading (0.506 seconds). After this second reading we gave Julie unlimited time to search for the errors.

This time Julie detected one more error than she had after her first reading. She pointed out, "It says 'boot' instead of 'boat.' Can I repeat the same one I mentioned before? It says *he* instead of *she*." As we mentioned, Julie fixated on *should of, though*, and *a part*, although she did not report these as errors in the story. She also did not fixate on "*the*" words, although she read the words (see Figure 4.3).

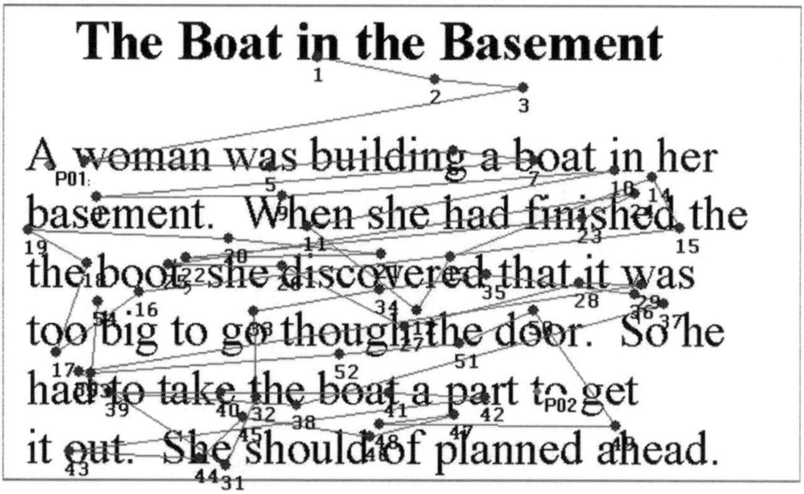

Figure 4.3. Julie's second reading of *The Boat in the Basement* with fixation points.

Julie made a number of regressions. For example, she produced a regression when she repeated "the boat" (Figure 4.4). Julie read the portion as "take the boat the boat apart" while her eyes were making a regression.

Other regressions did not result in repetition. Her eyes made regressions but she did not orally repeat the words. For example, she made a regression in reading the text portion: "she should *of.*" When she read it for the first time, she read it as "*should of.*" The second time however, Julie read distinctly "*should have,*" disconfirming the printed text (see Figure 4.5) as she substituted "*should have.*"

We asked Julie to take a look at the second sentence in the text to find an error other than *boot.* We decided to see what information Julie needed to detect the two "*the*" words in the text. She did not *perceive* the two *the* words, and she did not detect them even when she was instructed to "look closely" at the words in the sentence. In order to remove her intuitive sense of grammar to reject two *the*'s, we asked her to read the sentence backwards, word by word. When she did this, she detected the second "*the.*"

Gollasch (1980) and Xu (1998) also found in their research with older readers that the priority for readers is to construct meaning even when explicitly instructed to detect errors. Julie helped us understand that reading is a perceptual process by demonstrating, as Gollasch and Xu each found, that readers' first concern is to construct meaning, even when they are instructed to look for errors.

Janna

Janna was born and raised in China and had been in the United States for a little over two years when she read for us. She had minimal exposure to English and little experience with music prior to moving to the United States; however, through her participation in a music program at her

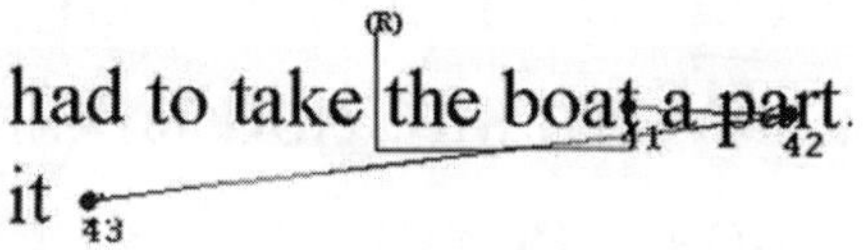

Figure 4.4. Repetition miscue accompanied by a regression.

Figure 4.5. Regression not resulting in repetition miscue.

school, she became highly proficient and competent in her use of English and her musicianship.

Janna's mother was present at our EMMA session. A sight-singing interview (Knox, 2003), based on the Burke Reading Interview (Goodman, Watson, & Burke, 2005), provided background information about Janna's views of music and their relationship to language. In Janna's words, "A big part of me learning to speak English was Mr. John [music teacher] and an English teacher. When they taught me the words and when I heard music, I could just use the words and express my own feeling."

Janna read two complete stories followed by sight-singing at the end of each story: *I'm the King of the Mountain* and *The Little Overcoat*. In both cases, the story was read first, followed by the sight-singing. She had not seen the books or the songs before.

Janna's reading of *I'm the King of the Mountain* contained minimal miscues. There is a repetitive phrase embedded throughout the story and in the music, "I'm the King of the Mountain, I'm the King of the Mountain." Although there was no indication or musical prompts within the written text that the phrases could or should be sung, each time the repetitive phrases occurred Janna sang them with exactly the same pitch, melodic contour, and flowing voice. Her eye movements were sporadic within the text as she created a flowing rhythm and made inferences and predictions about the text she read.

She then sang the song at the end of the story exactly as it should sound musically with the exception of one note. However, when Janna sight-sang the two repetitive musical phrases at the end of the story, she concentrated on the melody line with more hesitation and was slower reading the melody than when the same text phrases were embedded within the story. Her eye movements were more self-controlled at the end of the story sight-singing the song.

Underpinning her use of language, when reading written text, was a natural intuitive sense of the connection between language and music, a declamative rendering of music that supports text. In Janna's words, "I just made up my own music." A possible implication from her rendering a melody without the musical notations in the written text is that she involved her sense of what is referred to by Bernstein (1976) earlier as the universal melody.

Our findings substantiate that sight-singing utilizes the same processes and strategies as the reading of written text. The cueing systems, the cognitive strategies, and the learning cycles are the same; in other words, text reading strategies also apply to reading musical text.

Janna first read *The Little Overcoat* and then sight-sang the melody. Three of Janna's miscues are discussed next. Janna produced a partial miscue when she vocalized the beginning of a pitch and word, then sang the whole tone and word as shown in Figure 4.6.

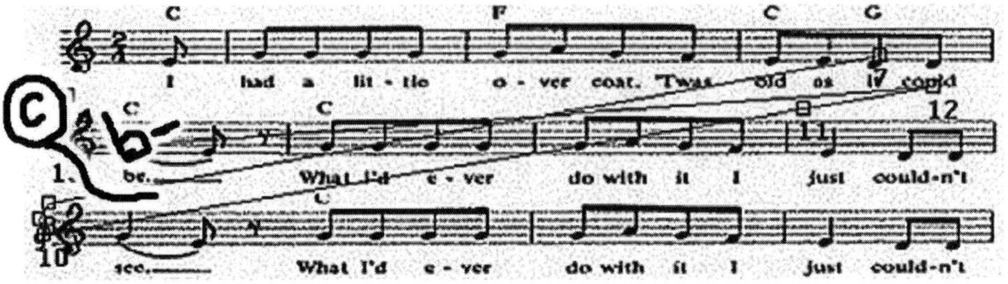

Figure 4.6. Janna's partial note and self-correction.

Figure 4.6 shows Janna's eye fixations as she sang a partial note and partial word, *be* (the fixation point number 7 at the end of musical line 1 and 8–10 at the beginning of musical line 3). She regressed back from musical line 3 to the end of musical line 1 (fixations 11, 12), then returned to fixation 13 at the beginning of musical line 2. She then corrected the partial note and word. It is possible that these rhyming words and their placement on the musical lines caused complications for Janna. However, this example clearly shows that the singer/reader integrates her background knowledge as she transacts with written and musical text to construct meaning. She searches graphic cues, both text and musical notations, to help her infer and predict the melodic patterns. She uses the strategy of confirming/disconfirming to correct the partial text sound and musical text.

Another example of a miscue is the omission of a complete phrase, both musically and textually. Janna first sang the phrase *What I'd ever do with it, I just couldn't see*, then omitted the repeated phrase, *What I'd ever do with it, I just couldn't see* (Figure 4.7).

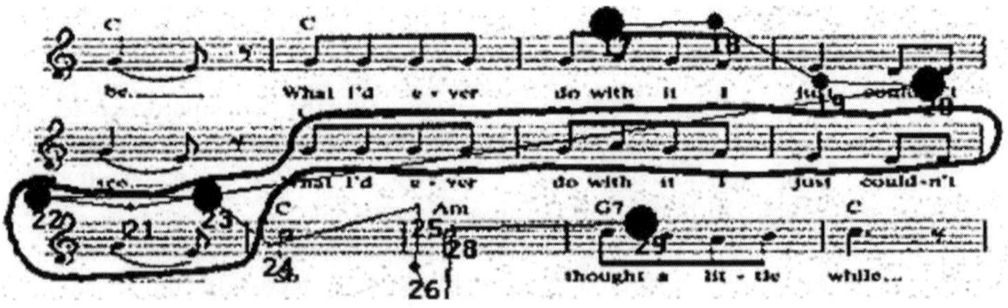

Figure 4.7. Janna's omission of a textual phrase and musical phrase.

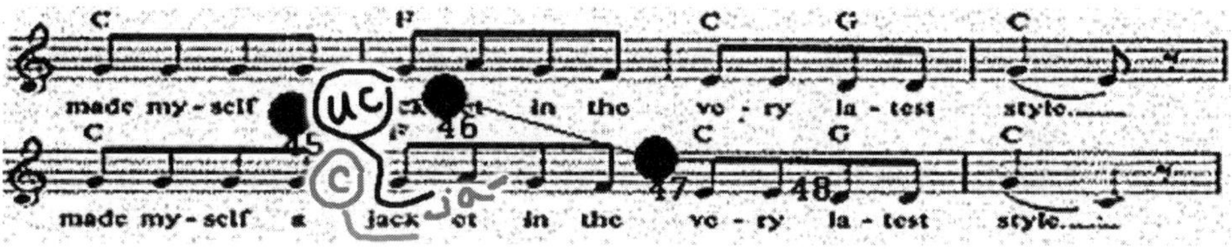

Figure 4.8. Janna's unsuccessful attempt to correct a musical notation.

This omission could be caused by Janna predicting a change in melody rather than a repetition of a phrase. The omission did not create change in meaning of the text or the melody. Janna did not disconfirm or self-correct this particular miscue omission because it did not cause any disruption of text or melodic change.

An unsuccessful attempt to correct (UC) a musical note is shown in Figure 4.8. Janna's eye fixations in this example are above the melody line, thus above the syllable and the note *G* (45). This placement of eye fixations continues above the melody line above the note *A* (46), between *the* and *ve-* (47) on the melody line, then on *E* on the melody line (48). During these eye fixations with no regressions, Janna substituted the note *B* in the original melody for the note *G* while singing the correct written text—*jă.* She then made a second substitution of the note *G* with a lower note of *A*, creating an unsuccessful attempt to correct the pitch to *G*.

Janna's Sight-Singing Using Two Semiotic Systems

Research by Knox (2003) on sight-singing and Levy (2001) on instruments for sight reading music concludes that adolescent readers/singers (sight singers) of music are engaged in the same process described by the Goodman model of reading (K. Goodman, 1996). EMMA research shows that young children such as Janna with at least 2 years of elementary musical experiences display the same processes and strategies as older sight-singers.

CONCLUSIONS AND FINAL THOUGHTS FROM OUR RESEARCH

Eye movement and miscue analysis (EMMA) research with young children provides answers for the questions we raised at the beginning of this chapter.

- Do readers look ahead as they read? Readers gain information by looking ahead. They spend varied intervals of time in different parts of a text. At times they gather more information (e.g., looking ahead in written text or musical notations or at illustrations), and at times they decide they don't need all the print information (skipping words, phrases and musical notations) that the text provides. They often orally read what they do not fixate on. Readers' voices follow the text sequentially while their eyes are moving sporadically across lines and from line to line. Readers of music also show similar strategies.

- Do readers sample text as they read? Readers' eyes often seek further information than what is available at the point of the difficulty. They move ahead to gather additional context or regress to previous parts of the text selectively. Readers' eyes often go beyond where their voice is. This also happens in musical text.
- What information do readers use to self-correct? Readers of written and musical texts use the strategies of scanning, inferring, predicting, confirming, correcting, and integrating. They use the three language cueing systems (graphophonics, syntax, and semantics) in an integrated way together with their contextual knowledge. Readers' substitutions, omissions, insertions, and corrections are indicators of the processes and strategies they use in reading. Musical miscues provide evidence of the same strategies.
- Is it okay to skip words and to orally repeat or look back over a text? Readers skip words orally, visually, and musically, especially when these behaviors maintain the structure of the written or musical text. Readers skip selected words and phrases, may repeat (oral repetition) and look back over text (regression). These strategies are helpful to readers in their construction of meaning. Self-correction, omissions, regressions, and repetitions have important implications for teachers and reading instruction. These strategies need to be understood and accepted in practice. And teachers should discuss with readers when such strategies are most helpful.
- Does the meaning a reader brings to a text relate to the ease with which it is read? Readers bring prior understandings about the structure and content of a written or musical text to their reading and, whether intuitive or learned, the reading is facilitated and therefore easier.

As a result of the EMMA research we report in this chapter and other EMMA and miscue analysis research, we expand on the answers to our original questions. Our two informants are young second-language learners. Second-language learners, as well as readers of languages other than English of all ages, utilize cognitive psycholinguistic strategies in similar ways. (Gollasch, 1980; Knox, 2003; Paulson & Freeman, 2003). The strategic nature of the reading process has been confirmed across languages through miscue analysis (Hudleson, 1981; Sloboda, 1984).

Readers, regardless of their ages, language background, or use of semiotic systems, utilize cognitive reading strategies and their language cueing systems to construct meaning while transacting with any form of written text. EMMA research contributes in important ways to knowledge about the role of eye movements during reading and adds to the understanding of reading as a sociopsycholinguistic, transactional, and meaning-making process.

The evidence we have presented clearly shows that young readers, including sociolinguistically and culturally diverse readers, are active constructors of reading as a meaning-making process. Young readers are cogenerators of text while transacting with authors. Meaningful reading instruction for young children must reflect such a view of reading.

REFERENCES

Bernstein, L. (1976). *The unanswered question: Six talks at Harvard*. Cambridge, MA: Harvard University Press.

Brown, J., Goodman, K., & Marek, A. (1996). *Studies in miscue analysis: An annotated bibliography*. Newark, DE: International Reading Association.

Cowley, J. (1993). *I'm the king of the mountain*. New York: Richard C. Owen.

Duckett, P. (2001). *First grade beginning readers' use of pictures and print as they read: A miscue analysis and eye movement study*. Unpublished doctoral dissertation, University of Arizona, Tucson.

Gollasch, F. (1980). *Readers' perception in detecting and processing embedded errors in meaningful text*. Unpublished doctoral dissertation. University of Arizona, Tucson.

Goodman, K. (1996). *On reading: A common-sense look at the nature of language and the science of reading*. Portsmouth, NH: Heinemann.

Goodman, Y. T. (1998). *The little overcoat*. Greenvale, NY: Mondo.

Goodman, Y., Watson, D., & Burke, C. (2005). *Reading miscue inventory: From evaluation to instruction*. Katonah, NY: Richard C. Owen.

Hudelson, S. (Ed). (1981). *Learning to read in different languages. Linguistics and literacy, series no. 1*. Washington, DC: Center for Applied Linguistics, Papers in Applied Linguistics. (ERIC Document Reproduction Service No. ED 198 744)

Kim, K., Goodman, Y., Xu, J., & Gollasch, F. (In press). A comparison of Chinese and English perceptions of embedded errors in written texts. In A. Flurkey & E. Paulson, & K. Goodman (Eds.), *Scientific realism in studies of reading*. Mahwah, NJ: Lawrence Erlbaum Associates.

Knox, M. (2003). *Reading music and written text: The process of sight-singing*. Unpublished doctoral dissertation, University of Arizona, Tucson.

Levy, K. (2001). *Music readers and notation: Investigation of an interactive model of reading*. Unpublished doctoral dissertation, University of Iowa, Ames.

Paulson, E., & Freeman, A. (2003). *Insight from the eyes: The science of effective reading instruction*. Portsmouth, NH: Heinemann.

Rinehart, C. (2004, November). Curtain call. *Neatoday*, pp. 20–29.

Sloboda, J.A. (1984). Experimental studies of music reading: A review. *Music Perception, 2*(2), 222–236.

Xu, J. (1998). *A study of the reading process in Chinese through detecting errors in a meaningful text*. Unpublished doctoral dissertation, University of Arizona, Tucson.

Chapter **5**

Letters and Numbers in Early Literacy

Emilia Ferreiro

As an introduction to letters and numbers in early literacy, it seems appropriate to present some general comments concerning the ideas that continue to guide my own research on literacy development. The aim of these remarks is to clarify my unique way of looking at literacy development, which allowed me, from the very beginning, to put in evidence some hidden facts that no natural observations could show, whether they be natural observations in classrooms or in family settings.

In the second part of the chapter, I present the results of a recent research project that lead to unexpected results, as unexpected as those of 20 years ago (Ferreiro & Teberosky, 1982), when colleagues and I studied the actions of young children in response to tasks about reading and writing. These results exemplify why I still believe in the importance of presenting specific challenges to young children in order to understand, through their actions and their comments, how they conceive our world of written signs.

No one can embrace all the cultural, sociological, psychological, and educational aspects related to literacy development. A methodological requirement of any research design consists of specifying research questions and finding appropriate ways to answer them. My research questions are not school-based questions. I am not interested in conventional knowledge—that is, right answers; I am not designing situations that could help children to improve their school performance. Some of my former students and collaborators are doing this, and I am proud of their work. However, the results I show have educational implications, as does all the research I have done during more than 20 years of searching in this field. The focus of my interest is to know how children conceive of written language, how they relate it to oral language, how they construct conceptual frames to grasp the structure of written marks and of written discourse.

INTRODUCTORY REMARKS

What does it mean to adopt a constructivist view of literacy development? It is, of course, a developmental view. But to establish a developmental pathway is not enough. The aim of a constructivist position is to show in what way acquisitions that correspond to a time 1 (T1) state (the very beginnings) of knowledge are related to the following states of knowledge at T2, T3.... Inversely, from a given state of knowledge, for instance at T3, the aim is to identify in what way the preceding acquisitions explain those acquisitions that appear at T3. Of course, it is not a state of knowledge that explains a subsequent state of knowledge. We are talking about a process and the intention is to grasp the dynamics of such a process. If everything is conceived to be preformed at time1, we are not in a constructivist interpretation, but in a nativist one.

A cognitive system is an open system in a social context, in permanent interaction with other persons and objects socially situated. However, these external influences cannot act by themselves. In order to act inside the cognitive system they always need to be incorporated, that is, interpreted by the psychological subject. This is the very deep meaning of the Piagetian concept of *assimilation*. If these external influences are conceived to act directly, without internal interpretation, we are in an empiricist position.

Children try to make sense of the print they encounter in various objects in their surroundings. They try also to make sense of the literacy events in which they participate. To understand that written marks are related to oral language is impossible outside specific social interactions where reading aloud takes place. However, reading aloud (and even phonic instruction) is meaningless unless an internal activity of the cognitive subject gives meaning to it.

Every individual history of literacy is, in a sense, singular. However, if we can find similar milestones during the development across various school traditions, across various social ways of being literate, across related and even nonrelated languages, and so on—what does it mean? It does not mean that we are confronting a biologically guided process. The opposition between biologically and socially guided processes is a false dilemma, at least in the case of literacy. It is not the case of denying some species-specific capabilities, but illiteracy among adults shows that it is not enough to belong to a literate society in order to become a literate person. To become a literate person means to acquire some socially defined skills sharing the values and meanings associated to it but it signifies, at the same time, to construct specific knowledge about the conceptual object that we call "written language." The ways to construct new specific knowledge are common to all human beings during their development and express some constraints the cognitive system imposes on the object in order to assimilate it. But, in turn, the resistance of the object to a distorted assimilation generates changes in the cognitive system, modifying sometimes the structure and always the content. A constructivist position is an interactive one and a dialectical one.

Constructivism acknowledges that literacy is a way of behaving in society, of assuming social positions related to social power and control. In this respect, we cannot deny that "to make sense of print" is not enough, because there is a socially validated way of defining the meaning of the verbs "to read" and "to write" in individual terms, and this social definition is related, in turn, to school failure or school success.

During their development, children learn about functions of literacy in society. I do not have proof that ideas about function are psychogenetically ordered. However, I know that some ideas related to function are particularly hard to grasp because they are linked to the understanding of social institutions: for instance, the idea of authorship as different from the idea of publisher.

To learn about functions and social values attached to print is, no doubt, very important. However, we cannot forget that any written text has precise graphic properties, and these graphic properties are also the object of children's inquiries. A written text is composed of a limited set of marks that are linearly ordered, and the distribution of the marks is not haphazard. For a written string to be an English, a Spanish, or a French text, it is not enough to share "the same alphabet." Some specific ways of composition need to be followed.

These ways of composition include the frequency of the use of letters; the estimated optimal length of the strings; combinations of letters allowed or prohibited at the beginning or at the end of a string; presence or absence of diacritic marks; distribution of upper case and lower case letters; and specific letter/sound values (Ferreiro, 2002). For instance, the written words "nation" and "constitution", in isolation, do not discriminate between English and French; when the context is provided and the decision is made, the corresponding letter/sound values are very different.

I discovered that children inquire about *formal* characteristics of writing well before specific instruction. These inquiries lead to conceptualizations that allow the organization of the data, the construction of several restrictions related to the conditions that a given string needs to fill in order to be "good for reading," and many other cognitive functions that I deal with elsewhere (Ferreiro, 1991, 1994). These conceptualizations are organized into a sequence that follows a psychogenetic pathway, independent of the evolution of ideas about the social functions of the system. Children are attentive to the forms of the letters used in their specific language environment but, at the same time, they start their way into literacy by discovering general principles that apply to any writing system (i.e., the linear organization of the letter's forms, internal variation of forms, limited number of forms in a given string).

A RESEARCH EXAMPLE

We have carried out quite a few research studies to understand how small children deal with the interpretation of written strings of letters and how they produce writing. Other researchers were more interested in the interpretation and production of numbers (Hughes, 1986; Sinclair, 1988). I found that it was time to put both things together, because the same child, at the same time, is solicited both by the environment and by school requirements to deal with letters and numbers.

We use the same verbs "to read" and "to write" for both kinds of marks, in spite of the fact that letters and numbers belong to very different writing systems. We use letters to write in an alphabetic writing system (in fact, this system is not entirely alphabetic in nature, but this is not the main point here). We use numbers to write in a system that is entirely ideographic. For instance, the written word *five* cannot be read as *cinco*. If I say "cinco" I am translating an English word into a Spanish word. On the contrary, the written sign *5* can be read "five", "cinco", "cinq", "cinque", and so on, without translation. The written sign *5* is an ideogram, not a logogram, not an alphabetic sign.

In what follows, it is important to keep in mind that numbers are written marks that belong to an ideographic writing system. Numbers are also conceptual entities with specific arithmetic properties. In addition, numbers could be named, and word numbers are part of the oral language. As linguistic entities, numbers have properties that do not follow from their arithmetic properties. For instance, English and French use a number system with 10 as a basis; in spite of this, French number names show evidences of a 20 basis: 80 is *quatre-vingt* = 4 times 20.

Usually, the names of the first digits are unpredictable. After 10 we found in English —as well as in Spanish —a small series with a peculiar final morpheme: The series of the *-teen* in English goes from 13 to 19; the series of the final *-ce* in Spanish goes from 12 to 15. At a given point in the series—from 16 on, in Spanish, and after 20, in English—number names become predictable. Knowing the names of the so-called "round numbers" (20, 30, 40,...), any number name inside these intervals is predictable (32, 43,...) because the compound names are formed following definite rules. The compound numbers show, in their very names, what is "inside" them (forty-six = "forty" and "six", etc.).

These regular numbers' words are "transparent". We may say that they exhibit *transparency*, a property that many other number names do not have ("eleven", for instance, is not transparent). In fact, transparency is not a property of the first numbers, in the order of counting (Nunes & Bryant, 1996).

We need also to take into account that numbers are used in our society for many purposes, some of them completely alien to the conceptual nature of the number system—for instance, numbers in the cars' identification plates, telephone numbers, and so on.

By far, the largest part of the research on number acquisition has been focused on the logic-mathematic aspects (Kamii, 1985; Piaget & Szeminska, 1941) or on the evolution of graphic resources for representing quantities. We decided to ask 4- to 5-year-old children to deal with number words outside a quantitative or a counting context, in order to focus on numbers as names. A student of mine, Monica Alvarado, took as a subject for her PhD thesis this very problem and in what follows I present some of the data she obtained thanks to her remarkable abilities to engage in dialogue with young children.

A familiar situation was proposed: to compose a list of "emergency phone numbers." In such a list any adult will use letters for the owners of the telephone numbers and numbers for the telephones. All the 4- to 5-year-old children in our sample did exactly the same.

The list was composed of five names (firemen, police, hospital, pizzas, mechanic) followed by telephone numbers with six digits each, organized in pairs according to the traditional way of "saying" telephone numbers in the country at the time of the research (see Figure 5.1). Names and numbers were dictated as they are written in an address book, for instance, "firemen, 36, 11, 25" (in Spanish: "*bomberos, treintaiseis, once, veinticinco*").

- Bomberos (Firemen)	**36** 11 **25**
- Policía (Policemen)	15 **82** 20
- Hospital (Hospital)	**18** 04 40
- Pizzas (Pizzas)	14 **39** **93**
- Mecánico (Mechanic)	12 **57** **63**

Figure 5.1. List of names and phone numbers dictated.

It is evident that we were not expecting right answers. In educational terms, our proposal seems to make no sense. However, it does exactly what we did years ago when we transformed the traditional question "What words do you learn how to write?" into the opposite request: "I know that nobody taught you how to write *butterfly* (or any other noun) but I am sure that you have some ideas about the way to write it." In understanding literacy development, the data obtained from asking children "to write what they haven't yet been taught to write" turned out to be crucial. We assume that something similar happens with the numbers. That is why we decided to ask children to write compound numbers (beyond the digits). This is the challenge we present to small children.

The list of two-digit numbers includes eight transparent name numbers (36, 25, 82, 18, 39, 93, 57, 63) and six nontransparent ones (11, 15, 20, 40, 14, 12). It included also a pair that was dictated as isolated numbers (04). All of the telephone numbers have one or two transparent number names, but never three.

Monica Alvarado interviewed each child individually. Why individual interviews? The crucial data item is not the piece of writing by itself but the process of writing with all the gestures and verbalizations that took place before, during and after the accomplishment of the task. In fact, with young children we never use an isolated piece of writing as sufficient evidence. Data, at these ages, must include: (a) the initial intentions; (b) the process of writing in all details; and (c) the justification—that is, the reading made by the child once she or he estimates that the task was completed.

Why did we choose a list instead of another kind of text? At the beginning of their literacy process, children could analyze isolated nouns better than statements. A coherent list is the best type of text in order to observe high levels of analytic performance at these ages. A list of nouns and a list of numbers were necessary in order to compare the conceptual levels about the writing system, already well known, with the performance with numbers. For that reason, children were selected according to definite criteria.

The study population consisted of 25 Mexican preschool children (boys and girls, average age 5 years, 2 months) attending two different middle-class schools in the city of Queretaro, the capital city of a state with the same name. The 25 children were not selected at random; we looked for 5 children at each of the levels indicated in Figure 5.2. In this table, and in what follows, "Syllabic 1" means children who write one letter for each syllable (quantitative correspondence), but any letter for any syllable (absence of qualitative correspondence); "Syllabic 2" refers to children who present both quantitative and qualitative correspondence. It is important to note that the presyllabic period covers a very large period of time. In fact, we chose children that were at the upper level of that period. That means that all of them were able to control the quantity of letters for a given name and

Age and writing level of interviewed children

Writing level	Number of children	Mean Age
Pre-syllabic	5	4;10
Syllabic 1	5	5;1
Syllabic 2	5	4;10
Syllabic-alphabetic	5	5;3
Alphabetic	5	5;6
Total	**25**	**5;2**

Figure 5.2. Age and writing level of interviewed children.

they all looked for a different combination of letters to write different names. The examples that follow help to understand it.

As I said before, each telephone number was a mixture of "transparent" and "nontransparent" word numbers. All children were sensitive to this dimension but they did not find the same solutions to the problem. For that reason, it is convenient to pay attention to the "transparency" variable when dealing with each example. In what follows, the analysis of each case replicates a previous publication (Alvarado & Ferreiro, 2002).

ANALYSIS OF CHILDREN REPRESENTATIVE OF EACH GROUP

Julian

Julian is 4 years and 8 months old (see Figure 5.3). He knows how to write his own name and also his age. He uses very few letter forms to write all the nouns; however, he never repeats a letter inside a given string and he never repeats a combination of letters in the same order to write different nouns (qualitative variations under control). He always uses four letters except on one occasion, where he uses five (he fixes the quantity of letters to concentrate on qualitative variations). It is a typical advanced presyllabic production and, as expected, the reading aloud is nonanalytic—that is, the word is not segmented into oral pieces and the pointing is continuous, without stops.

On the contrary, the writing of transparent numbers is more analytic. In the case of all transparent numbers, Julian wrote first the number that he was able to identify in the number's name (that corresponds in fact to the

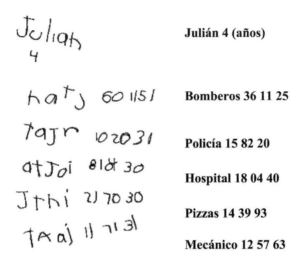

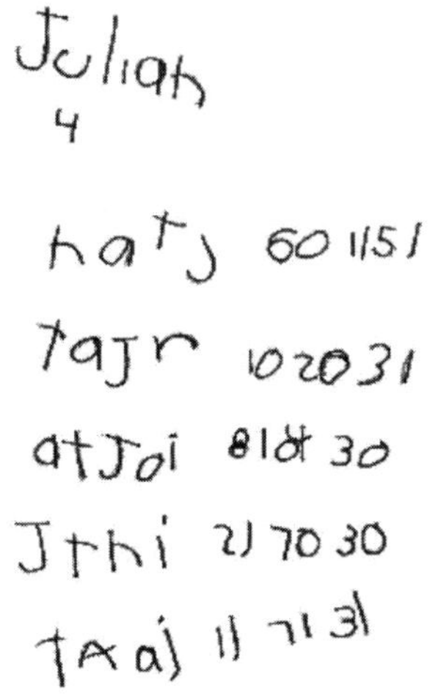

Julián 4 (años)

Bomberos 36 11 25

Policía 15 82 20

Hospital 18 04 40

Pizzas 14 39 93

Mecánico 12 57 63

Figure 5.3. Julian's productions—presyllabic.

units), and the numbers he wrote are correct (except in the case of 39 when he wrote a 7, because he doesn't know the form for nine). For instance, 25 is heard as "veinte y cinco"; "cinco" is known and is written first; "veinte" is not known; this part of the name needs another number and zero or one is a good candidate for it. In Julian's words: "*Entonces es de cinco* [5] *y asi* [1]" (*So, it is five* [writes 5] *and thus* [writes 1]). Julian is even more explicit, saying: "*Si es veintisiete le pones el siete, si es veintitrés le pones el tres y así, te fijas cuál dices*" (*If it is twenty-seven you write the seven, if it is twenty-three you write the three and so on, listen to the one you are saying*). It is then clear that Julian is making an analysis of each number into two parts.

With the nontransparent numbers Julian has more problems, because he is not able to identify, in the oral presentation, any reliable cue. So he chooses 1 and 0 in the three combinations [10], [01], and [11] as possible candidates to receive the wanted interpretation. Julian avoids the [00] combination, as all other children do. On three occasions another number appears and for different reasons in each case. Julian writes twelve (*doce*) as [21], saying "*es del dos* [2] *y asi* [1]" (*it is of two and thus*), treating this nontransparent number as if it was a transparent one.

In order to understand why Julian wrote [31] for twenty, an excerpt of the interview is needed. Julian was asked to write the police phone number (15 82 20). He wrote 15 as 10, saying "*es de estos…creo*" (*it is of those…I guess*). Next was 82 and he said: "*Es del dos* [2], *ves, ahora sí lo dijiste. Y este* [0]" (*It is two, now you have said it. And this one*). The last number was 20 and Julian immediatly complained: "*Ahora no lo dijiste*" (*You didn't say it now*). He tried the combination [01]. However, looking at the entire result

[102001] he objected: "*puro repetido*" (*the same all the time*). He replaced [01] by [31]. The final result is [102031]. The first use of 3 as a "dummy" was to avoid repetitions; at the same time, 3 became another possible "dummy" and it was used as such on another occassion. Forty was written as [30], while saying: "*Ahora lo difícil, yo creo...yo creo asi*" ("*the difficult now, I guess... I guess this*").

Julian is not an exceptional case. On the contrary, he is a good representative case of a consistent search followed by children of the presyllabic group (at its upper level). These children used two main criteria to write nouns: minimum and maximum quantity of letters (in Julian's case, no less than three; no more than five) and internal qualitative variations (i.e., they do not repeat a letter form in a given meaningful string). Even with a restricted amount of letters, they succeeded in writing each noun with a different combination of these graphic forms.

All children in this group wrote nouns from left to right. They also wrote two-digit numbers from left to right. With transparent numbers they started with the units (the 6 in 36, for instance) and then they added something that corresponded to the unknown part (the tens, in fact). However, what they added was not just any number. For instance, Julian (already cited) wrote exclusively zero and one in the second position. In fact, those numbers (0 and 1) were the most commonly used. We call *dummy numbers* those that are chosen to fulfill the place of the unknown part of the number, that is, numbers that could receive any value, according to the circumstances. In this presyllabic group, dummies were used 38 times: 1 was chosen 19 times; 0 was chosen 14 times and only on 5 occasions did some other numbers appear. One and zero were a clear preference for the entire group.

When children of this group were asked to read their written production they used similar strategies for nouns and for numbers: both were interpreted as a single unit, without distinction of constituent parts, so they never noticed that numerals used for the known part were not written at the right place. We did not observe corrections following the interpretation of the piece of writing, as we will observe in children of more advanced levels of writing.

Miguel

Miguel is the same age as Julian, but he belongs to the syllabic group (see Figure 5.4). Miguel writes three-syllable words with three letters, reading them syllabically: [EIM] = "*bom-be-ros*"; [ogi] = "*hos-pi-tal*"]. He writes four-syllable words with four letters, reading them syllabically: [IMUE] = "*po-li-ci-a*"; [EIUl] = "*me-ca-ni-co*". The only exception to this quantitative correspondence is the bisyllabic word "pizzas," which is written with three letters instead of two, due to the principle of minimum quantity usually followed by children.

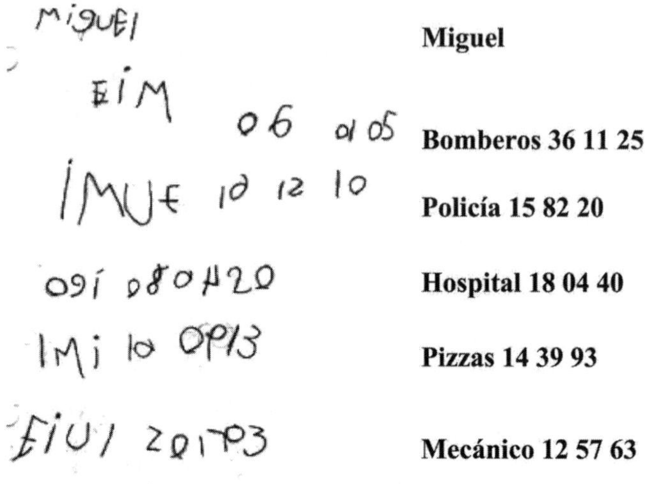

Figure 5.4. Miguel's productions—Syllabic I.

When dealing with numbers, Miguel shows his knowledge of the graphic form of all the digits, including 9. When writing transparent numbers, the numbers at the right position are all the right ones while the numbers at the left position are exclusively zero or one ("dummy numbers") (see Figure 5.5). These compound numbers are not read syllabically but morphemically: "*treintai-seis*," "*veinti-cinco*," "*ochentai-dos*," and so on.

Dictated numbers	Julian (pre-syllabic) 4;8	Miguel (syllabic -1) 4;8
36	60	06 ←
25	51	05 ←
82	20	12 ←
18	81	08 ←
39	71	09 ←
93	31	13 ←
57	70	17 ←
63	30	03 ←

Figure 5.5. Comparison of the writing of transparent numbers, same age, different level of conceptualization.

Dictated numbers	Julián (pre-syllabic) 4;8	Miguel (syllabic -1) 4;8
11	11	11
15	10	10
20	01--> 31	10
40	30	20
14	11	10
12	21	20

Figure 5.6. Comparison of the writing of nontransparent numbers, same age, different level of conceptualization.

Miguel wrote all transparent numbers from right to left (indicated by a → in Figure 5.5) and all nontransparent numbers from left to right (see Figure 5.6). Miguel's first comments to the dictated numbers are similar to those of Julian (presyllabic). For instance, he said "*veinticinco es de cinco* [5] *y asi* [0]" (*tweinty-five is five and thus*). The difference is that the known number is written at the right and this is so because Miguel, like all the children in this group, read the result looking for a correspondence between oral and written parts of the numbers. It is impossible for them to say "*cinco*" pointing to a zero or a one, because they know which one is the five; on the contrary, it is possible to say "*veinti*" (an unknown number) pointing to a "dummy" one.

All children at the syllabic levels made an explicit analysis of the nouns they intended to write. When these children wrote nouns, they made a syllabic analysis, paying attention to the first segment of the word, then to the second and so on. It was not until they found a graphic solution to the first oral segment that they proceeded with the next one.

On the contrary, the oral segmentation of number names do not proceed by successive syllables. Children first identify a familiar part ("*seis* [six]" in 36, for instance), write this number and return to the initial fragment ("*treinti-*," which is not a word number as "thirty" is). These children are sensitive to the correspondence between oral and written parts of both names and numbers. Although children at presyllabic level could consider [60] as a good representation of "36," no matter the place of the "6," children at the syllabic level would prefer [06], making similar use of "dummy numbers" but preserving the position of the known part of the compound number. In some cases they write from right to left (leaving by anticipation a space at the left); in other cases they write from left to write, but permute the position of the numbers when they read it. For instance, another child of the same group, Manuel (5 years, 8 months, Syllabic-1) wrote [60] for 36; when reading it, Manuel said:"*Treinta* [pointing to 6] *y seis* [pointing to 0] *Ay! No me quedó. Está al revés* [replacement of zero to obtain 06]" (*Thirty and six Oh! It is wrong. It is upside down*). In fact, in the entire group, 42 out of 80 transparent numbers were written from right to left.

In the entire syllabic group (Syllabic 1 and 2), "dummy" numbers were used 40 times when writing transparent numbers: Zero was used 24 times and the number 1 was used 15 times. (Only on one occasion was the number 7 used as a dummy.) In the presyllabic group both numbers 0 and 1 were used with rather similar frequency; in the syllabic group we observed a clear preference for zero.

With nontransparent numbers the written result obtained by this group of children is similar to the previous group (see Figure 5.6) but their way of reading is completely different. These children try to make a syllabic reading. For instance, Miguel read "quince" (fifteen), written as [10] syllabically: "*quin-ce*" and the same with "*vein-te*" (twenty), "*on-ce*" (eleven) and so on.

In the example of Miguel, the writing of nontransparent numbers is made initially with the same two dummies: 0 and 1. Then, another dummy is added: the number 2. The reason for the first 2 could be a need for differentiation: The sequence 10 was previously used to represent "twenty" and cannot be used to represent "forty" (the end part of the second and third telephone numbers); the reason for the second 2 is the same as in Julian's case: the name of "twelve" is, in Spanish, "*doce*, " starting with "dos," which is the very name of the digit 2. Many children write 12 with an initial 2 for this very reason, and Miguel is one of them.

Finally, we must state that the numbers 9 and 4 always present, in Miguel's case, an orientation that is not the conventional one. This is the way Miguel writes those numbers. We verified this by asking children who did not present numbers in a conventional orientation to write these numbers in isolation. The need to differentiate between nonintentional rotations and intentional ones is the key point to interpret the written productions of the next group.

Javier

Javier is 5 years and 11 months old. He belongs to the syllabic–alphabetic group (see Figure 5.7). The quality of Javier's handwriting is rather poor but his level of reasoning is very high. The syllabic–alphabetic group and the alphabetic group of children behave as a single group regarding the writing of compound numbers.

The great difference between this group and the previous one lies in two aspects, at first glance opposite: On one hand, these children know how to

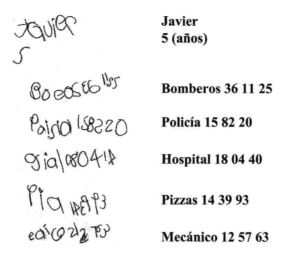

Figure 5.7. Javier's productions—syllabic–alphabet.

write conventionally more compound numbers; on the other, they invent a new solution for the unknown number—instead of making use of "dummy" numbers (that do not disappear but are dramatically reduced) they modify the graphic orientation of the written numbers corresponding to the tens, producing a 90° rotation on the vertical axis. These are intentional rotations. Let us see how these children justify this unexpected solution.

To write 25, Javier needs a rotated 2 that becomes close, as a form, to his way of writing 5 and he is uncomfortable with this. However, he explained: "*Es del veinti y del cinco, es del veinti que se pone como dos y del cinco porque dices veinti-cinco*" (*It is of twenty and five, it is twenty that is written like a two and five because you are saying twenty-five*). Then the interviewer asked: "*Entonces 25 se pone con 2 y 5?*" (*So, is 25 written with two and five?*) Javier answers strongly: "*No, con veinti y cinco*" (*No, it is with twenty and five*). We can assert that Javier made intentional rotations because he writes conventionaly isolated numbers 3, 2, 5, 4, and 6 (see Figure 5.8).

Johnatan

Johnatan (5 years, 4 months old, alphabetic group) is even more explicit. Johnatan was asked to write 36; he said:"*trein-ta-i-seis. Ah, es de seis* [6]. *Treintai…treinta es creo de tres* [rotated 3 at the left side of the 6]" (*thir-ty-six. Ah, it is six. Thirty…thirty I guess it is three*). The interviewer asked him to write a single 3 at the bottom of the page. He did it conventionally saying "*bien fácil*" (*so easy*). When the interviewer compared both performances of 3, Johnatan explained: "*este es de tres* [the isolated one] *y este del treintaiseis. Este solito es de tres, así solito tres y este de arriba cuando se parece a tres*" (*this is three* [the

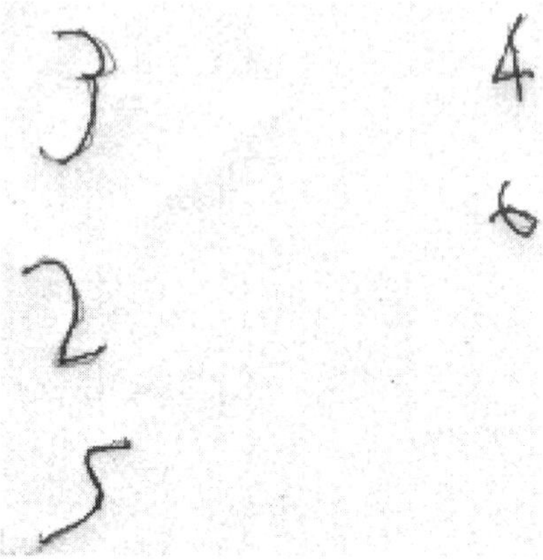

Figure 5.8. Javier's writing of isolated digits.

isolated one] *and this one is thirty-six. This one alone is three, this alone three and this up there when seems like three*). Then the interviewer asks: "*treintaiseis se parece a tres*?" (*Does thirty-six seem like three*?) and the boy answers: "*si dicen trein, trein, oyes?, se parece. Tre, trein, tres. Entonces es de los que se parecen a tres*" (*if you say* trein, trein, *do you listen?, it is alike.* Tre, trein, tres. *Then it is of those like three*). The same arguments were used by Johnatan in the case of many other compound numbers. Rotated numbers were used intentionally by him for the tens in 25, 39, 93, and 57.

These intentional rotations are relatively frequent in this group: We observed them in 29 cases out of 80 transparent numbers that were written (11 in the syllabic–alphabetic group and 18 in the alphabetic group). The writing of these transparent numbers from right to left is even more frequent than in the syllabic group (56 out of 80, i.e., 70% instead of 52.5% in the syllabic group). The only transparent number that all children, except one, wrote from left to write was 18. Many of them already know how to write it. However, this number was an occasion to observe the use of three digits: [108] was produced three times in this group and only one time in the syllabic group.

To know how to write a given number sometimes constituted an additional difficulty when we asked children to read them. This was particularly evident in the case of number 12. For instance, Monse (5 years, 7 months old, alphabetic group) wrote 12 conventionally but tried to read it syllabically: "*dos* [pointing to 1] *ce* [pointing to 2]. *Ay, no, cómo*?" (*dos-ce Oh no, how*?) The interviewer asked if it is well written and she answered: "*Si, pero no lo puedo leer, digo dos y no es el dos, está del otro lado*" (*Yes, but I can't read it, I say two but it is not the two, it is on the other side*).

The following graphics give a picture of three relevant aspects of this evolution. Figure 5.9 shows that the left position for the known part of the

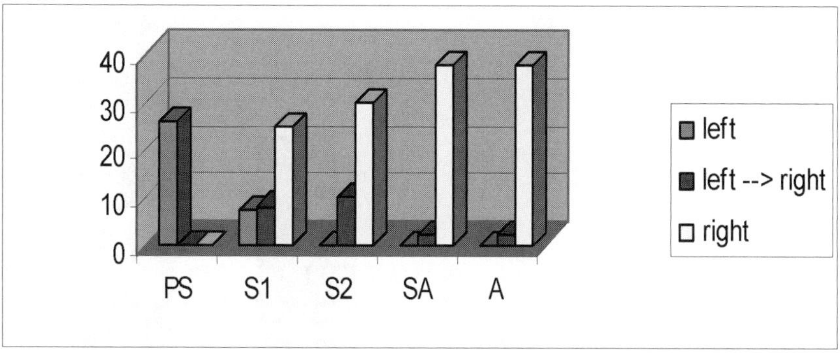

Figure 5.9. Placement of digits corresponding to units in bidigits transparent numbers (total frequencies).

compound transparent numbers is restricted to children of the presyllabic group and very few of the next group (Syllabic 1). It shows also that the left position is corrected to a right position when some children of both syllabic groups proceed to a reading aloud of the result (indicated as left —> right in the graphic).

Figure 5.10 shows the progressive preference for the use of zero as a dummy. Figure 5.11 shows that intentional rotations increase with the growing conceptual levels of interviewed children.

CONCLUDING REMARKS

The research example I have presented shows the complexity of the interactions between numbers and letters in early literacy, or more precisely, interactions between the alphabetical writing system (AWS) and the numerical writing system (NWS).

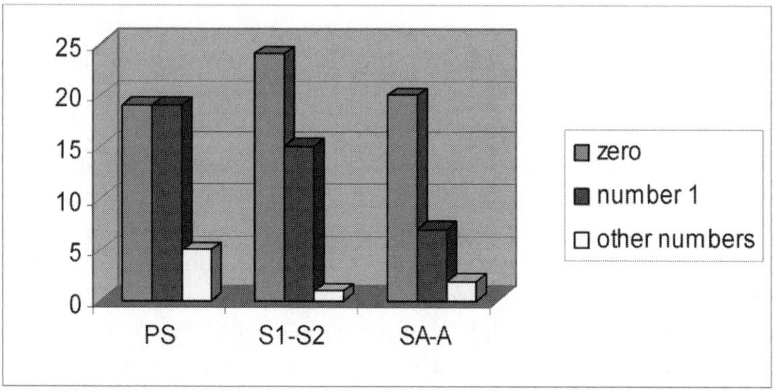

Figure 5.10. Numbers used as "dummies."

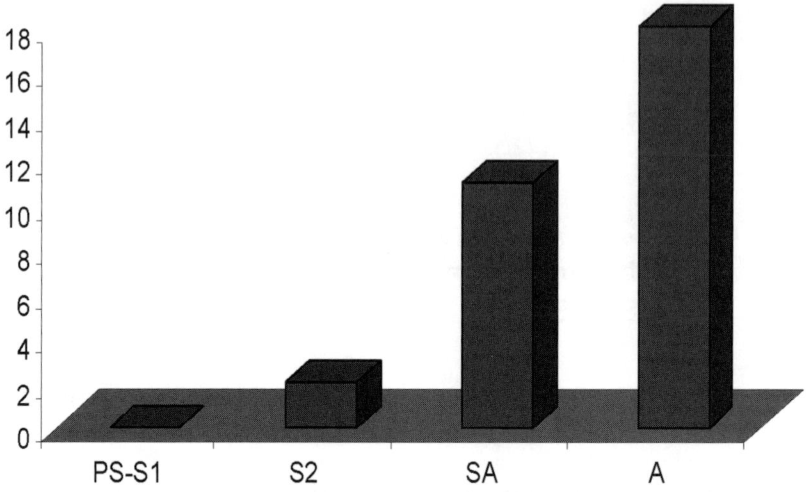

Figure 5.11. Intentional rotations of digits corresponding to the tens in bidigit transparent numbers (total frequencies).

At the beginning, children grasp more quickly the set of number graphemes than the set of letter graphemes. This is not surprising, because letters are subject to a number of typographic variations whereas numbers are not. In addition, each number has a name related to its numerical meaning, something that does not happen with the letters. Very early, children understand that any compound number is a result of a combination of basic numbers (i.e., the digits). All the children who participated in this study already knew that bidigits are a result of a combination of two digits, without knowing, of course, what are legal or illegal combinations.

However, not all children found similar solutions to the challenge of writing telephone numbers. Two important factors determine variations in the solutions children proposed: the transparency of the dictated numbers, and children's levels of conceptualization concerning the alphabetical writing system (AWS).

When dealing with *transparent numbers*, all children analyzed them into two morphemic parts that happened to be "a known part" and "an unknown part." For instance, in the oral name of 36 they identify the 6 plus "an unknown part" in need of an "unknown number." To indicate the "unknown part" children choose a dummy, that is, a number that could receive any value, according to the circumstances. It is remarkable that children consistently used a neutral deictic expression ("*y así,*" "*y este*") referring to a number not named as such. For instance, when writing 60 or 06 for 36 they say "*it is of six and this one,*" pointing to zero.

Children of all conceptualization levels put a 6 plus a dummy for 36. However, the position of the dummy differentiates sharply the solutions of the presyllabic group from the solutions of the syllabic group. Children from the presyllabic group wrote from left to right, first the known part (the 6) and then the dummy (0 or 1). Children from the syllabic group put the dummy in the first position or, more frequently, wrote these transparent numbers from right to left, whereas the nontransparent ones were written from left to right. This change of direction in the handwriting movement is remarkable for three reasons: first, because it is restricted to numbers and does not affect the nouns written with letters; second, because it is a solution selectively applied to transparent numbers; and third, because the dummy at the left allows a satisfactory reading aloud of the compound number as children say "*treinti*"—the unknown number—pointing to a dummy, and "seis" pointing to a 6.

Children of the more advanced levels, concerning the AWS, also may put dummies, but the important thing is that they are exploring a new solution, one that nobody could have suggested to them: They produce intentional rotations. Intentional rotations concern the 3 of 36 and 39, the 5 of 57, the 6 of 63 and the 9 of 93. Their oral justifications indicate clearly that, by doing this, they try to indicate that "*treinti*" is related to 3 but it is different from 3, and the same in the other cases. We may assert that these are intentional rotations because children who produce them write conventionally an isolated 3, 5, 6, or 9.

The evolution follows this path: First, children recognize two parts in the transparent number but these parts are treated as two separate pieces, without order. Then, they establish a definite order between the two parts of the transparent number. Finally, they take into account the quality of the unknown part through similarities between numbers' names. The use of intentional rotations seems related to a search for an equivalent of lower case/upper case letters. At least this was suggested by Paula, an English-speaking 5-year-old child reported by Brizuela (2004, chap. 3). Paula explicitly looked for "an upper case three" to solve the "thirty" part of 33. The more unexpected solution—that is, intentional rotations of numbers—proved indeed to be the more advanced one in cognitive terms.

What happens with *nontransparent numbers* is also worth noting. All children used dummies to guess the writing of nontransparent numbers. The numbers that are chosen to function as dummies are remarkable: We found almost exclusively the numbers 1 and 0, that is, the more problematic from a cognitive point of view. In children's terms, zero is not really a number because when we count we do not start with zero; one is not a real number because it does not indicate a quantity as the other numbers do. It is relevant, from an epistemological point of view, to indicate that, historically speaking, humanity had the same problems accepting zero and one as real numbers (Menninger, 1969). It is also remarkable that when two dummies are used for a nontransparent number, the combinations attested were 10, 01, and 11. No child used 00. In our situation, when dealing with the phone partial number 04, dictated as "*cero, cuatro,*" no child had difficulties, matching correctly the noun "zero" with the corresponding grapheme. Why do they avoid the 00 combination? A possible explanation could be the following. In counting situations, children usually refer to zero as "nothing."As a combination, 01 or 10 means probably "something" whereas 00 means probably "two times nothing."

Some children already know how to write some of the nontransparent numbers (12 or 20, for instance). None of the children who knew these conventional writings was able to justify them, and this is not surprising because the conceptual nature of this representation (place value) is still out of their reach. Instead, some of them—from syllabic levels on—tried to justify the compound number with a syllabic reading ("*dos-ce,*" "*vein-te*"). These syllabic attempts were restricted to nontransparent numbers.

Children made considerable cognitive efforts to understand such different systems as the alphabetical writing system and the numerical writing system. Both have presence in the social settings, and both are strongly valued in school terms. Some of the properties applied in the composition of letters are used also in the composition of numbers, but some are not. For instance, the principle of internal variation—that is, to avoid repetition of the same letter in a contiguous position—does not apply to numbers written in isolation. However, in our situation, when children saw a string of six numbers with some dummies repeated (e.g., 00), they replace one dummy for another, and this was the very reason for the use of the number 2 or 3 as dummies.

Some researchers might object that the task we propose to the children is an artificial one, as they are not able to cope with it, lacking specific information. My answer is that we were proposing that children invent solutions for a reasonable problem (in fact, all of them know that in their families some telephone numbers are written down in a specific notebook). The writing down of telephone numbers is one of the cases where dictation is socially validated, together with a precise need for accuracy. We aimed at putting numbers out of any reference to quantities to see how children analyze number nouns. Telephone numbers proved to be an excellent context for our purposes.

We aimed to observe the very moment when children invent a solution, putting into action the information already received but also their peculiar ways to make sense of this information. The invented solutions already described are not ideosyncratic. Children of similar levels of development share similar solutions. In addition, the solutions follow a psychogenetic pathway: First, children decompose transparent numbers into two morphemic parts; then, they find the right place to put dummies; finally, they try to replace dummies by numbers closer to the sound pattern of the unknown part of the compound number. Each acquisition becomes possible by the previous one; each solution obliges children to face new conflicting situations. However, the picture is incomplete unless we consider that these three levels are related with the way to conceive the alphabetical writing system. It does not seem appropriate to think of the development of numbers in an isolated module (Tolchinsky, 2003). Numbers and letters interact in several meaningful ways during the evolution.

REFERENCES

Alvarado, M., & Ferreiro, E. (2002). Four and five-year old children writing two-digit numbers. *Rivista di Psicolinguistica Applicata, II*(3), 23–37.

Brizuela, B. (2004). *Mathematical development in young children: Exploring notations.* New York: Teachers College Press.

Ferreiro, E. (1991). Psychological and epistemological problems on written representation of language. In M. Carretero, M. Pope, R. Simons, & J. I. Pozo (Eds.), *Learning and instruction: European research in an international context* (pp. 157–173). Oxford: Pergamon Press.

Ferreiro, E. (1994). Literacy development: Construction and reconstruction. In D. Tirosh (Ed.), *Implicit and explicit knowledge: An educational approach* (pp. 169–180). Norwood, NJ: Ablex.

Ferreiro, E. (2002). The distinction between graphic and ortographic knowledge. Its relevance for understanding literacy development. In J. Brockmeier, M. Wang, & D. Olson (Eds.), *Literacy, narratives and culture* (pp. 215–228). London: Curzon.

Ferreiro, E., & Teberosky, A. (1982). *Literacy before schooling*. Exeter NH: Heineman. (Original publication in Spanish: *Los sistemas de escritura en el desarrollo del niño*. Mexico: Siglo XXI Editores, 1979)

Hughes, M. (1986). *Children and number. Difficulties in learning mathematics.* Oxford: Basil Blackwell.

Kamii, C. (1985). *Young children reinvent arithmetic: Implications of Piaget's theory.* New York: Teachers College Press.

Menninger, K. (1969). *Number words and number symbols. A cultural history of numbers.* Cambridge, MA: MIT Press.

Nunes, T., & Bryant, P. (1996). *Children doing mathematics*. Oxford: Blackwell.

Piaget, J., & Szeminska, A. (1941). *La genèse du nombre chez l'enfant*. Neuchâtel: Delachaux & Niestlé.

Sinclair, A. (1988). La notation numérique chez l'enfant. In H. Sinclair (Ed.), *La production de notations chez le jeune enfant. Langage, nombre, rythmes et mélodies* (pp. 71–98). Paris: Presses Universitaires de France.

Tolchinsky, L. (2003). *The cradle of culture and what children know about writing and numbers before being taught.* Mahwah, NJ: Lawrence Erlbaum Associates.

Part **II**

LITERACY LEARNING IN THE CLASSROOM

> *For as hard as the school as an institution may try to focus children's attention on the neutral basics, young children are not driven by an interest in "the basics." They are driven by an interest in meaningful participation in classroom life. They link new kinds of communicative practices found in school with old familiar ones, so that they have some relevant resources and some basis for action, for participation. When children do this—when they reach for the old and familiar–they inevitably bring into the school their experiences and skills with talk, text, and symbols from the larger society. (Dyson, this volume, p. 154)*

The authors in Part II, *Literacy Learning in the Classroom,* invite us into the classrooms of knowledgeable and experienced teachers. Through their professional lenses we have a multidimensional view of the resources that children and teachers draw upon across literacy practices. These classrooms describe joyful busy places where children inquire into their "wonderings and wanderings" (Merriam, 1991), to expand on their potential, to take risks, and to develop ever growing concepts about literacy and the world. The teachers, confident in their abilities as literacy teachers of young children, and sometimes courageous enough to call themselves whole language teachers, engage their children in thinking and talking seriously about their world and in learning how to ask important and controversial questions. In such classrooms, children build visions about themselves as learners and develop positive views and concepts about their literacy learning and capabilities as readers and writers as they engage with teachers, their classmates, and a range of classroom resources.

We know that children are learning to read and write in all classroom settings, but unfortunately some children develop views of themselves reflected in a deficit view of learning that stands in the way of their developing confidence in themselves as readers and writers. There are classrooms in which some children learn that their family backgrounds, languages, and cultures are not valued, and they do not recognize the power of their own literacy histories and learning strengths. These children often say that they cannot learn or that learning to read and write is too hard. They become focused on "not messing up" rather than searching to make sense of the literacy in their world. This is especially true in a climate where administrators, teachers, and parents, in a concern to close "achievement gaps," rely mainly on tests and measurements to make decisions about children's performance and establish one-size-fits-all instruction that ignores what young children know.

Research for more than a century reiterates that the teacher in a classroom plays a most important role in children's successful literacy learning (Dudley-Marling, Abt-Perkins, Sato, & Selfe, 2006; Darling-Hammond, 2000). The authors in this part provide rich interpretations that build on theoretically based observations of literacy and literacy learning as socially, culturally, linguistically, and cognitively situated. They document children's diverse language opportunities and experiences and curriculum integration of writing, reading, storytelling, retellings, other symbol systems such as art, and drama, with lots of student-led conversations. They show how classroom experiences develop insights into the history of children's literacy knowledge and development. They provide profiles of children's language use, taking into consideration the influences of children's background knowledge, their cultures, and their languages—the funds of knowledge of their families and communities (Gonzàlez et al, 2005). Children's voices, sometimes in more than one language, become visible and central to understanding literacy development.

CRITICAL ISSUES RELATED TO LITERACY LEARNING IN THE CLASSROOM

- Knowledgeable professionals use kidwatching in classrooms to document children's learning through insightful observation, interaction, and evaluation.
- Teacher research is an ongoing process of kidwatching, self-reflection, and curriculum development.
- Researchers and teachers develop knowledge and understanding about literacy and literacy learning that provide them with evidence that children are learning literacy all the time.
- Children learn literacy in their classrooms as they learn about their world through a variety of subject areas.
- Children develop their views about literacy from the classroom environment, which may expand or narrow their concepts about literacy.

REFERENCES

Darling-Hammond, L. (2000). *Teacher quality and student achievement: A review of state policy evidence*. Educational Policy Analysis Archive. <http://epaa.asu.edu/epaa/v8n1/>
Dudley-Marling, C., Abt-Perkins, D., Sato, K., & Selfe, R. (2006, April). Teacher quality: The perspectives of NCTE members. *English Education, 38*(3), 167–187.
Gonzàlez N., Moll, L., & Amanti, C. (Eds.). (2005). *Funds of knowledge: Theorizing practice in households, communities and classrooms*. Mahwah, NJ: Lawrence Erlbaum Associates.
Merriam, E. (1991). *The wise woman and her secret*. New York: Simon & Schuster.

Chapter 6

Documenting Critical Literacy Development in Classrooms

Yetta Goodman

My research involves observing, analyzing, and working with teachers to document children's interactions with each other, the teacher and the written language in their classroom. These settings provide many opportunities to document the influence of printed texts on children's literacy learning especially with teachers who are effective at observing and analyzing what their children do with print. I call this process of teacher researchers' documentations and reflections *kidwatching* (an observational and analytical stance of children's learning) (Y. Goodman, 1985; Owocki & Goodman, 2002). Kidwatching is integral to teacher research; teachers use their learning from kidwatching to understand how their practice influences children's development and as a result to rethink their pedagogy and the environments they organize. As I participate with these teachers, I discover their expertise and document their learning as well as the learning of enthusiastic and engaged young children who often become co-researchers in the process. As teachers evaluate or assess the growth of their students and reflect on the impact of their teaching, they provide data that is an important aspect of interpretive research (Erickson, 1986) to be used as evidence for the educational community.

Examples from classroom settings make visible the influences of research on children, the role of the teacher and curriculum. I am usually cautious about applying research findings simplistically to classroom settings because theory, research and practice are most powerful when they inform each other. The classroom vignette that follows is an example of a teacher who is not simply a consumer of research but an integral contributor to ongoing educational research and theory building. By documenting vignettes from teacher research settings, it is possible to provide "key patterns in language and learning" for both teachers and children. (Harste, Woodward, & Burke, 1984, p. xix). Such "critical literacy lessons" involve careful analysis of what we learn from young children's language stories and in addition inform teaching and curriculum that value children's culture and their ways of knowing (Whitmore, Martens, Goodman, & Owocki, 2004). These are critical lessons because they allow children's voices to emerge, to reveal the power children have over their own learning and to highlight ways to organize environments that support such learning. Critical learning opportunities result in critical lessons that "shed light on the power structures [of literacy development] from a political perspective, a perspective that intentionally situates the event [the lesson] in the broader context of a triadic relationship between literacy, schooling and the sociocultural complexities of our real world" (Whitmore & Crowell, 1994, p. 6).

My purpose for presenting one language story of a teacher researcher is to encourage professional educators to develop and publish such vignettes in order to celebrate the learning of young children, value their construction of language and concepts, and use what we learn from literacy lessons to inform classroom practice and teacher education. In addition, such documentation should become common practice in professional development and at the same time illuminate the knowledge and experience of classroom teachers to be taken seriously as research evidence.

In classroom studies, teachers, researchers, and teacher researchers examine students' zones of proximal development and document children's learning as they mediate with the teacher, their peers and the context or learning environment. Literacy is learned continuously by the individual and that literacy learning continuously influences the social interactions in the classroom: the interactions of people, materials, space, and the multiple symbol systems available in an enriched classroom environment.

A CRITICAL LITERACY EVENT

This language story reveals the power of the language transactions that occur with a published text, the teacher, Wendy Goodman, an experienced bilingual primary grade teacher, and her first graders.

My discussions and documentation of this literacy experience began when I told Wendy about a book I had just read called *Ask Mr. Bear* (Flack, 1932/1971). I was excited about the book because it was predictable and had a plot with which children could identify. It was published in 1932 and is still in press. I believe that the author, Marjorie Flack, was part of a children's literature workshop in the early part of the 20th century at Bank Street College. Founded by Lucy Sprague Mitchell with a group of educational researchers, mostly women, the college developed from a research collective known as the Bureau of Experimental Education. At that time in the United States, early childhood researchers were carefully observing and documenting children's language and learning, influenced by the research and theories of Piaget and Dewey. The researchers were using their results to develop subject matter materials and children's literature to impact children's learning, and at the same time they were sharing their conclusions with classroom teachers (Antler, 1987; Mitchell, 1950).

As I analyzed *Ask Mr. Bear*, I realized that it had been designed based on understandings about language and the reading process. I also knew from miscue analysis research and Margaret Meek's concept that "texts teach what children learn" that when children and texts come together, the written text becomes a teacher (Meek, 1988). I wanted to document children's responses including their miscues to this unique text to gain insight into the influence of text construction on young readers. As children transact with a text, with the support of a teacher, a zone of proximal development is established for individual and groups of children (Y. Goodman & K. Goodman, 1992). I wanted to discover ways in which the text mediates literacy and literacy knowledge as readers engage actively with a well-constructed text. I shared my interest with this book with Wendy to see what her advice about using this book would be.

I was surprised to discover that not only did Wendy know the book but she had been using *Ask Mr. Bear* with first graders for a number of years. Wendy selected this text because she knew it had features that would help her young readers enjoy a well-written children's book, support them in making sense of the story, and at the same time give them many opportunities to talk about specific text features. She believed that such talk helped her children access a book that was more complex than other books they had been selecting in the classroom.

First, I tell the text story and talk some about the print and illustrations. Then, I discuss the interactions between Wendy and her students as they read *Ask Mr. Bear* and provide Wendy's commentary about her reading instruction.

Explication of the Text

The story is about Danny who wonders what he should give his mother for her birthday. He asks different farm animals: a hen, a goose, a goat, a sheep and a cow. Each animal suggests gifts that would be useful to Danny's mother: an egg, feathers, cheese, wool for a blanket, and milk and cream. Danny responds to each that his mother already has each product. The animal usually says, "Let's see what we can find then," and the growing group of animals move on to the next animal, which is bigger than the previous one. The cow, the last animal, tells Danny to ask Mr. Bear. Danny is willing to do so but the farm animals are not. Danny continues his journey alone, and finds and asks Mr. Bear. Mr. Bear whispers in Danny's ear. Danny thanks Mr. Bear and goes home. He asks his mother to guess what he has for her birthday. She guesses each of the items that the five farm animals suggested, which is not what Danny has in mind. The story ends with Danny giving his mother a big bear hug.

There are from one to eight lines of text, with a related illustration, on almost every page. On page 31, there is a summary of the language used in the story as the mother guesses, with Danny responding "No," to each guess. There are 12 lines on this page with no illustrations.

The first page of the story begins with the title of the book centered and in all capital letters. This is followed by two sentences formated one above the other. The illustration of a sad Danny sitting on a bottom step with his head in his hands is to the left and below the sentences.

Text: Once there was a boy named Danny.

One day Danny's mother had a birthday.

But then the author/designer spaces the third sentence in phrasal units. The sentence starts directly below the first two sentences:

Danny said to himself,

"What shall I give

my mother

for her

birthday?"

This print spacing of phrases from left to right with an indented organization continues with different language on 15 pages of this 32-page story, often involving dialogue in quotation marks. This format provides opportunity for perceptual and linguistic predictability as the story moves along through phrasal units.

On pages 2 and 3, Danny and the hen are shown in the illustrations facing each other, one on each of the two facing pages. The printed language uses the same order of introduction of each character. But on pages 4 and 5, the illustrations of the two are in a different order than in the written portion. The print says: "So Danny and the Hen" on the page with only the hen illustrated, whereas on the next page Danny is moving along in the illustration.

Young readers have to use the print as well as the illustrations to read the names of the characters. This helps the children build an understanding that illustrations and written text work together but not in a simple one-to-one correspondence. These features become a predictable pattern throughout the book. Because of repetitions of these patterns, I assume that these decisions were made consciously by the author/designer to allow the illustrations and the printed text to support the reader.

On page 5, where Danny is illustrated with his head separating the printed phrase, another interesting feature is introduced:

Text: all hopped along [Danny's head] until they met

On six of the pages, the sentence does not end on a page but with the phrase: "until they met" as just shown. These open-ended sentences are always on the right-hand page and constrain the reader to turn the page to continue reading. In overly simplistic children's literature, sentences often end with a period at the end of each line, often the only line and sentence on the page. This influences children to expect sentences to end when lines end. This causes miscues to occur when children read more complex print layout.

In *Ask Mr. Bear*, however, the author and designer expect that their readers are competent users of the language, so they construct a text that supports the reader with familiar language patterns and teaches children to wrap around a text at different places. They provide an unfamiliar aspect of written language within the familiar to support and extend readers' development. This book has only two pages that include a single line and sentence, but the diversity of numbers of lines and sentences throughout provides opportunities for children to predict diversity in formating to develop flexibility in their reading.

When teachers focus readers' attention mostly on letter-to-sound patterns or word recognition, it interferes with the features that a thoughtful author/text designer creates to help readers access a well-constructed literary work. I've heard children's literature author/illustrator Mercer Meyer say that he is concerned about teachers who tell children "Now pay attention here to the words" when the kids are excited about and exploring the illustrations. Such teaching does not encourage young children to attend to the power of the illustrations in telling the story and to learn how pictures and print work together.

Book walks, which are part of Wendy's reading instruction, often prior to reading, help children examine illustrations and appreciate the relation between page formats, the illustrations and the visible features of the print. *Ask Mr. Bear* is a predictable book with appropriate moments of nonpredictability and ends with a review of the language of the text as part of the story line. A well written predictable book includes nonpredictable elements that also become a predictable feature. Readers expect the language to change and expect to find surprise endings at the same time that they become used to the predictable language. If the written language, the actions, and the illustrations remain the same throughout a picture storybook, the text becomes formulaic and boring.

Ask Mr. Bear has many features to show that Marjorie Flack and her editors knew a lot about the reading process and how a well-written text engages and supports young developing readers. I now consider how a knowledgeable teacher like Wendy makes use of such a book in the reading development of her students.

Wendy and Her Students Read *Ask Mr. Bear*

Wendy Goodman is an experienced primary-grade teacher who often tapes her interactions with her students. She uses field notes and transcriptions to expand her knowledge about her children and to reflect on her own teaching. Her language lessons also inform and influence my research and theory.

Wendy is working with 5 children in a small group, keeping in mind the 24 other children working in pairs and individually throughout this busy classroom. The other children are engaged in a range of reading and writing experiences that they can do independently or quietly in small groups. The students come from a modest socioeconomic background and some of them are bilingual. Wendy knows her students and their families and continues to learn about the community in which they live. She honors children's inquiries and pays close attention to their language interactions, trying to understand the children's meanings and to document their learning. She selected the published text she is going to use thoughtfully.

Wendy works with her first graders in guided or directed teaching lessons. I selected a few examples to highlight the transactions that occur among the text, the teacher, and the children. Wendy's directed reading instruction involves a small group of children who she believes need a particular lesson focus. Her groups do not stay the same throughout the year. The young readers for this group were selected because they were reading in English but were choosing very simple books to read. Wendy wanted them to discover that they could read more complicated material. She included Fatima in the group because although she was reading much better in Spanish than in English, Wendy thought Fatima needed to be encouraged to see the relationship between her knowledge about Spanish reading and her reading in English. The interactions between Wendy and her students sound spontaneous, but it is obvious that the lesson proceeds based on the teacher's knowledge about her students, their language, the language of the text, and the reading process.

Each child and the teacher are holding a copy of the book.

Wendy: This book is very special to me because I remember when my first-grade teacher read it in class. I remember the cover and the pictures but most of all I remember going home that day and sharing what I learned with my mom.

The Text: *Story and Pictures by Marjorie Flack*

As they look at the title page some children read: written and illustrated...

Shawn: No that is not written and illustrated.

Wendy: Look at that, what do you think is happening there?

The children examine the print carefully in response to Shawn's comments and learn that "written and illustrated" can be said in different ways.

Wendy: Let's read the beginning of the story.

The children turn to page 1, look overwhelmed, and a number say: "That's a lot of words."

Wendy explains to the children that they have read many books that have only a few words on a page. She knows they can also read books with a lot of words and she wants them to find that out.

Fatima: Oh look there's the title again.

The children read in unison silently and out loud. Wendy describes what the children sound like: "It sounds like they are all reading the same thing at the same time but they are not at the same pace, sometimes they just hear each other and respond to each other with agreements or disagreements...they argue but keep reading because they are all interested in constructing their own meaning."

The Text: *One day Danny's mother had a birthday*. (p. 1)

Most of the kids read: One day Danny's mother had a birthday party

Shawn: No it doesn't say party just birthday.

The children agree with Shawn and read on.

The Text: *What shall I give*
my mother
for her
birthday? (p. 1)

The children are ready for the page to be turned.

Danny interrupts: What will he get her?
Wendy: Wait let's answer his question.

Wendy wants the children to think about the story. The children predict and talk about mother's birthdays and what they get her sometimes.

The Text: *Honk, honk, said the Goose. I can give you some nice feathers to make a fine pillow for your mother's birthday* (p. 7).
Claudia reads: I can give you some nice fresh to make a fine pillow.

The kids hesitate.

Wendy asks: Does that make sense? Can you make a pillow from fresh?
Claudia: Father?

Claudia, the children and the teacher laugh together and enjoy a short silly discussion about whether or not you can make a pillow from fathers.

Wendy: What else could it be?

Some kids say feathers and Wendy brings them back to the text.

Wendy: You decide.... Should we go back and try your ideas here or go on?

The class rereads the sentence with feathers and they continue the story. Wendy engages her students in discussing the language and attending to the print. As a teacher with knowledge and experience, she considers when to direct the kids' attention. She involves them in decision making to show them that they have choices of strategies to use. She responds to their personal inquiries and helps the children find their own answers to their questions. Wendy is a kidwatcher whose knowledge and experience help her monitor when to give an answer, when to push toward disequilibrium, when to ask "what do you think" and "why do you think so." She focuses the students on the language of the text in appropriate ways to discuss phonics, punctuation, the format of the print on the page, the grammar, but most of all she helps them focus on making sense. "What does it mean?" and "How do you know?" are questions she uses often. She waits for the children's answers and helps them learn to listen to and wait for each other. She wants her young readers to inquire into the reading process—to think about what it means to be a reader.

The Text:	*So Danny and the Hen and the Goose* (p. 12) ... *and the Goat galloped along until they met* (p. 13)

These two pages face each other. The goose and Danny are illustrated in movement on page 12, and the goat and the hen are on page 13. The children miscue on galloped with different responses: g'lopped (stress on second syllable); gallow (elongated o at the end); op-ed; giggled; jumped.

Shawn:	Can't be jumped because it has to be a /t/ at the end
Fatima:	No, that should have a /t/ and the -ed shouldn't be there.
Wendy:	Often in English with verbs they are spelled with ed but we say /t/ like walked and jumped. (She writes the familiar words she knows that children know on the board and has them pronounce and think about where they've read those words before).

At this point, the children decide they should continue to read the text knowing that they don't know "galloped." Two pages later, after they meet Mrs. Sheep and read "they all trotted together." Shawn calls out "galloped." The other students agree: "Yeah, it's galloped," as they go back to attend to the word on the earlier page. Most of the time when a child comes to the expected response, it is fascinating that the children seem to know what they know. This kind of behavior is documented in miscue analysis frequently. At this point Shawn talks more about galloped: "I kept thinking it had to be some way of moving." The children had used various sounding-out strategies during their first reading of "galloped," discovering that such strategies do not always help them with comprehension. Shawn keeps working, thinking about "that word" he didn't know. He helps the students focus on the grammatical function of the verb ("a way of moving") but also on its semantic meaning in this context. This story includes a rich array of past-tense verbs to show the farm animals and Danny moving along: walked; skipped; hopped; galloped; trotted; ran and ran. Wendy focused their attention on the relationship between the spelling of a regular past-tense verb (an orthographic feature of language) and its oral equivalent to help them continue to develop their knowledge of phonics.

Throughout the reading of this book, the children and the teacher discover and talk about many features of language. In one context, one of the children reads "Mr." for "Mrs." Another child says: "No. Look at the s."

Later when a similar miscue occurs, the focus is on syntactic and semantic information.

Fatima:	It can't be Mr. because it is a hen. You know if it was a Mr. it would have been a rooster.

The children explore the differences between Baa and Maa.

Shawn:	I thought goats said Baa and sheep go Maa.

Toward the end of the story the children talk about other metalinguistic insights.

The Text:	*"Hum, hum," says the Bear.* (p. 27)
Fatima:	Why does the bear go Hum, Hum.
Claudia:	Maybe its Um Um.
Shawn:	Maybe it's supposed to be Hmmmmmm! Hmm! It's probably written this way (points to Hum! Hum!) because somebody thought kids couldn't read Hmmm!

The children also discuss concepts they are developing about farm animals.

Shawn:	Goats give milk and you make cheese from the milk too.
Fatima:	Goats give milk? I thought it just came from cows.
Claudia:	At my grandpa's farm we drink goat's milk.

The children made intertextual ties when they remembered that they had read about sheep giving wool to make clothes in Tomie de Paola's *Charlie Needs a Clock* (1974). And they were chagrined and very worried that a little boy would go off into the woods alone looking for a bear.

From this language story, Wendy and I learned a critical literacy lesson: *The results of documenting children's transactions with an effective text, with each other, and with their teacher reveal the complexity and depth of their learning.*

As they work hard with the text, the children are thinking, questioning, moving into disequilibrium always with the goal of making sense of their world as they read. The dialogue in these environments supports children's continuous development as readers, engages them in taking risks, and supports them in building agency in their own learning.

In just over a half hour of a thoughtfully planned and constructed lesson, the children supported by their teacher examine English phonics, phonology, grammatical features, vocabulary, and the wording of the text. They talk about punctuation, formating, illustrations, spelling, important concepts and values about animals, and a range of other life experiences. They use new language to represent their new concepts and to reveal their knowledge constructions. They learn about how they use their language cueing systems and how reading strategies (predicting, confirming, reading on, self correcting, making inferences) help them make sense of print. They know that they are able to solve a range of problems that reading a good book poses for them.

CRITICAL LESSONS BUILD ON INSIGHTFUL DOCUMENTATION

Through the documentation and interpretation of the literacy event in Wendy's classroom, another critical lesson becomes obvious: *Very young children are capable of discussing sophisticated issues and developing oral and written language as a result of their engagement in critical dialogues.*

When there is documentation of the kinds of environments and interactions teachers organize that allow for and respond to children's questions and their wonderings, all members of the professional education community benefit. It becomes easy to demonstrate the amount of learning that takes place as teachers and children engage in meaningful language use in the classroom. Research in classrooms such as Wendy's reveals how dialogue in small groups and whole class brings children's families, communities, cultures, and histories into the classroom to help children build the concept that literacy is a common cultural practice that takes place at home as well as in school. Through the dissemination and sharing of such documentation, a range of people discover that young children are serious and thoughtful learners who want to share their concerns, their worries, and their excitement about the things they are coming to know.

In the public concern for better test scores and more effective instruction, there are teachers and administrators who focus on mandated methods and the direct teaching of abstract units of language, rather than on what children know and how they learn. In such settings, the role of learners in constructing their own knowledge is often forgotten. The focus on high-stakes tests does not provide lenses through which to view children's competence or to liberate their thinking and learning.

Careful analysis of classrooms, including in-depth case studies of individual learners, dramatically reveals children's voices, their constructions, and schema development of concepts and language. I call such constructions "inventions" to suggest that children who are doing the learning are inventing their own language within the context of conventional language use (Y. Goodman & K. Goodman, 1992). "Invented spelling" is an appropriate term because it suggests that children are engaged in using features of their language to construct and represent their own knowledge. In their transactions with literacy events, they explore whether their inventions work within the conventions of written language. In this sense, invention and convention are always in tension with each other. It is in the careful examination of the critical lessons of individual learners that inventions become visible, and at the same time their shifts toward convention also become visible as learners discover the need and purpose for convention in a socially constructed world.

Results of research that focuses on the microanalysis of the artifacts of classroom experiences—a range of written compositions, transcripts of talk about various topics and responses to literature, analysis of miscues, the interactions of children with each other and with their teachers—continuously demonstrate the power of teachers who recognize what children know and help them use their knowledge to become engaged learners. Children are always learning and becoming readers and writers (speakers and listeners) as a result. The varied experiences children have with literacy impact how they refine and adapt their reading and writing to new and unfamiliar experiences. These experiences are critical to children's learning because classroom experiences can be miseducative (Dewey, 1938).

There are growing numbers of books, professional journals, and dissertations that document the results of teacher research and collaborations between university researchers and teacher researchers (Whitmore & Crowell, 1994; White Soltero, 1999; Martinez-Roldon, 2003; Lopez-Robertson, 2004). As a research and teacher education community, we need to expand on this kind of research, but we especially need to actively make such works visible to parents, politicians, the general public and other researchers as well. These works need to become a major focus in discussions about school reform, in documenting successful teaching, and in demonstrating the rich literacy learning and development that take place in classroom communities with knowledgeable teachers. Kidwatchers have the knowledge and experience to use the lenses of their understandings to learn about their students and to provide rich opportunities for children to expand and extend their language and thinking. Descriptions of these experiences must be highly visible to all the stakeholders in the educational community.

REFERENCES

Antler, J. (1987). *Lucy Sprague Mitchell: The making of a modern woman.* New Haven, CT: Yale University Press.

dePaola, T. (1974). *Charlie needs a cloak.* New York: Prentice Hall.

Dewey, J. (1938). *Experience and education.* New York: Collier Books.

Erickson, F. (1986). Qualitative methods in research on teaching. In M. C. Wittrock (Ed.), *The handbook on research in teaching* (3rd ed., pp. 119–161). New York: Macmillan.

Flack, M. (1971). *Ask Mr. Bear*. New York: Aladdin Paperbacks. (Original work published 1932)

Goodman, Y. (1985). Kidwatching: Observing children in the classroom. In A. Jaggar & M. Smith-Burke (Eds.), *Observing the language learner* (pp. 9-18). Newark, DE, & Urbana, IL: IRA & NCTE.

Goodman, Y., & Goodman, K. (1992). Vygotsky in a whole-language perspective. In L. Moll (Ed.), *Vygotsky and education: Instructional implications and applications of sociohistorical psychology* (pp. 223–250). New York: Cambridge University Press.

Harste, J.C., Woodward, V., & Burke, C. (1984). *Language stories and literacy lessons*. Exeter, NH: Heinemann.

Lopez-Robertson, J. (2004). *Making sense of literature through story: Young Latinas using stories as meaning-making devices during literature discussions*. Unpublished doctoral dissertation, University of Arizona, Tucson.

Martinez-Roldon, C. (2003, May). Building worlds and identities: A case study of the role of narratives in bilingual literature discussions. *Research in the Teaching of English, 37*(4), 491–526.

Meek, M. (1988). How texts teach what readers learn. In M. Martin (Ed.), *The word for teaching is learning: Essays for James Britton* (pp.) Portsmouth, NH: Heinemann.

Mitchell, L.S. (1950). *Our children and our schools: A picture and analysis of how today's public school teachers are meeting the challenge of new knowledge and new cultural needs*. New York: Simon and Schuster.

Owocki, G., & Goodman, Y. (2002). *Kidwatching: Documenting children's literacy development*. Portsmouth, NH: Heinemann.

White Soltero, S. (1999). *Collaborative talk in a bilingual kindergarten: A practitioner researcher's co-construction of knowledge*. Unpublished doctoral dissertation, University of Arizona, Tucson.

Whitmore, K., & Crowell, C. (1994). *Inventing a classroom: Life in a bilingual whole learning community*. York, ME: Stenhouse.

Whitmore, K., Martens, P., Goodman, Y., & Owocki, G. (2004). Critical lessons from the transactional perspective on early literacy research. *Journal of Early Childhood Literacy, 4*(3), 291–325.

Chapter 7

Writing From a Personal Perspective: A Story of Two Classrooms

Barbara Cohen and Danielle Welner

> *The child lives in a somewhat narrow world of personal contacts. Things hardly come within his experience unless they touch, intimately and obviously, his own well-being, or that of his family and friends. His world is a world of persons with their personal interests, rather than a realm of facts and laws. (Dewey, 1902/1915, p. 5)*

More than 100 years ago, John Dewey (1902/1915) wrote *The Child and the Curriculum,* in which he stressed the important role that children's personal interests and experiences play in their literacy development. Today, as in the past, students may fail to see the relevance of what they are learning and lose interest when classroom instruction in reading and writing is disconnected from their lives outside of school. They may come to believe that what they do outside the classroom is not important and that their measure as literate individuals is unrelated to their personal lives. In the two classroom stories that follow you will see the positive impact that personal involvement in writing has on both adults and children.

PART I—THE GRADUATE CLASSROOM: BARBARA'S STORY

> Curriculum begins in voice...Personal and social knowing is the heart of the curriculum. (Short, Harste, & Burke, 1996, p. 50)

It's the spring semester and I'm sitting with the graduate students in my class, Reading and Writing Practices in Early Childhood and Childhood. We talk about the teaching of writing in their elementary classrooms. They share with me some of the frustrations they are experiencing: students who are unmotivated, lessons that are unproductive, published pieces that are uninteresting, and audiences that are uninterested. To deal with their concerns, I have planned a writing project that I hope will help them develop their own skills as writers as well as improve the teaching of writing in their classrooms. I call it the Zine Project.

What exactly is a zine? It's a type of magazine, a collection of original pieces of writing on a single topic that reflect an author's interests, experiences, and personalities. The term *zine* originated online, where nonprofessional writers published personal zines in order to share their points of view about topics of interest with a small community of readers. Today on the Internet there are numerous sites where readers learn about zines, locate books about zines, and actually read zines (Block & Carlip, 1998).

I adapted the zine concept for use in my classroom because it reminded me of the I-Search paper developed by Macrorie (1980) who suggested that research papers need not present information in a detached and objective stance but could, instead, be written in first person about topics of personal interest.

I was also influenced by the multigenre research paper developed by Romano (1995, 2000) and adapted by Allen (2001), which offers writers opportunities to put a "personal stamp" on their writing and "try out the lenses of poets, fiction writers, playwrights, and artists" (Romano, 2000, p. 57), as they explore the ways in which different genres shape their visions of the world.

Taking Up the Challenge

So I began the Zine Project by asking students to select topics for their zines that would focus on personal interests and experiences. It was a challenge from the very beginning. "You mean we have to come up with our own topics?" more than one student complained. "But I don't know what to write about" was a common cry. My students' concerns reflected one of the biggest problems in the teaching of writing. For so many years, "it hadn't occurred to most of us to ask young children to select their own writing topics. No, the children simply wrote about whatever topics we assigned" (Harwayne, 2001, p. 3).

A few students found topic selection relatively easy. A passion for ice cream led Heather to research and write about the pleasures of her favorite dessert. Joanna, on the other hand, selected a topic that was less about pleasure and more about frustration: dating and the single woman in New York.

There was one student, in particular, who was in a panic about selecting a topic. Jill explained that she was under a great deal of pressure because of the responsibilities of work and graduate school. Her biggest concern was that if she made a bad topic choice she would end up spending the precious time she had working on something she might ultimately hate. Long after all of her classmates had made their decisions, Jill finally came up with a most appropriate subject for her zine—*stress*! We all laughed. Her topic had been there all along and only the "stress" of the decision making had brought it to the fore.

This was such an important lesson for all of us. The students knew that because they had to "live" with their topic choice for the entire semester while they worked on their zines, it had to be something they were passionate about. They were beginning to understand the personal investment writers must have in order to spend weeks, months and years of their lives working on a piece of writing.

Providing Scaffolding for My Adult Learners

At the same time my students were considering the subject matter for their zines, I began sharing examples of zines and magazines that focused on a single topic and contained writing in a variety of genres. As Zinsser (1985) points out, "The best way to learn to write is to study the work of the men and women who are doing the kind of writing you want to do" (p. 128). We examined how the same topic can be represented in a variety of genres and we also looked for ideas on different ways of designing a cover, writing a table of contents, conducting an interview, and so on.

The class agreed that in addition to a cover, table of contents, "Dear Reader" letter, and "About the Author" page, they would write about their topics from different vantage points by including five different genres: interview, fiction story, nonfiction piece, personal essay, and poem. Cartoons, advertisements, and other optional pieces could be added according to their personal tastes.

As the writing got underway in earnest, a concern about the expectations for each of the required items arose. After fielding many questions, I came up with a checklist that the students found extremely helpful (see Figure 7.1). They were surprised that as adults they still needed structure and support from the teacher, and they realized how important this was for their elementary students.

The book *Wondrous Words: Writers and Writing in the Elementary Classroom* (Ray, 1999) became the centerpiece of our writing workshop. The students agreed that her words were indeed "wondrous" and we relied on her book throughout the semester for inspiration and practical teaching ideas. According to Ray, "Many of us who teach writing have learned to let authors...help us show our students how to write well" (p. 10).

We took Ray's advice and examined picture books that could teach us about the craft of text structure. Heather, who was writing her zine on the

Zine Project Checklist

1. Cover

_____ • includes title, author, graphics, illustrations or photographs

2. Table of Contents

_____ • includes title, genre, page numbers and a brief description of each piece

3. Dear Reader Letter

_____ • provides an overview of zine contents

4. About the Author

_____ • gives biographical information (family, schooling, hobbies, etc.)

_____ • may discuss interest in zine topic and include photo(s)

5. Interview

_____ • contains title, background information about interviewees

_____ • may focus on more than one interviewee

6. Poem

_____ • can be in any format (free verse, rhyming, acrostic, concrete, etc.)

_____ • includes title and information about the topic

7. Personal Essay

_____ • written in first-person with personal and factual information

8. Nonfiction Piece

_____ • provides factual information in a creative format

9. Fiction Story

_____ • includes narrative story elements focused on topic

10. Overall Presentation

_____ • typed, numbered pages, graphics, photos, color, etc.

_____ • proofread for spelling, punctuation, grammar

Figure 7.1. Zine project checklist.

joys of ice cream, used the book *A Poke in the I: A Collection of Concrete Poems* (Janeczco, 2001) as the inspiration for her poem "Savor Your Flavor." Donna's zine featured her favorite vacation destination—the Adirondack Mountains. Her nonfiction piece "Somewhere in the Adirondack Mountains" was modeled after the book *Somewhere Today* (Kitchen, 1992), which uses repetition of the title as the first line of each paragraph.

Alphabet books like *Illuminations* (Hunt, 1993) proved to be very popular; students used them as models for poetry, fiction, and nonfiction. Alison, for example, used the alphabet sequence for her nonfiction piece "An A-Z Guide to Wedding Gowns and Accessories," in which she combined text and photos whereas Christine wrote a poem "The ABCs of Adoption" for her zine. As the students began to use picture books as models for their own writing, they became excited about using these same books for mini-lessons with the children in their classes.

A Celebration of Writers and Their Writing

Not surprisingly, as the due date for the Zine Project came closer there was much trepidation among the students, especially those who had chosen their topics late and were anxiously trying to accomplish too much with too little time. Nevertheless, everyone completed the task on time.

The zines were amazing! The range of topics was broad—some were serious, others were humorous—but all of them were extremely personal and reflected their unique "writer's voice." Included among the titles were: *Aloha from Hawaii, International Adoption, SOS: Seeking Other Singles, Tiny Treasures: Yorkshire Terriers,* and *Adirondack Adventures.* Their creative and original cover designs were equally impressive (see Figures 7.2 and 7.3).

The pieces in the zines made fascinating reading. Joanna's fiction story "The Worst Date Ever" provided an amusing look at the singles dating scene, and Michelle's personal essay "Taking Things for Granted" spoke poignantly about the traumatic diving accident that left her father a quadriplegic. In her zine about the Adirondack Mountains, Donna first made us laugh out loud with her light-hearted look at skiing titled "Confessions of a Quitter" and then brought us to tears in "My Dad, My Hero," a touching story of a father-and-daughter mountain-climbing adventure.

Our writer's celebration had been planned from the outset. On the day that the zines were due in class the students created a display of their completed projects. For most of the class session these newly "published writers" were busy reading the work of their colleagues and responding on comment cards that had been placed next to each zine. Although at first the classroom was silent except for the occasional turning of pages, conversation and laughter gradually erupted as the students began asking questions

Figure 7.2. *Stress* zine cover.

and offering comments and congratulations. It was clear that despite spending several months together in class, reading one another's zines created a new level of intimacy and friendship among the students. They spoke openly about their newfound appreciation for the excellent writing and creativity reflected in their classmates' publications.

New Discoveries

After the writers' celebration in class, I took the zines home to read them and write my own my personal comments to each student. I was surprised at

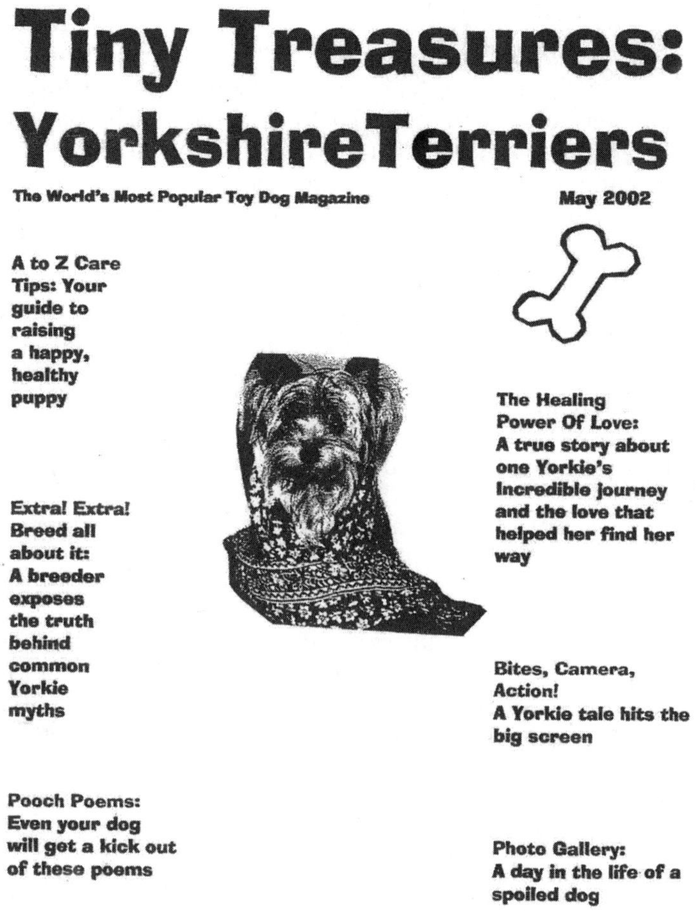
Tiny Treasures:
YorkshireTerriers
The World's Most Popular Toy Dog Magazine
May 2002
A to Z Care Tips: Your guide to raising a happy, healthy puppy
The Healing Power Of Love: A true story about one Yorkie's incredible journey and the love that helped her find her way
Extra! Extra! Breed all about it: A breeder exposes the truth behind common Yorkie myths
Bites, Camera, Action! A Yorkie tale hits the big screen
Pooch Poems: Even your dog will get a kick out of these poems
Photo Gallery: A day in the life of a spoiled dog

Figure 7.3. *Tiny Treasures* zine cover.

what I discovered. I found that Heather had a delightful sense of humor, Kerri had a flair for design, and Jill was a wiz at computer graphics. I recalled the words of John Dewey (1902/1915), who said, "There is all the difference in the world between having something to say and having to say something" (p. 56). If my students could write with passion and sensitivity about the important things in their lives, wouldn't it be wonderful if we could accomplish this same thing with children in the elementary school?

After the zines were completed, I asked the students to reflect on their experiences as writers. Kelly commented that she found some genres were easier to write than others; poetry writing for her was a pleasure whereas writing a personal essay was a much more difficult process. When it came to revision, Joanna stated, "I learned that I work best when I just go right to the computer. Prewriting is not for me."

Sharing these responses in class was such a valuable experience. It clearly highlighted the "idiosyncratic and recursive nature of the writing process" (Mayher, Lester, & Pradl, 1983) and helped everyone to become more understanding of the difficulties that their elementary students face as writers. Even more important was the pride and pleasure that each and every student felt about their final publications and experience as authors. Alice remarked, "I found out I enjoyed writing more than I thought I did. I never really considered myself a writer before."

When the final week of class arrived, the students were excited to take their zines home and share them with friends, family, colleagues and students. I was hopeful that this rich learning experience would continue on in the classrooms of my graduate students.

PART II—THE SECOND-GRADE CLASSROOM: DANIELLE'S STORY

> Writing is an act of faith: faith that what I have to say, how I see the world, are important.... My notebook is my filter of what's important and what's not. (Heard, 1995, p. 27)

Unfortunately, many school districts and teachers act as a filter determining what is important when it comes to a child's writing. Although we know that children's engagements with both reading and writing from the youngest ages represent meaningful activity in their social world (Martens, 1996), when they enter our classrooms they are often faced with limitations on the kinds of writing in which they can engage.

Prior to the course Reading and Writing Practices in Early Childhood and Childhood I had never even heard of the word "zine," and when faced with having to create one, I spent countless hours trying to think of a topic. It reminded me of my students' own frustrations in choosing topics. Although I knew that writers tend to write about things that are personally meaningful, it wasn't until I decided to create a zine that focused on Audrey, my Yorkshire Terrier, that this concept had personal relevance for me.

I knew that I wanted to give my second-grade students the same opportunity and creative control to produce their own zines and find their individual voices. Working on the Zine Project was going to be both a culmination and a celebration of our year of laughing, learning, and living together.

The Zine Is Born

Not long after completing my own zine project, I decided to adapt this project for my second graders. I realized that when children experience reading and writing solely for the purposes of fulfilling curricular requirements, meeting the standards, and pleasing the teacher, they miss out on the satisfaction of using language for personal and authentic purposes. They also may come away with a narrow perspective on the role that literacy plays in the world outside of school.

It seemed to me that the children would be better off working collaboratively in small groups so that they could divide up the work and have the support of their peers. I first shared my own zine, *Tiny Treasures: Yorkshire Terriers*, with my class. As I read to them, they became aware of many different types of writing: a "Dear Reader" letter, an "About the Author" page, an interview, a poem, a nonfiction piece, a fiction story, a photo essay, and a movie script. They loved my zine and asked me to read it over and over again.

Interestingly enough, many of my students seemed to know precisely what their topics would be. Their topics included everything from snowboarding to siblings and puppies to penpals. I created a chart of possible zine topics for some of my reluctant writers, and we discussed the importance of choosing topics not only that the children were interested in but also with which they had some experience.

After a long weekend to think things over, the students came in full of ideas. I asked each of them to write down their top two choices and then everyone came together to share. Amazingly enough, the children found that they had topics in common and were able to form groups quite easily.

It turned out that this was the year of the dog lovers; a majority of the girls and some of the boys expressed an interest in creating zines focused on puppies or dogs. The dog lovers gathered in one section on our carpet while others joined groups interested in bats, hockey, police officers, and New York City. Because of the tremendous popularity of the dog zine, I spent a little more time with this group, trying to narrow down the topic into more specific categories. This resulted in three separate zines: *Toy Dog Zine*, *Puppy Zine*, and *Doggy Times Zine*.

I was pleased to see that everyone was engrossed in their writing until one day a reluctant writer named Josh approached me. "I changed my mind!" he said, and sobbed that hockey just wasn't his thing. Knowing Josh, I was careful not to force him to choose one of the existing groups. Instead we spent lots of time talking about things that were important and relevant to his life.

Soon Josh realized that creating a zine about police officers, his father's profession, would enable him to write about something he knew a great deal about and, more importantly, it would be an opportunity to share something special with his father. Teddy, who was not yet in a group, volunteered to join Josh. He thought it would be cool to create an entire zine on police officers, especially after the bravery that so many of them had displayed just 8 months earlier on September 11, 2001. And so 5 days after the announcement of the Zine Project, all the children found topics that resonated with them and began writing.

Nurturing Young Writers and Their Writing

One of my initial goals for this project was to involve students in experimenting with different genres. We spent about 20 minutes per day looking at zines and discussing the different writing styles and creative layouts. I was fortunate to obtain copies of child-friendly zines such as *Animal Homes* (2000) and *Under the Sea* (1999), published by Scholastic. The children also had classroom time to check books out of the classroom and school libraries, to serve as models for their writing.

Because it was so late in the year, I narrowed the list of required genres to those I considered to be most appropriate for second graders. Each group received a checklist and a description of the requirements, which included a cover, a table of contents, a "Dear Reader" letter, and at least four different genres of writing. The genre choices were in the hands of the children; my job was to guide, model, and expose them to creative and interesting writing possibilities.

Over the next few weeks, we devoted roughly an hour each day to writing and shaping the zines. I was fortunate to work in a district where teachers like me had creative control to exercise professional judgment in teaching reading and writing using a meaning-centered and holistic approach. We were also fortunate to have access to quality literature and supplementary materials.

Big Lessons From Little Children

Zine writing took place as the children sat together in groups, of two to four members, where they planned their writing and experimented with different formats. Writing time became the most anticipated part of our day, and I realized that this unique opportunity for self-expression had a powerful influence on the children.

I spent part of our writing time conferencing with one group at a time. Although there were the occasional arguments, we found ways to work through them. The group working on the *Puppy Zine* (see Figure 7.4), for example, got into a tiff about who would be in charge of writing book reviews. Megan, Nadia, and Richard liked the idea of each member taking on a particular genre of writing, but problems arose when all three children wanted to write a review of their favorite fiction book. In the end, each student wrote a separate book review that showcased their individual talents and perspectives.

At one point, Josh, my most hesitant writer, stopped writing all together. I was concerned at first because although he had found a good topic, he couldn't quite figure out what to write about next. I was astonished when he approached me one day and explained that he had a great idea: He would interview his father, a police lieutenant, for his zine celebrating New York's bravest. As Josh

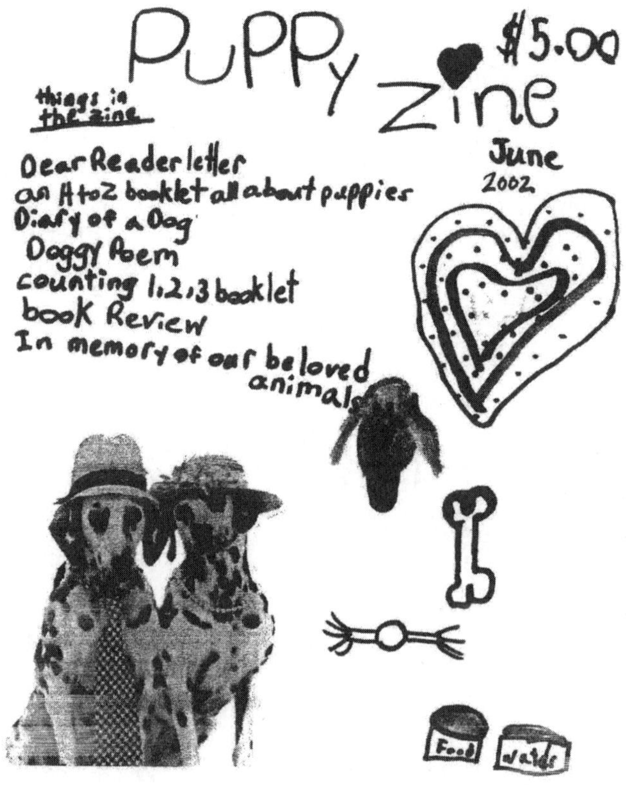

Figure 7.4. *Puppy Zine* cover.

demonstrated, the challenges of writing can be more easily dealt with if writers have access to information about the topics that interest them.

Even those children in my class who always loved to write were discovering new ways of using their words. For his *Hockey Zine*, Jesse was inspired by a concrete poem he had seen, and he carefully worked on creating a poem in the shape of a hockey stick. His writing partners, Michael and Danny, began collecting action-packed photographs of hockey players to include in their direction guide on how to play the game.

One of the published zines that I had shared with the children, *Animal Homes* (2000), provided a clear example of how to create a comprehensive diagram, including labels, of an animal. JohnPaul, Austin, and Thomas liked this idea and designed a "Close Up Look at a Bat" diagram for their zine *Blood Sucking Bats*. The question and answer book *How Do Bats See in the Dark? Questions and Answers about Night Creatures* (Berger & Berger, 2000) inspired the boys to create "Did You Know?," a compilation of facts that they learned during their research (see Figure 7.5).

The zines were not only informative, they were also poignant. In the zine *Things to See in New York City*, Cheryl recalls her feelings about the September 11 attacks. She writes, "This day we'll always remember the twin towers went down. This day my grandma will never forget. This day my grandma's friend died in the twin towers." Her writing partners, Nazia and Roshinie, added their own special perspectives on New York City. Born outside the United States, the two girls were eager to represent their perspectives on a city they had come to love. Their poem, with words printed against the

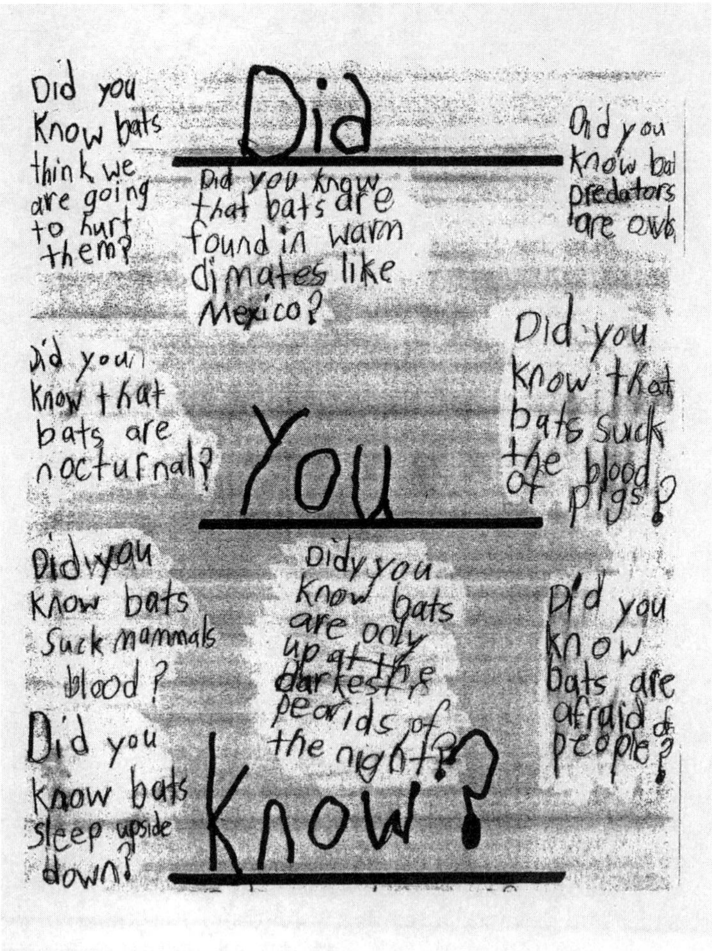

Figure 7.5. Nonfiction piece.

backdrop of a tall building, described "cars, interesting museums, Times Square, yelling, and kind people."

The Journey Ends, the Journey Begins

The last day before the end of the school year, the only thing on our agenda was to celebrate the children's work. The students proudly surveyed their zines sitting atop the empty bookshelves. The school's principal joined in the celebration as we witnessed these second-grade writers blossom into purposeful writers. One by one as each group shared its zine, sounds of laughter, cheering, and the occasional "oohhs" and "ahhs" filled the room. Watching the children smiling with zines in hand, I knew that this wasn't the end but actually a new beginning. Looking ahead to the next year with a different group of second graders, I couldn't help but think of the endless writing possibilities awaiting us.

The publications that resulted from this zine project affected my students the same way as my own zine affected me when I was in Barbara's graduate class. They were proud and even astonished at the quality of their writing. More importantly, they came away with new confidence in themselves and a desire to continue their work as authors in the future. As Georgia Heard (1995) stated:

> Writing is made of voices. Our single voices may seem to be lost in the bitter wind. But if we listen hard enough we can hear hundreds of voices trying to sing like us. Like threads weaving a cloth. Like the constellation patterns we draw to connect stars. Voices who have never dared sing before. (p. xi)

CHILDREN'S LITERATURE REFERENCES

Animal homes. (2000). New York: Scholastic.

Berger, M., & Berger, G. (2000). *How do bats see in the dark? Questions and answers about night creatures*. New York: Scholastic.

Hunt, J. (1993). *Illuminations.* New York: Aladdin.

Janeczko, P. (2001). *A poke in the I: A collection of concrete poems.* Cambridge, MA: Candlewick Press.

Kitchen, B. (1992). *Somewhere today.* Cambridge, MA: Candlewick Press. *Under the sea.* (1999). New York: Scholastic.

REFERENCES

Allen, C. A. (2001). *The multigenre research paper: Voice, passion, and discovery in grades 4–6.* Portsmouth, NH: Heinemann.

Block, F., & Carlip, H. (1998). *Zine scene: The do it yourself guide to zines*. New York: Girl Press.

Dewey, J. (1915). *The child and the curriculum and the school and society*. Chicago: University of Chicago Press. (Original work published 1915)

Harwayne, S. (2001). *Writing through childhood: Rethinking process and product.* Portsmouth, NH: Heinemann.

Heard, G. (1995). *Writing toward home: Tales and lessons to find your way.* Portsmouth, NH: Heinemann.

Macrorie, K. (1980). *Searching writing.* Upper Montclair, NJ: Boynton-Cook.

Mayher, J. S., Lester, N., & Pradl, G. M. (1983). *Learning to write/Writing to learn.* Portsmouth, NH: Heinemann.

Martens, P. (1996). *I already know how to read: A child's view of literacy.* Portsmouth, NH: Heinemann.

Ray, K. W. (1999). *Wondrous words: Writers and writing in the elementary classroom.* Urbana, IL: NCTE.

Romano, T. (1995). *Writing with passion: Life stories, multiple genres.* Portsmouth, NH: Heinemann.

Romano, T. (2000). *Blending genre, altering style: Writing multigenre papers.* Portsmouth, NH: Heinemann.

Short, K., Harste, J., & Burke, C. (1996). *Creating classrooms for authors and inquirers.* Portsmouth, NH: Heinemann.

Zinsser, W. (1985). *On writing well: An informal guide to writing nonfiction.* New York: Harper & Row.

Chapter 8

Monolingual Teachers Fostering Students' Native Literacies

David Schwarzer

The purpose of this chapter is to initiate a conversation about the roles of monolingual mainstream reading and language arts teachers related to the use of students' native languages in multilingual and linguistically diverse classrooms and to consider the following questions:

1. What knowledge must monolingual teachers possess to work in linguistically diverse and multilingual public school classrooms?
2. How should students' native languages in schools be viewed: as a "resource" or as a "liability"?
3. What are some unexamined misconceptions about monolingual educators teaching linguistically diverse students?
4. How might teachers foster their students' native languages and literacies?

After addressing these questions, I list 10 practical ideas to help monolingual teachers foster multiliteracy among their students.

WHAT KNOWLEDGE MUST MONOLINGUAL TEACHERS POSSESS TO WORK IN LINGUISTICALLY DIVERSE AND MULTILINGUAL PUBLIC SCHOOL CLASSROOMS?

The last U.S. census indicated that the number of language-minority students has increased dramatically over the last 10 years. There are more and more bilingual and multilingual children in U.S. schools. These children should be in bilingual programs designed and taught by certified bilingual teachers; or placed in classrooms designed and taught by second-language-certified teachers knowledgeable about second-language issues. However, the grim reality is that many language-minority children of immigration[1] (Suarez-Orozco & Suarez-Orozco, 2001) are being taught by well-intentioned teachers who are not well prepared to work with second-language learners.

Many researchers and practitioners agree that dual-language bilingual programs are the best possible option for language-minority students (Cloud, Genesee et al., 2000; Lindholm-Leary, 2001; Phillipson, 2000). However, many classrooms include second-language students from varied language groups where bilingual programs are not feasible because of the diverse nature of the languages involved. Because of the huge changes that have occurred in the demographics of the United States recently, school districts are often unable to keep up with the increasing number of second-language learners and their particular needs. Many of these students end up in "regular" classes that are already overcrowded. Therefore, it is imperative to redefine the role of the teacher to include a basic understanding of second-language issues and of the importance of fostering students' native languages as a national resource.

I make a distinction between a "large" language minority and a "small" language minority. Because of changing demographics, a large pocket of language-minority students may be present in one district while only a few of the same language-minority population are present in a nearby district. For example, Arabic speaking students may represent a large language-minority group in Detroit, MI, and a very small language-minority group in Ann Arbor, MI. For a particular Arabic-speaking student and his or her family, these different district affiliations may result in a well defined difference in the way they develop their native language: language maintenance through a well-developed bilingual dual-language program versus language loss in a "sink or swim" classroom. In most school districts, teachers deal with many different languages within the same class, with some of the languages represented by only a single student (Schwarzer, Haywood, & Lorenzen, 2003).

---

[1] According to Suarez-Orozco and Suarez-Orozco (2001) there is an important distinction between "immigrant children" (children born in other countries that immigrated to the United States), and "children of immigrants" (children born in other countries or in the United States to immigrant parents).

HOW SHOULD STUDENTS' NATIVE LANGUAGES IN SCHOOLS BE VIEWED: AS A "RESOURCE" OR AS A "LIABILITY"?

For many years, there have been voices in the field of education that have highlighted the importance of native languages as a national resource. Fishman (1980) cautions against the neglect of our own ecological language diversity: "Language resources are national treasures every bit as much as are mineral-, water-, and unpolluted air-resources. Once these resources are destroyed, they cannot be restored or recreated. We have been guilty of horrible neglect with respect to our language resources" (p. 170).

Since the bombing of the U.S. World Trade Center on September 11, 2001, the need for language-trained professionals in all fields, and in intelligence-related fields in particular, has become a national priority. Although it is not enough to think about native languages only from a utilitarian perspective, the United States is losing an important national resource every day as children and adolescents forget their native languages because they are not challenged to read and write in their mother tongue.

According to Ruiz (1984), language can be viewed as a problem, as a right, or as a resource. When it is viewed as a problem, it needs to be fixed. In many places, subtractive views of language learning are promoted (Valenzuela, 1999). Students gain English language proficiency, but lose their native language. When language is viewed as a right, it is a legal component of the school system and language diversity is viewed as one of our biggest assets, not a liability. For Ruiz, a second language is a resource that builds an additive attitude towards native language development (Valenzuela, 1999). Students, parents, teachers and administrators should encourage everyone in the school district not simply to maintain, but to foster students' native languages and literacies.

WHAT ARE SOME UNEXAMINED MISCONCEPTIONS ABOUT MONOLINGUAL EDUCATORS TEACHING LINGUISTICALLY DIVERSE STUDENTS?

According to Reyes et al. (1993), "Monolingual language arts teachers cannot tap into students' native languages because they do not have a working knowledge of other languages" (p. 659). I often discuss misconceptions monolingual teachers have about students' native languages in order for them to develop multiliterate classrooms. Then they decide for themselves how to address each misconception in their local communities.

Misconception. Monolingual language teachers cannot foster multiliteracy since they are not multiliterate.

Skutnabb-Kangas (2000) stated that:

> to what extent a monolingual teacher (or a teacher who does not know both languages involved in students' bilingualism) can support a student opti-

mally, has been extensively discussed... *A monolingual teacher teaching students who are to become bilingual or multilingual is by definition an incompetent teacher for those students,* except as an occasional guest speaker (Skutnabb-Kangas, 2000, p. 632' emphasis in the original)

Of course, a multiliterate teacher would be the best person to tap into all the resources available to multiliterate children; however, monolingual teachers may develop the sensitivity necessary to tap into the resources available in students' native languages, even if they do not have a working knowledge of those languages. Based on a growing number of multiliterate students in many school districts, teachers have no other choice. Rich language experiences that are good for the regular language learning—environmental print in the different languages, language use for authentic purposes, using authentic materials with authentic audiences, taking risks, and so on—are also good for multiliteracy development (Hudelson, 1987; Schwarzer et al., 2003). There are three positions in regard to the teaching of English to linguistically diverse children: teaching English at the expense of their native languages; teaching English regardless of their native languages; or teaching English while acknowledging, celebrating and fostering children's native language as a personal and national resource. This last option is the most supportive for language development but is still underdeveloped and basically unexplored.

Misconception. Only the classroom teacher is able to teach multiple languages in the classroom.

The role of the teacher in a linguistically diverse classroom that fosters multiliteracy is to become knowledgeable about the range of resources available in their learning community. The creation of such a community is possible when monolingual teachers orchestrate the classroom activity and are interested in involving the minority language community at large. Teachers can orchestrate different resources available throughout the school, the district, and the city to help students develop multilingual proficiency. Because language is socially constructed (Goodman & Wilde, 1992), the help of students, parents, siblings, elders, clergy, and other community members in a multilingual learning community is required. Tapping into students' linguistic community as funds of knowledge is crucial (Moll, Amanti, Neff, & Gonzalez, 1992)

Misconception. Teachers who do not know how to write in languages other than English cannot foster writing in the students' home languages.

Literacy in general and writing in particular are crucial abilities needed to attain high levels of multilingual proficiency (Fishman, 1999). Therefore, it is important for teachers to foster not only multilingualism, but multiliteracy (reading and writing in students' native languages) as well. To do so, monolingual teachers can enlist the help of parents, siblings, and other members of the school or district communities to provide students with rich multiliterate print environments in the classroom. For example, although monolingual teachers are not literate in languages other than English, they may ask parents or community members to buy or lend children's books in native languages for the classroom library. Teachers might also encourage parents to bring magazines, coupons, newspapers, and artifacts featuring native language print to give students real life experiences in their native languages. These are small changes in the classroom learning environment that have a big impact on students' appreciation and further development of their native languages and literacies.

Misconception. Teachers who do not know their students' home languages cannot assess their language proficiency in those languages.

It is not necessary to know Hebrew to assess whether or not a child reads Hebrew fluently. Experienced teachers know how struggling readers sound while reading in English. They sound exactly the same in Hebrew! When the child stumbles over every other word, looks for help, or sounds like a monotonous reader, these are likely to be signs that the child is not a proficient oral reader in his or her native language.

Another strategy used to assess students' native language reading proficiency is to ask students questions about the readings they have done in their native languages. If, for example, the child is reading a book like *Brown Bear, Brown Bear, What Do You See?* (Martin, 1992) in Korean, the monolingual teacher could ask the reader to point to the syllable or string of syllables that means "bear" in two different places in the book. If the Korean syllable does not look the same each time, the teacher asks the student for an explanation. By asking for particular words in context in several different places in the text, it becomes apparent that the child is not able to conventionally read the Korean text.

Misconception. Monolingual teachers cannot help children become multiliterate even if the teachers do not learn the heritage languages.

Modeling is central to any educational practice. If monolingual teachers want students to be interested in their native languages, they *must* provide a model for the children to follow. Teachers in the United States have wonderfully diverse cultural heritages (e.g., France, Germany, Poland, Italy, etc.). In central Texas, where the local teacher population is predominantly White and monolingual, many of the student teachers in our teacher education program are third- or fourth-generation German, French or Czech Americans. I discovered their language backgrounds by asking questions such as: *What do you call your grandmother? What kind of cookies does your family traditionally bake for Christmas? If your grandparents are alive, ask them what languages their own parents spoke, read or wrote.* Interviewing family members about their language backgrounds and constructing a family language use tree to display in their classroom is a feasible idea (Schwarzer, 2001). In a family language use tree, students explore their linguistically diverse backgrounds by asking family members (grandma, grandpa, mom and dad, etc.) about their family language backgrounds (see Figure 8.1). My students and I have been building family language trees for years. We are amazed to discover the varied language backgrounds of the students in the class who previously thought their families were monolingual English speakers.

Teachers and their students may learn to write their names in the writing system of their ancestry (Cyrillic, Hebrew, Arabic, Chinese, etc.).

HOW MIGHT TEACHERS FOSTER THEIR STUDENTS' NATIVE LANGUAGES AND LITERACIES?

Teachers' attitudes about native language instruction in the school falls into four basic categories: (a) to forbid, (b) to allow, (c) to maintain, or (d) to foster (Schwarzer, 2001).

	Grandmother	Grandfather	Grandmother	Grandfather
Called				
Language/s				
	Mother		Father	
Called				
Language/s				
	Me			
Called				
Language/s				
	Other family member/s			
Called				
Language/s				

Figure 8.1. Family Language Usage Tree, adapted from Schwarzer, 2006.

To *forbid* students' languages within the school setting may seem unusual in today's sociopolitical climate. However, there are states that have legislated English-only policies for their schools and there are unbelievable stories about teachers who penalize students for using their native languages in school. Many monolingual teachers in mainstream classrooms are unaware of their students' native tongues. Many teachers believe that their major responsibility is to foster English literacy development while disregarding students' native language resources (Ruiz, 1991). By ignoring or forbidding native language literacy, teachers are denying children the opportunity to become fully bilingual and biliterate.

In other contexts, there are those who *allow* students to use their native languages in some settings. For example, children may be allowed to use Korean during group work, and it is acceptable for one student to translate for another. In these settings, students' native languages are allowed for the purpose of the development of English. Thus, the creation of a primary language and a subordinate one is implied. Allowing native language usage "for a while" is looking at bilingualism and biliteracy as a "passing illness," such as getting the flu: You may cough for a while, but once you overcome "it" you will be completely cured (and become one of "us"—a monolingual English speaker and writer!).

The third option, to *maintain* students' mother tongues, is advocated by many language researchers and political activists (Fishman, 1980). Some language-minority groups have created private schools, weekend schools, and/or after school programs to maintain their children's native languages. Sometimes, even public schools and school districts under pressure from "large" language-minority groups hire qualified bilingual and biliterate teachers to teach during the school day in order to maintain students' mother tongues. However, these programs are considered extracurricular activity and available only for the language-minority students. Even when school districts take time and spend the money required for extracurricular maintenance programs, students still perceive a duality in their language learning—the school is mainly interested in developing English, whereas home and community settings are mostly interested in the development of English and the native language.

Many researchers advocate for bilingual and biliterate programs (Moll & Diaz, 1987; Moll et al., 1990), and others see the importance of native and heritage language instruction (Fishman, 1999; Skutnabb-Kangas, 2000). Others develop a strong case for mother-tongue language maintenance and for the need of a biliterate and multiliterate curriculum (Brisk & Harrington, 2000; Edelsky, 1986). However, such programs take place often outside of the classroom, as mentioned earlier. In a majority of classrooms that include second-language students from varied language groups with a monolingual teacher, bilingual programs are not always economically feasible. It is therefore crucial to engage monolingual mainstream teachers in understanding their critical role in the fostering of students' native languages.

I believe that the radical and still uncharted way to develop early multiliteracy is one in which monolingual teachers *foster* biliteracy or multiliteracy in their own classrooms. If the teacher only maintains students' native languages, the implication is that the native language should be "kept from disintegrating," kept in the same stage over a period of time. If the teacher fosters students' native languages, the implication is that the native language should be "improved" over the years of schooling.

TEN PRACTICAL IDEAS TO FOSTER MULTILITERACY

As a result of my work, I have adapted 10 ideas for monolingual teachers to use and adapt in teaching linguistically diverse students in their classrooms (Schwarzer et al., 2003).

1. *Create a multiliterate print environment*. Teachers, with the help of community members, can place multilingual posters throughout the classroom. These posters can include the alphabets or characters of the languages spoken in the class, key phrases such as *welcome, exit,* and so on, and the names of the children in the class written in their native languages and in English. One classroom teacher used transliteration for languages not written in alphabetic scripts in order to point at the written words while using them with her students.
2. *Use literature in students' native languages*. Children's literature in native languages becomes a bridge between the school and students' home cultures and is crucial to the development of students' native languages. Parents or siblings read a book in the child's first language for the whole class and students come to appreciate language diversity as a resource. Such readings send messages to the children who speak that language about the importance of their mother tongue. The classroom library should include books in the languages spoken by the children in the class and should be used during sustained silent reading or as resources for theme projects. The teacher might engage community members in developing audiotaped versions of the books for the children to use independently in the listening center.
3. *Create a multiliterate project to be conducted by a community member in the native language*. Dialogue journals, weekly individual literacy meetings in the native language, translation projects for the community, and letters to the grandparents or family members in the home country are only a few ideas to initiate the use of multiliterate projects with family or community members. Teachers and students can be in-

volved with these projects throughout the school year. The teacher orchestrates this activity while community members facilitate it.

4. *Create predetermined and relevant curricular language centers that are supported by multiliterate community members*. Teachers regularly invite multiliterate people from the community to help teach some of the curricular themes for the class in other languages. Not only extracurricular activities, but activities related to math, social science, natural science, and so on may be fostered in students' native languages by a family or community member. Teachers need to clearly communicate the expected outcomes to the community members involved. However, when children experience their native languages being used not only for "telling stories" but for "real science," it has deep effects on their conceptual development. In many communities, there are people who are untapped and unused resources.
5. *Create audiotaped cassettes with greetings, basic conversations, songs, stories, and so on in the students' first languages*. Teachers develop a community-produced collection of audio- or videotapes of community members singing; counting; telling about the daily weather; greeting the children at the beginning and at the end of the day. These audiotaped cassettes are coupled by a written version available to the students in the classroom multiliterate environment. Teachers then, during the daily routines of the class, listen to the audiotape while pointing at the written text. After a while, students from the different languages lead the daily morning routines while they make important literate connections between the spoken words in the audiotapes and the written words in the multiliterate print environment.
6. *Assess students' literacy in their first language*. Teachers need to know the students' linguistic abilities in their first languages in order to create a successful learning environment in which to foster children's multiliteracy. If teachers want to assess children's reading proficiency in their native languages and are unsure whether the children are creating their own idiosyncratic meaning from the written page, they may involve a community member in the assessment process. Moreover, if a child is able to read children's books alone, it is appropriate to challenge him or her to read the books in the classroom library independently while assessing his or her reading development over time.
7. *Start learning words and phrases in the students' first languages as well as your own heritage language*. Modeling is very important in language development. If teachers show they are learning their own family heritage language as well as that of their students, that modeling makes a significant impression on their students. Teachers learn simple phrases such as *How are you? Good job!* and *See you tomorrow* in their heritage language and in their students' native languages. To encourage

students to take risks with their own heritage languages and literacies, teachers should model their own risk-taking. This modeling has a profound impact on students' understandings of the importance of their native languages.

8. *Involve the community as active participants in the class.* Appreciating language diversity as a resource is a necessary first step in developing and fostering a multiliterate learning community. Parents, community activists, clergy, volunteers, and staff personnel become valuable resources for creating such a community. Moreover, by using family language trees, students' awareness of language is encouraged.
9. *Find ways to translate school letters and formal information sent to parents into all of the languages available in the learning community.* Teachers do not need to translate all the school letters and formal communications sent to parents on a weekly basis. However, it is important to create a letterhead in all the languages available in the classroom community for the formal communications of the school and/or the classroom teacher to the parents. The letterhead could include a phrase such as *Hello* in all the languages represented in the classroom. Also, the weekly folder sent home to showcase students' learning achievement should include at least a sentence written in students' native languages, such as *Great job! I am proud of you! Keep up the good work!* Moreover, it is important to have at least one formal letter per year sent to the parents in their native tongue to reassure them of the school's commitment to the development of students' native language and literacy proficiency. These activities involve the students, their families, and community members in creating a language bridge between the home and the school communities.
10. *Use the students' culture and experiences as a catalyst for multiliteracy development.* By inviting students to share with the class, issues related to their cultural backgrounds, their native languages become part of the classroom curriculum throughout the year. When students talk about their cultural traditions, they use their native language (e.g., *bar mitzvah, quinceñera, fajitas, kinaaldá*, etc.). Teachers who use students' backgrounds and cultural assets as a catalyst for curriculum purposes find students exploring their native literacies (Schwarzer, 2001). The students generate lists of cultural relevant words and concepts that are followed by the English explanation and posted for the whole class to see.

In this chapter, I have set forth the importance of engaging early childhood educators in considering how to respect and foster multiliteracy development in every classroom. Even as you read these lines, many children are losing precious words, phrases, and sentences in their native tongues. Reflective monolingual teachers fostering early multiliteracy development create sanctuaries in their classroom in which students' native literacies will flourish.

REFERENCES

Brisk, M. E., & Harrington, M. M. (2000). *Literacy and bilingualism: A handbook for ALL teachers*. Mahwah, NJ: Lawrence Erlbaum Associates.

Cloud, N., Genesee, F., & Hamayan, E. (2000). *Dual language instruction: A handbook for enriched education*. Cambridge, MA: Thomson Learning Order Fulfillment (PO Box 6904, Florence, KY 41022-6904).

Edelsky, C. (1986). *Writing in a bilingual program: Habia una vez*. Norwood, NJ: Ablex.

Fishman, J. A. (1980). Minority language maintenance and the ethnic mother tongue school. *Modern Language Journal, 64*(2), 167–72.

Fishman, J. A. (1999). *Handbook of language & ethnic identity*. New York: Oxford University Press.

Goodman, Y. M., & Wilde, S. (1992). *Literacy events in a community of young writers*. New York: Teachers College Press.

Hudelson, S. (1987). The role of native language literacy in the education of language minority children. *Language Arts, 64*(8), 827–41.

Lindholm-Leary, K. J. (2001). *Dual language education, bilingual education and bilingualism*. London: Multilingual Matters Ltd.

Martin, B. (1992). *Brown bear, brown bear, what do you see?* New York: Holt.

Moll, L. C. & Diaz, S. (1987). Change as the goal of educational research. *Anthropology and Education Quarterly, 18*(4), 300–311.

Moll, L.C., Amanti, C., Neff, D., & Gonzalez, N. (1992). Funds of knowledge for teaching: Using a qualitative approach to connect homes and classrooms. *Theory into Practice, 31*(2), 132–141.

Moll, L.C., Vélez-Ibáñez, C., & Greenberg, J., Whitmore, K., Saavedra, E., Dworin, J., and Andrade, R. (1990). *Community knowledge and classroom practice: Combining resources for literacy instruction* (OBEMLA Contract No. 300–87-0131). Tucson: University of Arizona, College of Education and Bureau of Applied Research in Anthropology.

Phillipson, R. E. (2000). *Rights to language: Equity, power, and education. Celebrating the 60th birthday of Tove Skutnabb-Kangas*. Mahwah, NJ: Lawrence Erlbaum Associates.

Reyes, M. L., Laliberty, E. A., & Orbanosky, J. M. (1993). Emerging biliteracy and cross-cultural sensitivity in a language arts classroom. *Language Arts, 70*(8), 659–668.

Ruiz, R. (1984). Orientations in language planning. *NABE: The Journal for the National Association for Bilingual Education, 8*(2), 15–34.

Ruiz, R. (1991). The empowerment of language-minority students. In C. Sleeter (Ed.), *Empowerment through multicultural education* (pp. 217–227). Albany: State University of New York Press.

Schwarzer, D. (2001). *Noa's ark: One child's voyage into multiliteracy*. Portsmouth, NH: Heinemann.

Schwarzer, D., Haywood, A., & Lorenzen, C. (2003). Fostering multiliteracy in a linguistically diverse classroom. *Language Arts, 80*(6), 453–460.

Skutnabb-Kangas, T. (2000). *Linguistic genocide in education, or worldwide diversity and human rights?* Mahwah, NJ: Lawrence Erlbaum Associates.

Suarez-Orozco, C., & Suarez-Orozco, M. M. (2001). *Children of immigration*. Cambridge, MA: Harvard University Press.

Valenzuela, A. (1999). *Subtractive schooling: U.S.–Mexican youth and the politics of caring*. SUNY Series, The Social Context of Education. Ithaca, NY: SUNY Press.

Chapter **9**

Nurturing Reflective Readers in Primary Grades Through Over the Shoulder Miscue Analysis

M. Ruth Davenport and Carol Lauritzen

In a one-on-one reading conference, Ruthi, the first author, asked third grader Hillary to explain her thinking about a miscue she had made during oral reading.

Ruthi (Teacher):	Which one were you stuck on?
Hillary:	(She points to the word "touch")
Ruthi:	"Touch"? OK, what did you think it was?
Hillary:	I thought it was like "thought" or something
Ruthi:	"Thought," OK, and how did you get "touch"?
Hillary:	I don't know really

This response, typical of young readers, shows Hillary's difficulty in articulating her problem-solving strategy. Her classroom experiences have not encouraged her to develop an ability to think about her reading and, therefore, to have conscious control of her own reading process. In an era of skill-based instruction, children may develop narrow views of literacy, rather than taking ownership of reading as a meaning-making process.

We have developed Over the Shoulder miscue analysis (OTS) (Davenport, 2002; Davenport & Lauritzen, 2002) to provide the context for a teaching conversation in which students are empowered as readers and develop metacognitive awareness of their own strategies and processes during reading. Using OTS miscue analysis also gives educators the information they need to make teaching decisions that support children as readers. Our goal is to nurture reflective learners who are able to express their actions as readers.

The purpose of this chapter is to establish the role of OTS miscue analysis as a tool in early literacy instruction that helps young readers develop metacognitive language and control over their own reading process. We describe OTS miscue analysis and provide evidence that it promotes metacognition in early readers.

WHAT IS OVER THE SHOULDER MISCUE ANALYSIS?

OTS miscue analysis is a tool for writing down information about the reader, her miscues, and her retelling, and it allows teachers to make notes about miscues, strategies to teach, or observations to share with the reader. [*Note.* For ease of description, we identify the reader as female, the teacher as male.] To conduct OTS miscue analysis, the reader brings any text she is currently reading to a conferencing setting. The teacher and student sit side-by-side to enable the teacher to read the text as well. It is not necessary to have a second copy of the text or to make copies of what the student has read. The teacher reminds the student of the type of notes he will be writing on the OTS miscue analysis form (see Figure 9.1); then the student is invited to read. Upon hearing a miscue, the teacher writes three things: (a) what the reader said, (b) what the text said, and (c) a check mark in one of the columns regarding self-correction or meaning change. These columns are: (a) self-corrected, (b) uncorrected with no meaning change, and (c) uncorrected with meaning change. Teachers return to the form after the conference to make the check marks in the graphic similarity columns. The conversations are not taped, so some miscues will inevitably be missed. However, the teacher still gains a wealth of information about the reader based on the miscues that are on the form. The OTS miscue analysis form should *never* become a place in which miscues are merely counted and presented to the reader as "mistakes" (Davenport, 2002).

At the heart of OTS miscue analysis is the teaching conversation. The teacher may occasionally stop the reader at the end of a sentence and ask for a discussion of the reader's actions and possible reasons for a particular miscue. He may also present, model, or scaffold reading strategies that may be helpful in the future. It is important that these interruptions do not occur too frequently and that they focus on significant teaching or a celebration point. Teaching conversations also occur after the reading. The student is invited to retell the passage and a discussion ensues to clarify misconceptions, to help the student understand any unfamiliar concepts or vocabulary she may have encountered, or to develop comprehension strategies. The

Over the Shoulder Miscue Analysis and Teaching Conversation
Davenport 2002

Student____ **Grade**________ **Date**________________

Selection Read_________________________________ **Type of Text**_______________________

Amount Read_______________ **Comments on Text**_____________________________________

Notes from TEACHING CONVERSATION – Scribe as much as possible

Here are **suggestions** for the conversation, which **may** include **any or all** of the following (**or other discussion**):

- Tell me about what you just read – Anything you'd like to add? – Do you remember what happened here? (if something significant was omitted) – Does this remind you of anything? – Do you have any questions about this?
- Take back to OTS form – Discuss patterns of miscues – Go back to individual miscues (teacher-selected or student-selected) - What were you thinking when you said…? How did you get that?
- Go back and clarify concepts or words where meaning may have been lost
- Select a brief Teaching Point – Model or remind student of a strategy – Suggest something to work on
- End with a Celebration Point – Point out what the student is doing well

Figure 9.1. Over the shoulder miscue analysis and teaching conversation form.

(continued on next page)

OVER THE SHOULDER MISCUE ANALYSIS FORM

Student____________________ **Date**________ **Selection Read**________________________________

Reader Said	Text Said	Self - Corrected	Uncorrected - No Meaning Change	Uncorrected - Meaning Change	Graphic Similarity			Self-Corrected during Conversation
					High	Some	None	

Figure 9.1. Continued.

(continued on next page)

TOTALS FOR THIS PAGE	Miscues:							
		SC	Unc No Chg	Unc With Chg	H	S	N	SC During Conv.
Overall Totals								
Percentages								

Cannot code for graphic similarity: Complex miscues, omissions, insertions, partials

Observations about Comprehension

Mentions important information______________________________

Able to summarize, gets the gist ______________________________

Able to synthesize text information – Gains a new perspective – Combines ideas - ____________________

Able to extend understanding through connections to self__________ to the world__________ to other texts (or movies)__________

Refers to making visual images of the text during reading______________________________

Able to analyze the author's craft (interesting words, metaphors, similes, colorful images)____________________

Asks questions____________________Makes inferences and predictions____________________

Figure 9.1. Continued.

(*continued on next page*)

Global Observations

_____ **Reader is self-monitoring their reading and constructing meaning**

High number of self-corrections, uncorrected miscues don't change meaning (*it's* for *it is*, *Mother* for *Mom*)

_____ **Reader needs to be more concerned with the construction of meaning**

High number of uncorrected miscues that change meaning, accepts nonwords

_____ **Reader is over-relying on print – Sounding out is strategy most commonly used**

Graphic similarity is high on miscues that change meaning (*house* for *horse*)

Additional Insights about this Reader and Suggestions for Instruction

Figure 9.1. Continued.

discussion also includes the OTS miscue analysis form, the reader's observations of her own reading process, specific miscues, potential reasons for the miscues, and strategies she has or could use. In addition, the teacher shares new strategies.

The talk that takes place during these individual conferences provides empowerment for readers, allowing them to take ownership of their own reading process. Teaching conversations allow the teacher to gain substantive assessment information and insights into the reader and help the student acquire the metacognitive awareness and metalinguistic language that will help her become better able to share what she observes about herself during the reading process. The teaching conversations provide a rich context in which the teacher helps the reader move forward in her ability to be an independent, efficient reader.

What Is the Rationale for Over the Shoulder Miscue Analysis?

We believe it is important for classroom teachers to know each individual student well as a reader. In order to do this, one-on-one reading conferences offer an opportunity to listen to each child read, assess her comprehension, examine her miscues, and teach the strategies used by effective and efficient readers (Goodman, Watson, & Burke, 2005). Miscue analysis enables teachers to look at the nature of the changes readers make in the text as they read orally and to examine whether the reader's miscues affect the author's intended meaning.

The teacher should proceed from, and help the reader develop, an understanding that reading is a process of constructing meaning from print, based on information from the language cueing systems: syntax, or sentence structure; semantics, or word meanings; graphophonics, or the relationships between symbols and sounds; and pragmatics, the cueing system that informs the reader about how language is used in varying social contexts.

Once teachers have gained this sociopsycholinguistic view of the reading process (K. Goodman, 1996) and learned to conduct miscue analysis (Y. Goodman et al., 2005; Wilde, 2000), inevitably they gain "miscue ears" (Watson, 1999). That is, they notice and interpret changes in the text during oral reading as valuable information about what the reader is doing with language and what strategies would be helpful to teach a particular reader.

What Evidence Do We Have That Young, Early Readers Can Be Metacognitive About Their Reading Within the Context of an OTS Miscue Analysis Teaching Conversation?

The OTS miscue analysis framework provides an expanded lens on readers and the reading process by combining analysis of miscues with a teaching conversation. It is through these discussions that young children reveal their metacognition. The following examples emerge from our work with 10 readers in Grades K–3 over 4 months. Hannah shows the level of awareness that a first grader can achieve.

[Before reading a book about bumper cars.]

Carol (Teacher):	After you read the title do you do anything special before you start reading?
Hannah:	Yeah, look at words and look at the picture at the same time.

Hannah knows that she can activate prior knowledge after considering the title and that she gets meaning clues from the pictures. After reading, Carol commented on one of her miscues.

Carol:	Do you know what was very interesting to me? I wanted to ask you how you figured out something...you weren't sure what that word was and then you got it because you asked me for help, but down here you got it all by yourself. How did you figure that out?
Hannah:	'Cause when I looked on that one and that one and that one (pointing to the word "car" each time it appeared on the page), I looked on these three. I said a word in my brain says "car" so I figured it out.

Although Hannah expresses her strategy in the language of a 7-year-old, it is apparent that she realized that the word "car" was repeated three times on the page and she used that repetition to figure out the word when it appeared again. Michael, another first grader, used a different strategy to figure out a word.

Carol:	This one kind of puzzled you. What is that?
Michael:	It seems like "creek." It was kind of hard because I figured out that two ee's are "e."
Carol:	Do you know what that word means?
Michael:	Maybe like one time we went to Wolf Creek and my brother's party was there. I guess a creek is like a mountain or something or like a little...we went to this one river that was like a creek.

Carol:	You did a good job of figuring it out from your experience.

Both these young children demonstrate that they, like others of their age, have metacognitive awareness of their reading, although they have not yet developed precise language for communicating their process.

Austin, a second grader, self-corrected the miscue of "certain" for "curtain." Ruthi asked him to explain.

Ruthi:	How did you get "curtain?"
Austin:	I knew that "certain" didn't go with "went up" and I went, like, "cur-tain."
Ruthi:	Okay, you put it in chunks.
Austin:	And then it made sense.

Austin was aware of semantics when he stated that "certain" didn't go with "went up" and recognized that reading is supposed to make sense. He also demonstrated how attention at the word level moves a reader to understanding at the text level. Littia, another second grader, reveals a "skip and go on" strategy.

Littia:	[Reading, gets stuck and stops, skips "many" and reads "things." Then she goes back and says "many."]
Ruthi:	You're so smart! Tell me how you got that!
Littia:	I sounded it out. I thought it was "man" but that didn't make sense, so I just read the rest and came back and I got it.

Not only does Littia have a strategy for pronouncing words, she is aware of and articulates that strategy. In her head, she first tried the "sounding it out" strategy, but she knew to cross-check for meaning. When it didn't make sense, she switched to a second strategy of using the syntax and semantics of the sentence to solve the word puzzle. It is notable that both Austin and Littia state that reading must make sense.

Third-grader Julián demonstrated a different metacognitive strategy. Although he was quite familiar with the book, he was not articulating the words clearly. Ruthi asked him what he was doing.

Ruthi:	You are doing so great, but you know what I'm hearing?
Julián:	What? Mumble, mumble, mumble?

Ruthi: Yeah, exactly.
Julián: I've been reading this book to myself. I'm thinking I can just hear it in my head.

Ruthi took him back to several key words that he had not articulated clearly, and found that he understood them. Julián realized he didn't have to read orally to understand the text, and he was aware that he was mumbling rather than pronouncing the actual words. Julián also cleverly demonstrated metacognitive awareness by volunteering to record Ruthi's miscues on an OTS miscue analysis form when she was reading to him.

How Can OTS Miscue Analysis Facilitate Young Readers' Development of Metacognition?

Some students need assistance in acquiring the language of metacognition. Both of us provide children with this language by labeling the readers' processes for them. Carol had Daniel examine his completed OTS miscue analysis form.

Carol: This column means you changed it but there was no meaning change. Look! You did two of that. You said "McGiffey" for "McGuffey" but it doesn't really matter the exact name of the book.... You started doing what a good reader does—self-correcting and the ones that didn't change the meaning, you left alone. Wasn't that smart?

Other times the labeling may occur during the retelling.

Carol: You said they wanted to train them (horses). How did you know they wanted to train them? That was a smart inference. What clues did you have for that?
Daniel: Well, I know what "breaking" means. When you ride them a lot and put on a saddle.
Carol: So you used the clue "breaking a wild horse" and said that meant to train them, so you made an inference and that is what good readers do.

Experience with this labeling allows children to acquire the language needed to explain their own processes. Other children benefit from coaching that allows them to acquire new strategies for reading. Second grader Caylyn was able to articulate her initial strategies in this way: "I sound it out" and "I skip what I don't know and I move on and I figure it out and go back to it.

'Cause if you skip a word, you can go to the other one and it can kind of tell you." Evidence for using a "sound it out" strategy occurred in every reading conference with her. The following excerpt is from the seventh conference:

Carol:	When you got right here, you paused for quite a while and then you said it was "decided." How did you figure that out?
Caylyn:	I saw the d-e-c and then I cut that part off and it said "ided."

Evidence for the "skip it and go on" strategy, which occurred less frequently, is illustrated by the following example:

Caylyn:	I read to the end of the sentence in my head.
Carol:	How did that help?
Caylyn:	'Cause it kind of told me at those parts, I figured it out.

It seemed that Caylyn did not know the "placeholder" strategy, as she would often pause for several seconds, and eventually ask for help. Therefore, Carol started coaching her to think about meaning and to put in a word that would make sense. Finally, in session 7, she miscued "mean" for "brainless" in "You are brainless copycats." This was a deliberate miscue on her part, taking advantage of the "placeholder" strategy. Caylyn was able to use a "meaning-making" strategy when she gave herself permission to be less print-bound. She was aware she had done this because she commented on using "mean" when she was retelling, indicating that it was a word she had used, although it wasn't the word in the book.

Kindergartner Logan provides a good example of how metacognition develops over time through coaching. In initial conferences, he demonstrated that he "could read" by pronouncing the words on the page. Logan, an impressive decoder for a 5-year-old, showed his willingness to rely on pronouncing sounds without constructing meaning when reading the last page of *Tina's Taxi* (Franco, 1994). The text read: "She washes her taxi until it shines. And then Tina goes to visit her friends." Logan read: "She washes her taxi until it sells. And then tells $gots to $vers her friends." (A $ indicates a nonword.) When asked, "If you were going to tell someone about this story who had never read it before, what would you tell them?" Logan replied, "I would tell them to never, ever read this story without me." When asked why people read he said, "Because of the books…the books are there." For Logan, the reason for reading a book was like the reason given for climbing a mountain—it's there! Logan recognized many words and sounded out many others, but OTS miscue analysis revealed that he had little understanding of the purpose of reading. Therefore, in each session, Logan's attention was drawn to the idea that reading is supposed to be meaningful. When reading a story about Halloween candy he had dictated, Logan miscued "haven't any chocolate bunch it's not good for me" for "haven't any chocolate because it's not good for me."

Carol:	What word would make sense right there?
Logan:	"Because"
Carol:	That word would make sense, wouldn't it? And when we read it's supposed to make sense.
Logan:	[agreeing] Yeah!

When Logan was reading the words he had dictated for the wordless book *Tuesday* (Wiesner, 1991), he was again reminded of meaning.

Carol:	You were able to read all the words that you wrote last time and those words tell the meaning of what's on that page, don't they?
Logan:	Ye-es!
Carol:	And even if you weren't here to read it for somebody, they could read your words and they would know what the meaning was on that page.

After eight instructional sessions emphasizing meaning, Logan made his first self-correction.

Logan:	...the bird stared...started to fly.
Carol:	You know what I really like that you did there? "Stared" didn't make sense so you changed it to "started." That was a really smart thing to do.
Logan:	[no comment but continues to read and then comments about the following page] Hey, that's not right. It should say "they floated to the house."

Again Logan connected the text with meaning. He did this again several pages later when he commented on the frogs floating "by his house" as opposed to "in his house." He continued to read until the frogs got inside the house and then he said, "I told you they'd get inside the house." Although Logan still had not articulated that reading is a meaning-making process, his comments and interactions during the OTS miscue analysis sessions indicated that he was starting to make sense of print, instead of just saying the words.

The young children in our study provide evidence that early readers are metacognitive and are in control of their own reading processes, leading to self-regulated learning. "Self-regulated learning, as the three words imply, emphasizes autonomy and control by the individual who monitors, directs, and regulates actions toward goals of information acquisition, expanding expertise and self-improvement" (Paris & Paris, 2001, p. 89). The OTS miscue analysis procedure scaffolds even the youngest reader toward viewing reading as a meaningful process. When Ruthi first began working with Littia, she was a reader who solely relied on the "sound it out" strategy. Now, she is a reader who clearly takes charge of the construction of meaning and uses a variety of strategies when encountering an unfamiliar word.

Additionally, the OTS miscue analysis teaching conversations help readers see what they are doing well as readers and help them realize that making miscues is part of the reading process. Teachers keep the focus on the student's construction of meaning while examining patterns of miscues, and empower students by helping them develop metalinguistic language.

> Working with a supportive teacher who is interested in what students are doing as they read, readers come to appreciate their own strengths. They become more confident and use their meaning-centered strategies more often and weaker strategies less. And they take responsibility for their reading, knowing they are responsible for constructing meaning in a text for themselves. (Martens, 1995, p. 42)

What Are the Critical Issues in Early Literacy Addressed Through OTS Miscue Analysis?

The positive effects of retrospective miscue analysis have been reported for third graders (Martens, 1998; Moore & Brantingham, 2003) and older readers (Y. Goodman, 1996; Y. Goodman & Marek, 1996; Moore & Aspegren, 2001; Moore & Gilles, 2005). Research in metacognition also reveals that older readers demonstrate control of their own strategies (Paris & Paris, 2001). Arabsolghar and Elkins (2001) report that "as children get older and learn about themselves and reading strategies, teachers can help them to be strategic readers by teaching the use of cognitive and metacognitive strategies in their classes and providing opportunities for practicing these" (p. 156). Our research indicates that we do not have to wait for children to get older. We can help very young children approach reading as a meaningful process in which they have ownership of their own strategies. However, we need to have the patience to model, coach, and support their learning and we must create the learning environment that scaffolds this ownership.

OTS miscue analysis has to occur within a rich literacy learning environment in which learners feel safe and are willing to take risks. Creating a community of learners in which we view "literacy as mutual aid" (Taylor, 2004) must be a priority. Mary Diener, third-grade teacher, achieves this community by giving children opportunities to demonstrate their miscues to the whole class. This allows students to be "showcased." They learn to observe themselves and others as readers. In this environment, readers not only are willing to have their miscues examined by their teacher but also are willing to be models for the whole classroom. They enjoy figuring out what other readers are doing and why, and they enjoy taking on the role of teacher (M. Diener, personal communication, January 20, 2004). "This is the kind of responsive teaching–learning relationship that moves the learner into the zone of proximal development by creating an environment where the learner's worth and potential as a reader is validated" (Moore & Aspegren, 2001, p. 503)

In the current political climate, children are being subjected to increased levels of assessment. Too often the purpose is to collect data to demonstrate achievement to outside audiences rather than to facilitate students' learning. OTS miscue analysis, on the other hand, is an effective tool that supports assessment *for* learning, not just of learning (Stiggins, 2002). OTS miscue analysis creates an interaction between the teacher and child that focuses on the learning process before, during and after reading. Looking at the whole process is critical for understanding a young child's learning (Ferreiro, 2004). OTS miscue analysis emphasizes taking a positive view of what readers *can* do, rather than a deficit view of what readers are unable to do. It also allows assessment to occur as part of the daily routine of the classroom so that the learner realizes that looking at oneself as a reader is part of becoming a good reader. Situating OTS miscue analysis within individual reading conferences provides assessment that is authentic, easy, and pleasurable.

Dyson (2004) has asked us to consider the "real basics" in literacy learning and how our beliefs shape our practices. We believe the basics must include children embracing literacy as meaningful and pleasurable. Therefore, we incorporate into our practice Over the Shoulder miscue analysis, which provides a context that keeps our focus on meaning and enjoyment. We know a reader like Daniel has attained the "real basics" when he says in a teaching conversation, "I would like to grow up and read my life away."

REFERENCES

Arabsolghar, F., & Elkins, J. (2001). Teachers' expectations about students' use of reading strategies, knowledge and behaviour in Grades 3, 5 and 7. *Journal of Research in Reading, 24*, 154–162.

Davenport, M. R. (2002). *Miscues, not mistakes: Reading assessment in the classroom.* Portmouth, NH: Heinemann.

Davenport, M. R., & Lauritzen, C. (2002). Inviting reflection on reading through Over the Shoulder Miscue Analysis. *Language Arts, 80*, 109–118.

Dyson, A. H. (2004, January 24). *Written language in childhood spaces: A critical perspective on the "basics."* Paper presented at the Critical Issues in Early Literacy Conference, University of Arizona, Tucson.

Ferreiro, E. (2004, January 24). *Critical literacy issues: The acquisition of written language.* Paper presented at the Critical Issues in Early Literacy Conference, University of Arizona, Tucson.

Franco, B. (1994). *Tina's taxi.* New York: Scholastic.

Goodman, K. S. (1996). *On reading: A common-sense look at the nature of language and the science of reading.* Portsmouth, NH: Heinemann.

Goodman, Y. (1996). Revaluing readers while readers revalue themselves: Retrospective miscue analysis. *The Reading Teacher, 49,* 600–609.

Goodman, Y. M., & Marek, A. (1996). *Retrospective miscue analysis: Revaluing readers and reading.* Katonah, NY: Richard C. Owen.

Goodman, Y. M., Watson, D. J., & Burke, C. (2005). *Reading miscue inventory: From evaluation to instruction.* New York: Richard C. Owen.

Martens, P. (1995). Empowering teachers and empowering students. *Primary Voices, 3,* 39–42.

Martens, P. (1998). Using retrospective miscue analysis to inquire: Learning from Michael. *The Reading Teacher, 52,* 176–180.

Moore, R. A., & Aspegren, C. M. (2001). Reflective conversations between two learners: Retrospective miscue analysis. *Journal of Adolescent & Adult Literacy, 44,* 492–504.

Moore, R. A., & Brantingham, K. L. (2003). Nathan: A case study in reader response and retrospective miscue analysis. *The Reading Teacher, 56,* 466–474.

Moore, R. A. & Gilles, C. J. (2005). *Reading conversations: Retrospective miscue analysis with struggling readers, grades 4–12.* Portsmouth, NH: Heinemann.

Paris, S. G., & Paris, A. H. (2001). Classroom applications of research on self-regulated learning. *Educational Psychologist, 36,* 89–102.

Stiggins, R. (2002). Assessment crisis: The absence of assessment FOR learning. *Phi Delta Kappan, 83,* 758–765.

Taylor, D. (2004, January 23). *Literacy for the common good: Teaching in the cracks for a more just and caring world.* Paper presented at the Critical Issues in Early Literacy Conference, University of Arizona, Tucson.

Watson, D. J. (1999). A whole language journey: Are we there yet? In A. M. Marek & C. Edelsky (Eds.), *Reflections and connections: Essays in honor of Kenneth S. Goodman's influence on language education* (pp. 51–66). Cresskill, NJ: Hampton Press.

Weisner, D. (1991). *Tuesday.* New York: Scholastic.

Wilde, S. (2000). *Miscue analysis made easy: Building on student strengths.* Portsmouth, NH: Heinemann.

Chapter 10

Influences on Retellings: Learning from High and Low Retellers

Prisca Martens, Pat Wilson, and Poonam Arya

Retellings have been used for language-based inquiries for over 75 years (Kalmbach, 1986). These inquiries provide evidence, for example, that repeated instruction with retellings raises comprehension (Gambrell, Koskinen, & Kapinus, 1991), that mediated story retellings benefit children with learning disabilities (Morrow, Sisco, & Smith, 1992), and that comprehension is related to children's sense of story (Barnhart, 1990). Studies also show differences between the retellings of good and poor readers (Weber, 1990), and that retellings may be used to strengthen student responses and to learn subtle difficulties students may be having (Kalmbach, 1986). The National Reading Panel (2000), too, found a "firm scientific basis" (p. 4–42) for the effectiveness of retellings (recall of story) on building comprehension.

Our past research led us to study children's readings and retellings more deeply. In this chapter we provide an in-depth analysis of the highest and lowest retellings and the associated readings of second graders in different reading programs. Focusing on these readings and retellings clearly highlights their unique features and relationships. The data we report is drawn from a larger study that used both qualitative and quantitative techniques to examine the impact of three second grade reading programs on children's understandings and perceptions of reading and their reading strategies (Arya et al., 2005; Wilson et al., 2003). Two were commercial reading programs that use explicit and systematic phonics instruction as central to early reading instruction: Reading Mastery (RM) (Engelmann et al., 1995) and Open Court (OC) (SRA/McGraw-Hill, 2000). The third was a literature-based program, labeled Guided Reading (GR), wherein children were taught to use multiple strategies to focus on the meaning of what they read.

WHAT WE DID

The 84 children in the larger study attended schools in urban settings, were matched on percentages of free and reduced lunch programs (87–100%), and were not receiving special education or English as a second language services. The children had also been in their respective schools and reading programs for at least 2 years. We worked one-on-one with each child in two separate sessions. Both sessions were audiotaped and transcribed. We counterbalanced the sessions to eliminate any effects of the session order. In one session we used an adaptation of the reading interview (Goodman, Watson, & Burke, 2005) to learn the children's beliefs about reading, the strategies they use, and perceptions of themselves as readers. We also administered the Woodcock Johnson Psycho-Educational Battery–R (WJPE–R), Word Attack subtest (Woodcock & Johnson, 1990) to assess the children's knowledge of phonics application to pseudo-words in isolation.

In the other session, we asked the children to read and retell a complete text following standard miscue analysis procedures (Goodman et al., 2005). The texts were authored trade books that had been leveled according to Fountas and Pinnell's (1996, 2001) criteria. We considered both a child's reading accuracy and the quality of the retelling when determining whether to move the child to a more advanced level book.

When the children finished reading, we asked them to tell the story in their own words. Each of these retellings consisted of two parts. First, in the unaided retelling, the children shared, without being interrupted, what they remembered from the reading. Then, in the aided retelling, we asked questions that were rephrasings of the readers' comments (without giving information about the text) or that were general prompts, such as "Tell me more about…"

Data Analysis

To analyze the miscues we followed the classroom procedure of miscue analysis (Goodman et al., 2005), with at least two researchers coding each child's miscues (inter-rater reliability of .90). We scored the WJPE–R Word Attack Subtest according to the test's procedures.

To analyze the retellings we adapted the quantitative retelling protocol established by Morrow (2001). We scored evidence of setting, characters, plot episodes, story cohesion, and inferences/connections on a scale of 0 to 2, with

0 indicating no evidence and 2 indicating strong evidence, and calculated the number of points earned over the total possible points to gain a percentage score. Two of us coded each retelling, and in cases of disagreement a third researcher resolved the differences (interrater reliability of .95).

High and Low Retellers

To identify the retellers for this study, we ordered the children's retelling scores from highest to lowest across programs and located natural breaks between scores. These breaks fell at 75% for readers with high retelling scores and at 38% for those with low retelling scores. High and low retellers were represented in all three programs but not equally. We then looked for natural breaks in the ordered scores within each program to create more equal representations of readers. For the high retellings this meant that we adjusted the score for Open Court to 71%. For the low retellings we adjusted the Reading Mastery and Open Court scores to 33% and the Guided Reading score to 45%. With these scores we identified 17 high and 16 low retellers (6 high and 5 low from RM, 5 high and 5 low from OC, 6 high and 6 low from GR). These 33 retellers represent about 38% of the children in the larger study.

We began our analysis of the high and low retellings with the retelling content (setting, characters, plot episodes, and inferences/connections) that we'd previously analyzed for the larger study (see Figure 10.1A). To further analyze the data we followed Lincoln and Guba's (1985) process for reading the retellings of these 33 children to find emerging themes. The overall theme that emerged from our readings related to the forms of the retellings. The forms fell into two broad categories: the organization the reader used for the retelling, and the types of language features the reader used (see Figure 10.1B). We determined subcategories for each of the forms. Organization refers to whether or not the student retold using *scattered details* (no order or "big ideas"), a *gist* (the basic plot with no elaboration), or a *story* (a narrative) and the cohesiveness of the retelling (high, some, or none). Language refers to whether the student *stuck to language in the text,* included *transition words* (i.e., "after that...," "in the beginning...," etc.), "translated" the text to use *personalized language* or dialect, integrated *dialogue* from the story into the retelling, and used *complex sentence structures* (i.e., independent and dependent clauses rather than simple sentences). Once we determined the subcategories for each form, two of us independently coded the retellings and compared our results (interrater reliability of .96).

THREE READING PROGRAMS

To contextualize our findings, we first describe each of the programs.

Reading Mastery

The Reading Mastery (RM) site uses a scripted reading program (Engelmann et al., 1995), in which children are homogeneously grouped based on program assessments. The phonics instruction is explicit and systematic, and draws on synthetic phonics as defined in the National Reading Panel report (2000). Comprehension is explicitly taught through repetition, with questions asking for specific answers, and skill exercises. For example, when reading a factual selection, children read one to two sentences, the teacher asks text explicit questions, and sometimes the teacher gives information for children to repeat. Materials include a second-grade anthology written by two authors who use a controlled vocabulary and incorporate general information intended to build children's knowledge base.

Open Court

In the Open Court (OC) program for initial reading instruction (K–2) children read a literature anthology containing both classic and contemporary literature organized in thematic units. Decoding skills are taught systematically and explicitly. In the second grade program there is a shift from decoding skills to reading fluency and comprehension taught through teacher directed literal and inferential questions (SRA/McGraw-Hill, 2000). The teachers are advised to follow a three-part scripted instructional plan for both word study and comprehension. The children in this program are homogeneously grouped for reading based on program assessments.

Guided Reading

Based on her interpretation of Fountas and Pinnell's (1996) work, the school reading specialist designed this literature-based program for the GR site, which she called "Guided Reading." Although there are similarities to the work of Fountas and Pinnell (1996), the GR program diverges from that work in significant ways, one being the homogeneous grouping of the children for reading across second grade classrooms on the basis of running record accuracy scores. During reading instruction, the teachers use authentic texts and, when the children encounter difficulty, encourage them to: "Read that again so that it sounds good"; "If you don't know it, skip it and come back"; and "Use the sounds and the picture to figure out the word" (Jordan, 2002). Stories are regularly discussed and children are encouraged to connect what they are reading to their personal experiences. The teachers support children's growth in comprehension through such strategies as timelines and story maps. Skills and phonics are taught primarily in meaningful contexts, not in isolation. Instruction in using graphophonic cues, for example, involves asking the children to find words in the text they are reading that begin or rhyme with the sound of a target word.

OUR RESULTS

Analysis of Retelling Content

The high retellers, as expected, score higher than (or, in one instance, equal to) the low retellers in each area of retelling content (see Figure 10.1A). It is notable that in making inferences and connections both the GR high and low retellers are considerably stronger (63% and 47%, respectively) than the RM (50% and 0%, respectively) and OC (25% and 25%, respectively) retellers.

Figure 10.2 and Figure 10.3 display excerpts from two RM retellings of *Flossie and the Fox* (McKissack, 1986), one high (Andrew, 82%) and one low (Bethany, 23%). Andrew (see Figure 10.2) names characters (i.e., Flossie, the fox, the mother/grandmother) and includes a range of details from the plot. Bethany (see Figure 10.3), on the other hand, names characters (i.e., Flossie, the fox) and makes few references to the storyline.

Analysis of Retelling Form

Organization. In organizing their retellings, most of the high retellers at OC (75%) and GR (83%) provide the gist, whereas most RM high retellers (83%) use a story-like (narrative) structure (see Figure 10.1B). In contrast, no low retellers organize their retellings as a story. The high retellers in all three programs are strong in cohesiveness, but only GR low retellers show any cohesion. Andrew (see Figure 10.2), for example, tells a story with cohesion (score: 1 out of 2), whereas Bethany provides scattered details with no cohesion (see Figure 10.3).

Language. Although all of the high retellers use both personalized language and complex sentence structures, they vary in their use of transition words (range of 67% to 83%) and dialogue (range of 25% to 83%) (see Figure 10.1B). Among the low retellings, there is no consistent pattern. For example, no RM low retellers use transition words or dialogue, but those in the other two programs do (see Figure 10.1B). When comparing across the three programs we find that the GR low retellers have higher percentages than the RM and OC low retellers in the use of transition words, personalized language, dialogue, and complex sentences. No GR low reteller sticks to the language of the text; that is, they all use personalized language.

Andrew and Bethany provide examples of the high and low retellers' use of language. Andrew (see Figure 10.2) uses transition words (i.e., "when she

A.

Retelling Content:	RM Retellers High	RM Retellers Low	OC Retellers High	OC Retellers Low	GR Retellers High	GR Retellers Low
Setting	81%	42%	100%	67%	100%	83%
Characters	100%	83%	94%	50%	94%	50%
Plot Episodes	86%	23%	72%	23%	79%	33%
Inferences/Connections	50%	0%	25%	25%	63%	47%

B.

Retelling Form:	RM Retellers High	RM Retellers Low	OC Retellers High	OC Retellers Low	GR Retellers High	GR Retellers Low
Organization						
Scattered Details	17%	100%	0%	80%	0%	40%
Gist	0%	0%	75%	20%	83%	60%
Story	83%	0%	25%	0%	17%	0%
Cohesion	75%	0%	100%	0%	81%	33%
Language						
Sticks to the Text	0%	40%	0%	60%	0%	0%
Transition Words	83%	0%	75%	40%	67%	80%
Personalized Lang.	100%	60%	100%	40%	100%	100%
Dialogue	83%	0%	25%	20%	67%	40%
Complex Sentences	100%	20%	100%	40%	100%	100%

Figure 10.1. Content and form (organization and language) included in the high and low retellings.

Researcher (R): Alright, Andrew...retell me *Flossie.*

Andrew (A): Flossie, she is a girl and she is taking Ms. ____ a basket of eggs.

R: Excellent. Okay.

A: And she meets a fox and the fox wants the eggs. (R: Mm-hm). And she won't give the fox the eggs because they are for, um, Ms. __. (R: Go ahead...) And, when she was on her way, the fox followed her and he was trying to prove that he was a fox. (R: Mm.) And the fox said, "If I prove to you that I am a fox, will you give the eggs?" and she said, "That's only if you prove to me that you are a fox." (R: Mm-hm) And, when she got to the last page, she told the fox that, "You have big teeth. I know one of Mr. J.W.'s hounds have big teeth and he is looking at you right now and all over you." (R: Mm-hm) And, when it first begins, she, her mom called her, when her mom called her, she hurried up and put her little stuffed doll in a tree trunk. (R: Mm-hm). And when she got to her mother's house, ...

Figure 10.2. Excerpts of Andrew's retelling of *Flossie and the Fox* (McKissock, 1986).

got to the last page"), dialogue (i.e., "If I prove..."), personalized language (i.e., "stuffed"), and complex sentences (i.e., "when she was..."). Bethany (see Figure 10.3), however, only uses language from the story and simple sentences, with no transition words, personalized language, dialogue, or inferences/connections.

Analysis of Miscue and Strategy Patterns

Figure 10.4 contains the miscue analysis scores that are representative of the patterns we found between the high and low retellers in each program. Figure 10.4A contains selected scores related to meaning construction. The "meaning construction no loss" pattern is the "comprehending score." This score indicates miscues that are fully acceptable in the story or, if they are unacceptable, they are successfully self-corrected. Comprehending scores indicate students' reading proficiency by determining the quality of readers' miscues and readers' ability to successfully focus on meaning *during* the

Researcher (R): ...Bethany, ... Tell me about [the story].

Bethany (B): *Flossie and the Fox.*

R: ... What's it about? ...

B: She was going to take some fresh eggs. (R: Okay...) She put a cat in the log and the cat __ branches. (R: ...Okay...) The fox kept on going where she was going...There were chickens there.

R: Why'd the fox keep going where she was going?

B: Keep asking questions.

Figure 10.3. Excerpts of Bethany's retelling of *Flossie and the Fox* (McKissock, 1986).

reading (Goodman, 2003). This differs from the comprehension score (indicated by the retelling scores), which focuses on meaning *after* they've finished reading. The "meaning construction loss" pattern calculates the reader's unacceptable miscues that are not successfully corrected, thereby causing the reader to lose meaning (Goodman et al., 2005).

The meaning construction patterns in Figure 10. 4A show that although the high retellers have higher retelling scores, the low retellers have comparable, even slightly higher, comprehending scores. In other words, although there are stark differences in their comprehension *after* they read, the high retellers (comprehending scores of RM: 34%; OC: 32%; GR: 30%) and low retellers (comprehending scores of RM: 39%; OC: 39%; GR: 32%) show similarities in comprehending *while* they read. This indicates that they read with similar patterns of fully acceptable miscues or correction of unacceptable miscues. The meaning loss scores indicate that the OC (57%) and GR (49%) high retellers lost more meaning while reading than did the low retellers (OC: 48%; GR: 44%).

Figure 10.4B primarily shows readers' use of graphophonics. "Sound similarity" and "graphic similarity" reveal the children's use of sound and graphic cues in context, whereas the "phonics pseudo-words" score (Woodcock & Johnson, 1990) shows their use of phonics out of context. "Miscues per hundred words" (see Figure 10.4B) indicates the readers' accuracy as they read.

The graphophonics patterns show that the low retellers in all three programs make more use of sound cues than do the high retellers (see Figure 10.4B). The use of graphic cues is similar between low and high retellers re-

A. Meaning Construction

	Retelling Mean Scores		Meaning Construct. No Loss (Comprehending Score)		Meaning Construct. Loss	
	High	Low	High	Low	High	Low
RM	82 %	25 %	34 %	39 %	36 %	50 %
OC	76 %	26 %	32 %	39 %	57 %	48 %
GR	83 %	37 %	30 %	32 %	49 %	44 %

B. Graphophonics

	Sound Similarity		Graphic Similarity		Phonics Pseudo Words		Miscues Per Hundred Words	
	High	Low	High	Low	High	Low	High	Low
RM	75 %	85 %	92 %	89 %	42 %	57 %	12.0	8.6
OC	81 %	93 %	87 %	92 %	33 %	45 %	12.6	9.7
GR	87 %	90 %	94 %	92 %	32 %	48 %	12.1	8.9

Figure 10.4. Mean miscue analysis scores for the high and low retellers at the Reading Mastery (RM), Open Court (OC), and Guide Reading (GR) sites.

gardless of program. The most dramatic difference in scores for the high and low retellers is with the test of phonics using pseudo-words (see Figure 10.4B). Whether they are receiving systematic explicit phonics instruction or phonics instruction in context, the low retellers in all three programs (RM: 57%; OC: 45%; GR: 48%) score considerably higher than the high retellers (RM: 42%; OC: 33%; GR: 32%). In standard scores (Woodcock & Johnson, 1990) the low retellers' scores (RM: 117; OC: 110; GR: 110) are considerably above the high retellers' scores (RM: 104; OC: 101; GR: 99), with a score of 100 being on grade level. The low retellers, then, are much better at sounding out and reading nonsense words than are the high retellers, regardless of instruction. The low retellers are also more accurate readers than the high retellers.

Reading samples from two GR students, Benjamin (high reteller: 86%) and Cameron (low reteller: 29%), who read the first chapter of *A Cricket in Times Square* (Selden, 1960) illustrate the similarities in the high and low retellers' patterns of reading strategies. Both readers use prediction strategies, correction strategies, and most of their miscues are fully or partially syntactically and semantically acceptable. The following text sentence provides an example.

Text:	"From above, through the iron grills that open on to the streets, he had heard the thrumming of the rubber tires..."
Benjamin:	"From above, through the iron grills that open on to the streets, *and*..."
Cameron:	"From above, *those*..."

The miscues of both readers demonstrate that they are integrating language cues and predicting meaning. Benjamin substitutes "and" for "he," predicting a compound phrase, and Cameron substitutes "those" for "through," predicting the subject of the sentence. Although their miscues are not acceptable in the complete sentence, they are partially acceptable because they make sense from the beginning of the sentence up to and including the miscue.

Another example is found in this sentence:

Text:	"Birds, the pigeons of New York, and the cats, and even the high purring of airplanes above the city Tucker had heard,..."
Benjamin:	"*The* birds, the pigeons of New York, the cats, ..."
Cameron:	"Birds, the pigeons of New York, and the cats, even the high purring of the airplanes above the city..."

In this example Benjamin inserts "The" before "Birds" and omits "and" after "New York" and Cameron inserts "the" before "airplanes" and omits "and" after "cats." Both readers make miscues that are fully syntactically and semantically acceptable and do not change the meaning of the text, demonstrating that they are comprehending and focusing on meaning as they read.

WHAT WE'VE LEARNED

As we reflect on the profiles of the high and low retellers we are struck by several findings. The first is that as they are reading, the low retellers do not *sound* that different from the high retellers. The two groups read similar material, use similar strategies, and are comprehending in comparable ways. Yet there are stark differences in their retellings. With one exception, the high retellings are told in gist or story form with some cohesion and include descriptions of the setting and characters, most of the plot episodes, and some inferences/connections, transition words, and dialogue. In addition, all of these retellers use personalized language and complex sentences.

The low retellings, on the other hand, involve primarily scattered details (some as a gist) with descriptions of the setting, characters, and plot episodes and, in some cases, transition words, dialogue, personalized language, and complex sentences. These differences in the quality of the students' retellings is not the result of differences in the students' readings, however, because they are comprehending in similar ways.

Second, we find that the children in the Open Court and Reading Mastery programs who receive systematic explicit phonics instruction do not have higher scores in phonics or comprehension than the Guided Reading children who receive phonics instruction in the context of meaningful reading and discussions. Both the low and high retellers in the GR program have scores similar to the low and high OC and RM retellers when using graphophonic cues in context or in reading pseudo-words in isolation. The retelling scores for the high retellers at GR and RM are similar, whereas the low retellers at GR score substantially higher than the low retellers at OC and RM. This finding runs counter to the conclusions in publications such as *Put Reading First* (Armbruster, Lehr, & Osborn, 2001), which states, for example, that "Systematic phonics instruction results in better growth in children's ability to comprehend what they read than non-systematic or no phonics instruction…regardless of [children's] socioeconomic status" (p. 14).

Finally, we are struck by the influence of the reading programs on the students' retellings. The high retellers at RM and OC look very different than the low retellers at RM and OC (see Figures 10.1 and 10.4). In contrast, the GR high and low retellers are similar in many ways. The numerous opportunities these children have to openly discuss the reading process and strategies in contextualized and meaningful ways, as well as to discuss literature, rather than answer questions, likely enhance their language use in their retellings.

FINAL THOUGHTS

This study has several limitations. The research was done in one site representing each program, with five to six high and low retellers in each program. In addition, although students from all three programs were strongly represented in the high and low retellers even in the initial ordering of scores, the GR students were more familiar with retellings than the RM and OC students. This unevenness in familiarity may be a factor in the findings.

Nevertheless, this research enriches our understandings of retellings by revealing the web of interwoven complexities that influence retellings as an aspect of comprehension. As Davis, Sumara, and Luce-Kapler (2000) state, "Complexity Theory would want to know something about the many systemic relationships that exist within and outside the reader and the act of reading. It would be curious about everything and the way that all components of a reading experience are influential to and co-emergent with one another" (p. 277). In this time of accountability and focus on developing good readers, being curious about and understanding these and other complexities of retellings and how reading instruction affects comprehension is critical.

REFERENCES

Armbruster, B. B., Lehr, F., & Osborn, J. (2001). *Put reading first: The research building blocks for teaching children to read*. Washington, DC: Partnership for Reading.

Arya, P., Martens, P., Wilson, P., Altwerger, B., Jin, L., Laster, B., & Lang, D. (2005). Rethinking the direction of literacy instruction: Systematic phonics or literature-based? *Language Arts, 83*(1), 63–72.

Barnhart, J. (1990). Differences in story retelling behaviors and their relation to reading comprehension in second graders. In J. Zutell & S. McCormick (Eds.), *Literacy theory and research: Analyses from multiple paradigms,* Thirty-Ninth Yearbook of the National Reading Conference (pp. 257–266). Chicago: National Reading Conference.

Davis, B., Sumara, D., & Luce-Kapler, R. (2000). *Engaging minds: Learning and teaching in a complex world*. Mahwah, NJ: Lawrence Erlbaum Associates.

Engelmann, S., Bruner, E., Hanner, S., Osborn, J., Osborn, S., & Zoref, L. (1995). *Reading Mastery*. Columbus: SRA/McGraw-Hill.

Fountas, I., & Pinnell, G. S. (1996). *Guided reading: Good first teaching for all children*. Portsmouth, NH: Heinemann.

Fountas, I., & Pinnell, G. S. (2001). *Guiding readers and writers (Grades 3–6): Teaching comprehension, genre, and content literacy*. Portsmouth, NH: Heinemann.

Gambrell, L., Koskinen, P., & Kapinus, B. (1991). Retelling and the reading comprehension of proficient and less-proficient readers. *Journal of Educational Research, 84*(6), 356–362.

Goodman, K. (2003). Miscue analysis: Research on the reading process. In A. Flurkey & J. Xu (Eds.), *On the revolution of reading: The selected writings of Kenneth S. Goodman* (pp. 105–116). Portsmouth, NH: Heinemann.

Goodman, Y., Watson, D., & Burke, C. (2005). *Reading miscue inventory: From evaluation to instruction*. Katonah, NY: Richard Irwin.

Jordan, N. (2002). *Teaching reading and learning to read: The guided reading school*. Unpublished manuscript.

Kalmbach, J. (1986). Getting at the point of retellings. *Journal of Reading, 29*(4), 326–333.

Lincoln, Y. S., & Guba, E. G. (1985). *Naturalistic inquiry*. Newbury Park, CA: Sage.

Mathison, S. (1988). Why triangulate. *Educational Researcher* (March), 13–17.

McKissack, P. (1986). *Flossie and the fox*. New York: Scholastic.

Morrow, L. M. (2001). *Literacy development in the early years: Helping children read and write* (4th ed.). Needham Heights, MA: Allyn & Bacon.

Morrow, L. M., Sisco, L. J., & Smith, J. K. (1992). In C. Kinzer & D. Leu (Eds.), *Literacy research, theory, and practice: Views from many perspectives*, Forty-First Yearbook of the National Reading Conference (pp. 435–443). Chicago: National Reading Conference.

National Reading Panel. (2000). *Teaching children to read, an evidence-based assessment of the scientific research literature on reading and its implications for reading instruction*. National Institute of Child Health and Human Development, National Institutes of Health.

Selden, G. (1960). *Cricket in Times Square*. New York: Bantam Doubleday Dell.

SRA/McGraw-Hill. (2000). *Open Court, teacher edition*. Columbus, OH: Author.

Weber, R. (1990). The construction of narratives by good and poor readers. In J. Zutell & S. McCormick (Eds.), *Literacy theory and research: Analyses from multiple paradigms,* Thirty-Ninth Yearbook of the National Reading Conference (pp. 295–301). Chicago: National Reading Conference

Wilson, G. P., Pitcher, S., Altwerger, B., Arya, P., Jin, L., Lang, D., et al. (2003). *The impact of four reading programs on children's reading strategies: Research summary report*. Towson, MD: Towson University Literacy Research Center.

Woodcock, R., & Johnson, M.B. (1990). *Woodcock Johnson Psycho-Educational Battery –R*. Riverside Publishing.

Chapter **11**

Literacy "Basics" in Childhood Spaces: A Critical Perspective on the "Basics"

Anne Haas Dyson

In this essay, I feature a self-involved capital B, an impolite pronoun, and a future tense that is rapidly losing touch with reality. There is, perhaps, something odd about these featured characters. Strip them of their mating with human values, substitute evaluations with a disinterested tone, and one has a mere list of textual elements and errors of convention (e.g., a misplaced capital letter, an incorrect use of a pronoun, an inaccurate tense). That is, one has part of the seemingly neutral "basics" of learning and teaching to write.

These "basics" are receiving increased attention within the current political context of accountability and standardization. To maintain its public respect (and its accreditation), a school may need to post "adequate" yearly progress on a basics skills test. At the early grade level, such tests (e.g., The Iowa Test of Basic Skills) emphasize reading skills more than writing; of the latter, emphasis is placed on transcription (e.g., spelling, capitalization and punctuation, and grammatical usage).

In this essay, I am not going to argue against children learning the "basics." But I am going to argue that stripping away human meaning and values from those basics is, in practice, impossible. School lessons on even the seemingly most straightforward of skills—"matching" speech sounds and written graphics, editing for "correct" grammar, even brainstorming "good" topics for writing—all link the technical aspects of language with the cultural and ideological; that is, all mate the purely linguistic with the circulating worldviews of power-saturated, human societies (Bakhtin, 1981).

This ideological linking happens because the school as a public institution is situated within the complex economic, cultural, and linguistic contexts of a society (Levinson, 2000). Ironically, one may see this macro relationship between the official public sphere of the school and the politics of the wider society by paying close attention to the microdynamics of young children's school lives.

For as hard as the school as an institution may try to focus children's attention on the neutral basics, young children are not driven by an interest in "the basics." They are driven by an interest in meaningful participation in classroom life (Dyson, 1989, 1993). They link new kinds of communicative practices found in school with old familiar ones, so that they have some relevant resources and some basis for action, for participation (Miller & Goodnow, 1995; Vygotsky, 1978). When children do this—when they reach for the old and familiar—they inevitably bring into the school their experiences and skills with talk, text, and symbols from the larger society.

In turn, the school traditionally responds by being highly selective in its choices of what kinds of linguistic and cultural resources are appropriate for use "in public," that is, in the official or teacher-governed sphere, including the enacted curriculum (McNaughton, 2002; Moll & Gonzalez, 1994; Williams, 1965): "We don't speak that way"; "we don't write about that"; "we don't talk about that in school." Thus, the school language arts curriculum functions as a kind of ideological filter.

In the essay sections to follow, I consider the relationship between societal diversity, as evident in children's social and symbolic actions, and official and public efforts to teach them to write. The sections are organized around the *B*, the "me," and the "will be," so to speak. Those textual characters star in vignettes drawn from an ongoing study of child writing in a regulated, that is, test-monitored, central city school. Through the ongoing project as a whole, I aim to contribute to efforts to reconsider the "basics" (i.e., the foundational aspects of children's entry into school writing; The New London Group, 1996).

In the end, our conceptions of the "basics" link to our notions of the kinds of publics—the kinds of "we's"—that should be fostered in and beyond the classroom. If these are to be intellectually thoughtful, socially inclusive, and humanely transformative publics, schools should not be places that teach children to be officially deaf and blind to the humanly complex world in which they live.

In the following, I briefly describe the project from which I am drawing my vignettes, and then I turn to the first of my featured textual bits, the egocentric capital B.

LOCATING THE "BASICS": THE PROJECT SITE

The human characters featured herein were all members of Mrs. K.'s first grade in an elementary school in a mid-sized, Midwest central city. The school's children were primarily from low-income homes but from diverse ethnic heritages, defined as African American, Mexican, White, and American Indian. (Eighty-five percent of the school's children qualified for the federal school lunch program.) I am a middle-aged White woman with extensive (35 years) experience teaching and studying in central city primary schools.

Mrs. K., who was White, had spent her entire teaching career of over 20 years at this school site, teaching through many curricular upheavals but, throughout all, continuing to sing, read, tell stories, and laugh with her children. She had participated in the district's professional in-services on writing workshop pedagogy (i.e., on children drafting and editing their own texts). And she had also attended the district meetings on mandated textbook-based lessons.

Mrs. K.'s writing activities reflected this history; they incorporated textbook exercises on basic skills, extended child writing (for which topics were modeled but not required), and teacher-led editing conferences to reinforce taught skills. During the daily "journal" time, Mrs. K. modeled writing and editing her own story, and then the children wrote and as many as possible edited their work with Mrs. K., before they all took turns reading their entries to the class. During the school year, Mrs. K. had a student teacher, Ms. H., Mexican American and in her twenties. Ms. H. closely modeled her teaching practices on those of Mrs. K.

I was a regular observer in Mrs. K.'s class over the course of an academic year. Twice weekly I observed and audiotaped Mrs. K., Ms. H., and the children on the playground and in the classroom, especially during literacy activities. In addition, I photocopied all written products produced during "journal time" (N = 1,512). In this essay, I feature that daily journal time. Two of the child participants, Tionna and Ezekial, were the focus of intense weekly observations. I chose them because they drew on different linguistic resources, had overlapping but distinctive circles of chosen companions, and, also, had varying responses to the teaching of the "basics." In this essay, it is not their distinctiveness that matters as much as their common intention to use written symbols to participate in the official classroom public (and also the unofficial or peer-governed one).

Tionna was Black and a speaker of African American Vernacular English. Her close friends were Janette, Mandissa, and Lyron (all of African American heritage). Ezekial was of Mexican heritage and monolingual in English; he used common features of nonstandard vernaculars (e.g., "ain't," "he don't"). He interacted widely in the classroom but his most consistent companions were Lyron (also a friend of Tionna's) and Joshua (of American Indian and Mexican American heritages). In addition to the preceding children, Elly (of European American heritage) and Jon (of Mexican American heritage) also make recurrent appearances herein.

In my analysis, I am paying attention to the enacted definitions of official "skills," the nature of children's unofficial or nonacademic cultural and textual resources (e.g., vernaculars, play practices, valued texts), and, most importantly, how children used those resources to interpret or make sense of (or around) literacy lessons. From this analysis, then, come the vignettes featuring "B," "me," and the future tense. I chose these vignettes because they were densely situated within official and unofficial worlds and thus were theoretically rich.

Within each section to follow, I begin with a child's product, situate that product within classroom vignettes, and finally consider how the vignettes illustrate the relationship between the official public and the nature of children's resources. I weave, throughout the sections, the project's evolving theoretical frame on "the intersection of language and human beings" in a social and political world, that is, the intersection of written language and societal ideology (Woolard, 1998, p. 3).

SITUATING THE "BASICS" IN A CONTESTED SOCIAL WORLD: EZEKIAL AND THE CAPITAL B

> Today is my mom's
>
> Brthday

The preceding text is the beginning of one of Ezekial's journal entries. It might seem, at first glance, a simple expression of personal news, with an impressive apostrophe and a misplaced capital B. Sometimes a misplaced capital is nothing more than that (as I was reminded when I proofed this text). However, it was something more than that in this case. To make a connection between Ezekial's production of this text and the social and ideological nature of classroom life, that capital B is key. And to use that key, I have to view the text, and Ezekial's composing of it, from a certain theoretical angle.

Guided by sociocultural views of literacy (e.g., Hanks, 1996; Street, 1993), Ezekial can be seen as participating in a literacy practice, that is, in a recurrent, culturally valued activity—the official daily journal time. Moreover, informed by Bakhtin's (1981) dialogic theory, Ezekial's participation, his writing, becomes a kind of conversational turn. Ezekial orchestrates his resources, including his knowledge of written conventions, and writes in response to, and in anticipation of, others' desires, expectations, and judgements.

To what "state of affairs" in the classroom public was Ezekial responding (Volosinov, 1986, p. 95)? On the day of the capital B, Mrs. K. had sat in her usual place in front of an easel, as the children had gathered on the rug to watch her write her own piece. She made a "quick sketch" of a store and then wrote about going shopping to buy her daughter a Halloween costume. As she wrote, she called the class's attention to her spaces between words, her periods, and her capital letters, including a capital H on Halloween (because "it is a holiday"). After she was done, one child after another raised a hand to report on their holiday costumes and their trick-or-treating plans. Ezekial raised his hand too and told about his mother's birthday and about how he would have her take him to Chuck E. Cheese, a kid-friendly pizza place. (A bit off topic, I had thought.)

Back at their seats, many children began to write about Halloween, and Ezekial began to write about his mother's "Birthday." When Mrs. K. inquired about that capital B on birthday, he explained that birthday was "the name of a holiday."

"It's a special day at your house, isn't it, when it's someone's birthday?" she replied. But "is it a special day at Tionna's house because it's your mother's birthday?"

Ezekial gave her a wide-eyed, somber look. "Probably not," said Mrs. K. in a sympathetic voice. She explained that a holiday would be a special day, not only at his house, but at other people's houses too. Ezekial erased the apparently self-involved capital B and substituted the more socially sensitive lower case one (see Figure 11.1).

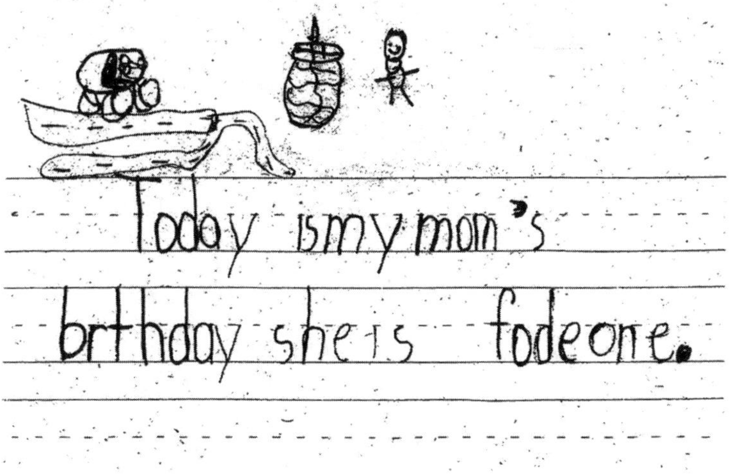

Figure 11.1. Ezekial's text about his mother's birthday: "Today is my mom's birthday she is fodeone."

"That was sad for him," said Mrs. K. to me as she passed by. But why *did* he seem so sad that his mother's birthday was not a holiday?

The next week when I returned to the school, many children were again writing about Halloween. Ezekial was writing about Christmas. As he worked, his table mate Tionna wrote that "me and Brittany are...goin to look the same on walloween!" Then she began to draw herself and Brittany wearing their unicorn costumes, complete with "pointy heads," to which Ezekial responded, in a teasing voice:

Ezekial:	I do not like when people have some pointy heads. That gives me a headache.
Tionna:	Oh oh! Well, we're gonna give you a headache, 'cause you're gonna get poked.
Ezekial:	AHHHHH!
Tionna:	(in a straightforward tone) But you're not gonna see us, 'cause you don't celebrate Halloween.
Dyson:	You don't celebrate Halloween? (also in a straightforward voice)
Tionna:	No, he don't celebrate Halloween.
Ezekial:	'Cause that's celebrating to the devil. (continuing the matter-of-fact tone)

Ezekial's capital B on *birthday*, then, seemed to be his way of participating in the classroom public, in which a holiday was the valued currency of the moment. He responded to the Halloween scene by writing himself into the ongoing conversation with another holiday—if not his mother's birthday, then Christmas! (Ezekial wrote about Christmas during another day of intensive Halloween activity. But after Halloween was over, so was his interest in Christmas, at least for about 6 weeks.)

Graphic Conventions in the Classroom Public

Ezekial's experience with the capital B illustrates the dialogic frame evolving herein. That misplaced capital B suggested a misunderstanding of a rule and then a misunderstanding of the nature of a holiday itself. Ezekial seemed to need to look beyond the importance of a day in his own family to understand the concept of a holiday.

And yet, Ezekial *was* looking beyond the importance of a day in his own family. He was drawing on an experiential resource that might allow him participation in the classroom public. For him, the "write-in-your-journal" task became a complex social event and an instantiation of a recurrent practice that was itself a part of a constellation of practices constituting school literacy (Hanks, 1996). Those practices included being read to (e.g., about

Halloween), teacher modeling (e.g., of composing a conventionally correct text about Halloween), group singing (e.g., about Halloween), and sharing children's writing (e.g., often about Halloween). These interrelated practices involved children in the "public" values of the school.

In that public, there was an explicit valuing of writing conventions and an implicit one of recognized holidays—and the two were linked through a capital letter. Ezekial, though, did not become a writer of texts about Halloween; that is, he did not abandon his complex identity as a member of important social spheres other than school (e.g., his family and his church). Instead, he drew on his experiences to find a special day associated with treats, and he marked it with a capital letter. That capital B on *birthday* was an indicator of his social desire to be included. In a similar way, other children may appropriate and blend linguistic, textual, and experiential resources from out-of-school social worlds in order to participate in school (Dyson, 1993, 2003).

Thus, within the dialogic theoretical frame of this project, children's texts are a means for negotiating a place for themselves in an ideologically charged public, a public with differing values about what and how to speak or write. Moreover, in this negotiating, written conventions are not just collections of rules but potential communicative resources.

In regulated schools like Ezekial's, the curriculum includes lists of skills (like capitalization and punctuation) that are to be mastered at certain grade levels and tested in a standardized way. But using an allographic variation (like capital and lower case letters) is at least potentially a matter of choosing from one's symbolic repertoire. There *are* regularities of conventional use. But there are always new contexts for that use and new meaning possibilities.

Consider, for example, the greeting in a birthday card I just purchased. The card depicts two pugs and, inside, it reads: "Hope your Birthday goes without a wrinkle." Or consider how apparently simple rules about capitalizing proper nouns (and, of course, first words in sentences) change across languages or even across the text of a single book. In Ezekial's classroom library, book characters sometimes shouted out their words in CAPITAL LETTERS (and those words were not even holidays!). When Ezekial himself wanted to shout out how cool it would be to play soccer with his classmate Jason, he wrote:

.C.O.O.L. P.L.A.I.N.G.

"Why did you put all the periods?" I asked.

"Because I want all of 'em capitalized," he explained (i.e., he was following the rule that a capital letter comes after a period).

The pedagogical point here is not that teachers should refrain from helping children learn capitalization conventions. Rather, I am arguing that, from a dialogic perspective, the basic unit within which to examine composing is not the rule nor even the product; it is a child participating in a situated event, negotiating a place in the goings on. And a key quality—a foundational "basic," perhaps—of engaged participation in a complex world is not rigidity or some notion of written language as a static collection of rules; it is flexibility, a willingness to recontextualize one's resources in response to situational demands and, thereby, to learn about the constraints and possibilities of that recontextualization (cf. Clay, 1975; Dyson, 2003; Miller & Goodnow, 1995).

To further such a quality, educators might first work to be open to and explicit about differing ideologies, values, and beliefs in the classroom public. Such openness might help educators widen their own and children's "socioideological consciousness" and sense of communicative space (Bakhtin, 1981, p. 290). Second, to support children's participation in that space, they might give maximum scope to children's alertness to print in and out of school, acknowledging what children themselves notice about the graphic options used by composers of signs, cards, comics, web sites, books of all kinds, and on and on. (For particular curricular suggestions, see Y. Goodman, 2003.)

The interest herein is in ideological gaps revealed by, and flexibility and adaptability in use of, not only written conventions but also the very voices that animate children's lives—the particular and typified genres, registers, dialects, and languages. This variability illustrates most vividly how the classroom public situates itself relative to the diverse resources of children's everyday worlds. To help me do my own conceptual stretching to these broader dimensions of written language use, I now bring Tionna center stage.

DIALOGIC COMPLEXITIES OF "HOW WE SAY THAT": TIONNA AND THE MISBEHAVING "ME"

Lyron is the best boy in the
class he is cute to me and Janette
we will both live with him
when we grow up me and Janette
like him he side [said] oh pless [please] he
is verry cute to me and Janette.
(unedited text by Tionna, February of school year)

Lyron is the best boy in the
class**.** **H**e is cute to me and Janette**.**
We will both live with him

Janette and I

when we grow up. **[crossed out *me and Janette*]**

like him. **He said "Oh please." He**

is verry cute to me and Janette.

(text after editing [in bold] with student teacher, Ms. H.)

The first text just shown, written by Tionna in February, displays assorted basic skills (e.g., capitalizing names, and ending [the text, if not each sentence] with a period). I focus, though, on that coordinated subject, which Tionna originally (and, like her peers, almost always) rendered as "me and" somebody, in this case, "me and Janette."

Near the end of the school year, when I asked Tionna to reread journal entries for me, she tripped up on the edited and "properly" linked agents:

Tionna:	(reading) "Lyron is the best boy in the class. He is cute to me and Janette. We will both live with him when we grow up. Me, Janette, and I, and Janette—Me, Janette, and I" (pause)
Dyson:	I think that's where Mrs. K. was doing that editing.
Tionna:	(sigh) "We will both live with him Janette and I when we grow up. Me, Janette and I and Janette!" Supposed to be Mandisa in there too. "And I did—did [inserted] like him. He said, 'Oh please!' He is very cute to me and Janette." Where's Mandisa? I ain't put her name in there just once.
Dyson:	...Why would Ms H. and Mrs. K. cross [those words] out?
Tionna:	I don't know.

Tionna's confusion was notable because she did not have a general aversion to Mrs. K.'s editing of her texts. Tionna even used a carat symbol for inserts when she noted a missing word and adjusted old texts by crossing out what she judged as not sensible words. Why, then, did Tionna seem to ignore the editing and, instead, look for the missing Mandisa (i.e., for "Me, Janette, **and Mandisa**")? Just as importantly, why (or how) did "me and Janette" matter to Mrs. K. and Ms. H.?

To consider these questions, I return to my project's evolving frame, which now needs some complicating dimensions. Within this dialogic frame, when speakers (and writers) address others, they situate themselves within layers of stratification—of difference, even if they share a common language, like English (Bakhtin, 1981). You can hear this stratification in a language's spoken varieties or vernaculars; these exist because different social groups bring to their "common" language different histories, geographies, and cultural traditions. Thus, language vernaculars index social and cultural differences. Age may be indexed as well, as cohorts may share developmental features of speech, as well as lexical items common to their time (e.g., Pokemon characters).

Interwoven with this societal stratification is genre stratification, that is, a repertoire of practices or ways of using language in particular situations, for example, telling stories, providing directions, engaging in arguments, and offering apologies. The meaning of any utterance, then, may vary depending on the practice and also on how speakers and listeners are positioned in the larger society.

Thus, contingent on the social and power relation between speaker and listener and on the framing practice, the subject "me and Janette" might mean a representation of joint agency; a developmental phenomenon of English-speaking children's syntax; a feature of many nonstandard vernaculars (grammar in the descriptive sense); an informal register of the ever-changing "standard" English; or just "improper" or even impolite usage (grammar in the prescriptive sense) (Wolfram, Adger, & Christian, 1999).

Within the school setting, Mrs. K. tended to respond to the conversational meaning of children's utterances. But by December, editing conferences had begun; and, in this context, she and Ms. H. attended to any and all perceived grammar (i.e., language usage) errors. Their actions were compatible with district curricular guidelines, the Iowa Test of Basics Skills, and the district's "daily oral language" texts, which provided written sentences like the following for children's oral correction:

> me and dan didnt see them (Leik & Altena, 1993, p. 16)

In all these sources there was simply correct or incorrect usage. There were no situational subtleties (Hymes, 1972), no vernacular complexities (Smitherman, 2000), no age-related progressions (Lindfors, 1987), just a homogeneous "we," as in "this is how we say that correctly" or "this is how we can make it sound better." Ms. H. tended to say, "This is how we can say that different"; but, because saying it "different" meant changing the text, that phrasing did not seem to have any distinct meaning.

In contrast, for 6-year-old Tionna, as for young children generally, words and how they were arranged and articulated seemed inextricable aspects of how varied "we's" talk, that is, of situated voices (e.g., Garvey, 1990). When playing in the unofficial or child-governed world, Tionna could assume the distinctive language styles and vocabularies of people in varied social roles—a radio star, a fast food worker, a teacher, a preacher, and even a love counselor:

Tionna: (to her work table companions, as her peer Elly sits and cries softly over Brad's "dumping" her) [Elly]'s thinking about all the days that she having fun with Brad.... That has changed. She want that to go back together. She don't want that to break up.

Brad: (quietly to Tionna, who sits right next to him) I still like Elly....

Tionna: Just say um, "Elly I didn't mean to say it. I was just in a bad mood." I say it for you. (louder voice) Elly, Brad say, he was just in a bad mood.

Tionna's "Lyron" text had, in fact, been written during the peak of unofficial boyfriend/girlfriend play. The play was "fake," as Tionna explained, because first graders were "too little." Its emotional ramifications, though, were not fake, as just illustrated. By February, the unofficial "like play" was entering into children's writing through unofficial love notes and official journal entries.

In Tionna's case, Lyron, Janette, and Mandisa had been showing up in each other's journals since the beginning of the year, as they were friends. But now they were redefining their relationship to one of a boyfriend with several girlfriends. On the day Tionna wrote her "Lyron" text, the "gender play" had begun as Lyron and Tionna sat playing Legoes together (Thorne, 1993). Tionna had been building her home when Lyron implicated himself into her house!

Tionna: This is my small room 'cause I got parts to my house. Soon as you walk in there's a part right there—

Lyron: My picture's on the wall, when you walk in.

Tionna: Yeah. This is *my* room, and this is my living room....

Lyron: Where's *my* room?

The location of Lyron's room is settled and, then, Tionna explicitly states what has now been implied:

Tionna: I'm marrying Lyron. I *will* marry Lyron. I will *marry* you Lyron. I will.... Me and Janette will. Then you'll have two girl friends. You know Janette likes you.

And Lyron agrees:

Lyron: Both of you guys can marry me.

When the children return to their seats for writing time, Lyron again begins the play:

Lyron: (turning to Tionna, who sits across from him) I know what you're gonna write about.
Tionna: What?
Lyron: Me.

Tionna begins to draw Lyron "looking all happy." And then she draws herself (with a heart on her full skirt) (see Figure 11.2).

Tionna: Now there's me and Lyron…
Lyron: And Janette.

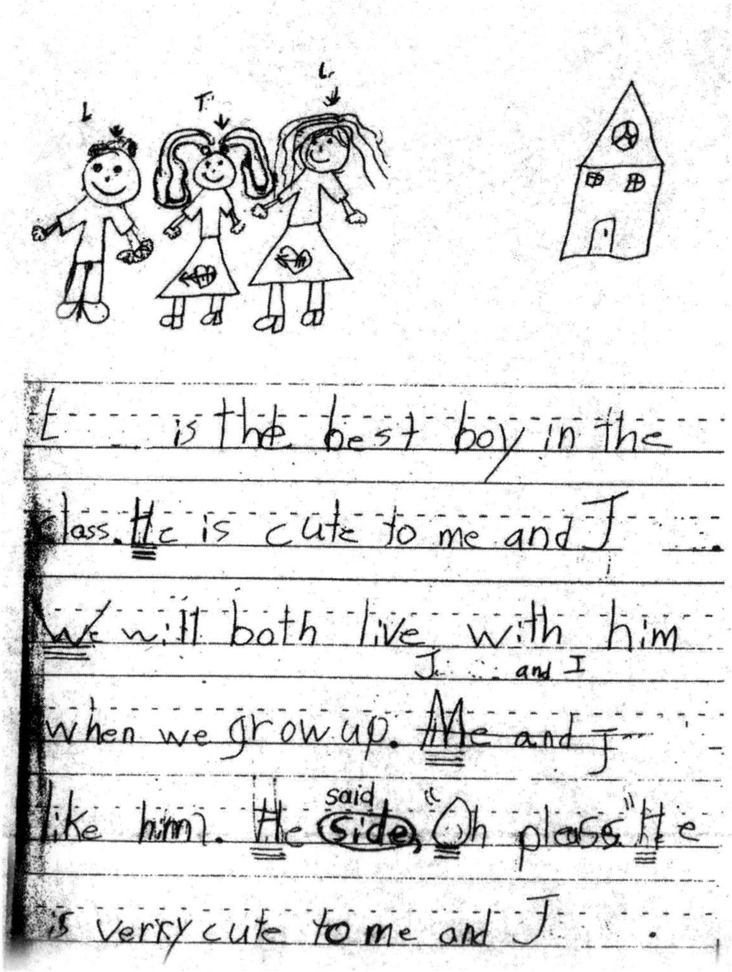

Figure 11.2. Tionna's "Lyron" text.

Tionna:	Me and Lyron and Janette—nobody else.
Lyron:	Mandisa! (i.e., "Don't forget about Mandisa," who sits separately from Tionna, Lyron, and Janette at the other of the two classroom table clusters)
Tionna:	She'll be in there next time.

Finally she writes her text, and soon Ms. H. comes by her table and zeroes in on that "me and Janette":

Ms. H.:	How can we write "me and Janette" different? (And when Tionna does not respond) We do it every morning, sometimes [in the daily oral language exercise]. "Janette and [pregnant pause]"? What's another way to say "me"? (No response is forthcoming). One letter.
Tionna:	You? ["u"]
Ms. H.:	No. "Janette and..."
Tionna:	I.
Ms. H.:	So right up here write "Janette and I."

And Tionna does so.

During the class sharing time that follows, Tionna reads her piece (struggling with and eventually skipping the edited "Janette and me/I" section). Mrs. K. joins in the class's audible enjoyment of the text:

Mrs K.:	You never know who you're gonna marry. I always thought I was gonna marry this boy that lived behind me.... But you know what? Never did marry this boy that lived behind me....We're still friends though.

Like Ezekial, then, Tionna had a strong desire to participate in the interrelated official and unofficial life of the classroom. Moreover, her focus when she reread her "gender play" text with me—4 months later—was on what might seem an impolite omission of her good friend Mandisa from the text. Any textual improprieties, much less social ramifications, of "me and Janette" did not seem clear to her.

Usage and the Classroom Public

Tionna's use of "me and Janette" (and, more markedly, her use of African American Vernacular English) might suggest a child who, analogous to Ezekial, had to look—or, more accurately, listen—beyond her own family's speech; she had to learn how "we" say things when "we" are at our language best. But Tionna's talk and writing made evident that she did look and listen; she had an ear for situated language—for the ways that varied "we's" sound.

Indeed, over the course of the academic year, Tionna relied increasingly on explicitly revoicing talk in her texts. Mrs. K., in fact, thought Tionna became an unusually strong writer precisely because "there's lots of talk" in her home. Tionna wrote about what her dad or her grandma said; she replayed the words of her auntie, her friends, her cousins, and even her teachers. In one entry, for example, Tionna wrote about a cousin who

> always copy cat me and **I say** aren't you tier [tired] of copycating me **she say** no am [I'm] not that is my favord [favorite] so plese stop ascking [asking] me mame [ma'am] I get tier of that[,] calling me mame so I will call her mame.

The assertive back and forth of Tionna's written dialogue and her explicit feelings and conversational present tense ("she say" and "I say") contrast with the more descriptive, syntactically complex, and formal prose of her texts based on her teacher's talk. For example:

> Yesterday Mrs. K wint to the doctor she had to leav for the rest of the after non because **she said** her son Kelly had a bump on his arm **she said** they had to remove it.

Moreover, the fact that she, like all class members, never wrote "ain't" suggests some sense of language features marked generally as "unofficial" and non-academic.

Tionna's "ear," though, was not accompanied by any inclination—nor official opportunity—to explicitly discuss variations in language use, which may not be surprising for such a young child (Gleason & Ratner, 1993). And yet, looking to the future, the curricular "basics" in her school emphasized mastery of rules—be they capitalization or prescriptive usage, not flexible, aesthetically alert, rhetorically powerful ways with words (Martin-Jones & Jones, 2000). Tionna's access to the latter understanding was dependent on the human and media voices of her everyday world.

To return to a variant of this essay's refrain, the pedagogical point is not that children should not talk about, and have the opportunity to learn, the edited English of wider communication (Smitherman & Villanueva, 2003). Rather, I am pointing out, first, that "basic" matters of "usage" are complex developmental, social, cultural, and political matters (Clark, 2003; Rickford, 1999). Second, a curricular valuing and promoting of communicative flexibility, and of the use of different language varieties as options and resources, seems critical. It matters in allowing children equal access to familiar voices as resources for learning to write. And it also matters in furthering socially, politically, and aesthetically sophisticated language use. As novelists and other verbal artists demonstrate, and ethnographers of communication in and out of the classroom document (e.g., Martin-Jones & Jones, 2000), such sophistication is necessary both to render and to participate widely within "a contradictory and multi-languaged world" (Bakhtin, 1981, p. 275).

A curriculum for flexibility might even marry a curricular attention to graphic symbols with the meaning-making qualities of human voices. (Recall Ezekial's desire to have his words shout out in capital letters; Tionna herself liked exclamation points, which made her words "sound happy," she said.) Through role plays, literary study, and performative play throughout the elementary school, those meaning qualities might extend to the explicitly acknowledged heritage dialects and languages, and the linguistic options, of speakers and writers (Delpit & Dowdy, 2002).

Having considered now the self-involved capital B and the impolite "me," and the flexibility and generativeness of writing conventions and human voices, I have one last grammatical form to briefly consider—that future tense rapidly losing touch with reality. That feature helps me highlight the link between individual flexibility in written language use and agency in a complex culture.

REFRAMING CHILD LITERACY: A TENSE LOSING ITS GRIP

> I am going to have
>
> fun at my birthday party
>
> Brad and
>
> Manny and
>
> Joshua and
>
> Ezekial are coming to my party It will
>
> be fun and Lyron will come.... (written by Jon in March; edited for ease of reading)

Jon's text is seemingly a straightforward rendition of a personal plan or, as Mrs. K. phrased it, evidence of how children write a kind of "life story." Her children wrote their eager anticipations of important happenings: "This is what I am going to do...." Mrs. K., like Ms. H., saw such life stories, whether plans or narrative reports, as a basic in writing workshop pedagogy; all of their modeled texts during journal time were life stories.

But the children's future-tense plans were anything but straightforward. Planned home birthday parties, trips to "all-you-can-eat buffets," and weekend play dates at friends' homes were seldom mentioned after the anticipated date had arrived. When I inquired about how the party, for example, had gone, children would report that for one reason or another (e.g., unknown addresses, mothers saying no), the plans did not work out.

Jon too was anticipating a party that was not to be. What was the purpose of such plans? To answer this question, I need to return to my evolving theoretical frame, this time highlighting the cultural world of childhoods themselves.

Within this project's frame, a literacy practice is a kind of social dialogue, and it exists within configurations of other practices that constitute a shared cultural world (Bakhtin, 1981; Hanks, 1996). Indeed, cultural groups adapt written language to their evolving practices and needs (Street, 1993).

School children themselves form cultures. Schools bring a critical mass of children together of a similar age and historical moment, and those children use shared practices—including play practices—to organize themselves in an unofficial cultural world (Corsaro, 1985; Dyson, 1989, 1993). If children have some time and space for decision-making in official writing activities (e.g., choice of topic, opportunity to talk and share with peers), their unofficial play practices may come to frame their writing decisions (e.g., as in Tionna's "gender play" text). In this way, children's official literacy practices become a resource for unofficial childhood cultures. So, over time, not only do individual children develop as skillful participants in literacy practices but cultures—configurations of shared practices—themselves develop.

Consider, for example, those personal plans that proliferated in Ezekial's and Tionna's room. Mrs. K. herself regularly modeled her own composing about plans for, or reports of, weekend activities, which could involve, for example, shopping, dinner, movies. The children seemed to have appropriated from this modeling a kind of social dialogue (i.e., anticipating "fun" events, to use Mrs. K.'s common word), linguistic markers of that practice (i.e., the future tense, particularly "I am going to..."), and, ideologically, its implicit valuing of the worthiness of a busy life and, more particularly, evening and weekend plans.

Indeed, a half of all journal entries from January through mid-June (N=1042) included the phrase "I am going to...." When children's outside-of-school plans involved in-school friends, the plans functioned as a kind of play; instead of girl friend(s) and boy friend(s), or fast food counter clerks and cooks, the children could be, for instance, party givers and invitees.

In late March, Jon's planned birthday started in a common and relatively contained way. He wrote about his upcoming party and named many (but not all) male class members as invitees. But soon pressure came to bear on Jon from the girls who sat around him in his table cluster, particularly Mandisa and Elisha; on the other table cluster, pressure came too from Elly, who now openly "liked" him (in addition to Brad), and from Janette, who was on his after-school hockey team. Ezekial, Elisha, and Janette even wrote their own texts anticipating Jon's birthday. Jon responded to the pressure with more written plans, naming different combinations of children.

On the day of his actual birthday, Jon's party spilled beyond the borders of the imagined. This had not happened before—nor did it happen after; there had been many planned parties, play dates, even trips to California, all of which faded into the next affair. But, this time, the negotiations and anticipations had reached unusual intensity. When the get-ready-to-go-home bell sounded, and the children from Jon's table cluster went out into the hall to retrieve their coats from their lockers, Janette, Ezekial, and Elisha immediately gathered around Jon. They wanted to know if they could come home with him for the party.

Jon said that they could not come, because his little brother would be in the car with his mother when she came to pick him up. There would be no room for extra children.

But the extra children persisted. Maybe, said Jon, Ezekial and Janette could squeeze in the front seat. Elisha started to cry. Jon reconsidered: They could all squeeze in. As this negotiating was going on, children from the other table cluster were rounding the classroom doorway, heading toward their lockers. One of those children was Manny, who, hearing the conversation, announced that he too would be getting into the car. Also newly in the hall way was Elly, who, standing by her locker, said in a plaintive, high-pitched voice, "Hope I can come to the birthday boy's party tonight."

Jon went back into the classroom and asked his teacher if he could "call my mom to see if some of my classmates can come to my party?" It was too late for that, his teacher said.

"You should have given out invitations," said Mandisa, and Elisha agreed.

Jon went home and the disappointed others eventually went to the after-school care program (but only after a couple had phoned their mothers in the office and, unsuccessfully, sought parental permission to go to Jon's house).

Text Types and the Classroom Public

Like Ezekial's B and Tionna's "Me and Janette," then, Jon's "future-tense" text was not in and of itself meaningful. Seemingly a "life story" in the literal sense, it was rather a life story in the virtual sense. That is, it figured into, and helped construct, the ongoing cultural life of the children. The purpose of nearly all such plans for peer gatherings outside of school was to socially participate inside of school, in the unofficial world.

As the children situated "I am going to" texts within their unofficial world, their own social relations were newly realized as they adapted a variety of interconnected literacy practices that they had learned about in and out of school. For example, not only did written plans for a party give rise to oral negotiations and others' written intentions, but they also gave rise to the exchanging of written names, phone numbers, and bits of addresses. Moreover, written plans could provide the impetus for compiling lists of invitees for one function or another.

The sense of flexible options children displayed was thus not so much a *quality* of *a* child's writing as a dynamic *outcome* of agency in a complex culture. And, once again, this flexibility was in some tension with a more rigid official public. During the spring semester, when pretend plans were at their peak, the children began an official study of neighborhoods, maps, and addresses, which was the next topic set in the required first grade social studies text. The maps were of fictional neighborhoods; the addresses on the related worksheets belonged to the "green house" or the "yellow one"; following sidewalk paths to the right or left took the pencil-pushing children nowhere in particular. The children were to be learning skills and acquiring information that would be important for their end-of-year standardized test and, moreover, that would be expected by their second-grade teachers.

During writing time, though, numbers began to appear on drawn houses, which accompanied written plans for not-to-be get-togethers. Relative location was considered when children planned whether just walking or a parent with a car was required. The cultural practice of composing plans for get-togethers thus became potentially more complex and interrelated with other practices needed in the local circumstance.

To return now to this essay's refrain, the point is not that modeling is not a good instructional strategy, nor that personal experience is not a reasonable source of textual material. Rather, the point is that a text type, like a capital B and a "me and you" phrase, becomes meaningful only as it figures into communication and symbolic options in a social world. Moreover, children's texts too are situated in the social and political complexities of childhoods themselves. Teachers alert to children's agendas can interpret their texts as situated in practices, on which they can build or to which they can respond. For example, children may need to explicitly discuss what they already know about the pleasure and pain of public inclusion or exclusion. In the official public, we—teachers and children—have opportunities and obligations that relate to the common good. It is this notion of the common good in a socioculturally diverse world that, in fact, is motivating *my* grappling with the basics.

ON A "BASIC" CONTRADICTION

I began this essay with a vision of school literacy informed by the politics of accountability. This vision highlighted a curricular emphasis on identified basics. Such curricula tend to explicitly put forward a monologic view of language and, by implication, of the social world it indexes. To properly use a capital B, a "me" with a "you," a future tense, children should not look or listen to the possibilities of language use around them but, rather, keep "on task," mastering the designated skills, following the rules for how proper written language should look and sound.

At the same time, I have contradicted this curricular focus, arguing that young children make tasks meaningful precisely by looking around and contextualizing tasks and texts within social events and cultural practices (Miller, 1996). Implicit in the vignettes, and explicit in the evolving theoretical frame, has been a vision of language, oral or written, as meaningful only against a larger landscape (Bakhtin, 1981)—the chosen graphic conventions against an existent repertoire (Hall, 1997); one's register, dialect, or language against the backdrop of sociolinguistic possibilities (Hymes, 1972); the enactment of certain genres or practices against the constellation of a particular field of action (Hanks, 1996). This is, in fact, the fundamental contradiction that bespeaks the problem of the traditional "basics"—those basics belie an attempt to reduce the essential dialogic nature of language itself, and this cannot be done, unless one is aiming for mimicry, not for control of communicative possibilities.

Indeed, in my own project, Mrs. K. was highly sensitive to context in how she responded to children (e.g., recall how she joined in to appreciate Tionna's Lyron text, not focusing on that child's usage in the whole class forum). Like many skilled and sensitive teachers, she made adjustments in action; but she had been provided no professional opportunity to understand her own flexible use of language, much less to consider how such flexibility mattered for and to her students.

Surely it is time for those interested in multiple languages and language variants, in diverse cultural practices and worldviews, in the expanding symbolic repertoire of our time, to appropriate and reaccentuate this word "basics." Reimagined basics must include differentiating the multiple dimensions of written language as a symbol system (from letter font to text type) and expanding one's means of flexibly adapting them to an expanding repertoire of interrelated communicative possibilities. In these new basics, diverse languages "and the cultural practices and views of the world[s] in which they are embedded" (Hornberger, 2000, p. 354) are resources for individuals and groups. Without such redefining work, those languages and practices that differ from the narrow prescribed ones are only deficits to be overcome in order to tidy up children for their public appearance in school—a public that is alienated from children's worlds and also from the complex and constantly changing social and language worlds in which we all live.

I close, then, with a call: Me and you, like other educators, should respond to the seemingly precarious future of our young by raising questions about the true Basics, an inclusive and public-minded Basics, spelled, of course, with a capital B.

AUTHOR NOTES

Children's and teachers' names are pseudonyms.

I thank Yanan Fan, my energetic and insightful research assistant, and acknowledge the College of Education, Michigan State University, which provided funds to help me begin research in area schools. The project has continued and expanded with the much-appreciated support of the Spencer Foundation. The findings and opinions expressed are, of course, my sole responsibility.

REFERENCES

Bakhtin, M. (1981). Discourse in the novel. In C. Emerson & M. Holquist (Eds.), *The dialogic imagination: Four essays by M. Bakhtin* (pp. 259–422). Austin: University of Texas Press.

Clark, E. (2003). *First language acquisition*. Cambridge, England: Cambridge University Press.

Clay, M. (1975). *What did I write?* Auckland: Heinemann.

Corsaro, W. (1985). *Friendship and peer culture in the early years*. Norwood, NJ: Ablex.

Delpit, L., & Dowdy, J. K. (Eds.). (2002). *The skin that we speak: Thoughts on language and culture in the classroom*. New York: New Press.

Dyson, A. H. (1989). *Multiple worlds of child writers: Friends learning to write*. New York: Teachers College Press.

Dyson, A. H. (1993). *Social worlds of children learning to write in an urban primary school*. New York: Teachers College Press.

Dyson, A. H. (2003). *The brothers and sisters learn to write: Popular literacies in childhood and school cultures*. New York: Teachers College Press.

Garvey, C. (1990). *Play* (enl. ed.). Cambridge, MA: Harvard University Press.

Gleason, J. B., & Ratner, N. B. (1993). *Psycholinguistics*. New York: Harcourt Brace.

Goodman, Y. (2003). *Valuing language study: Inquiry into language for elementary and middle schools*. Urbana, IL: NCTE.

Hall, S. (Ed.). (1997). *Representation: Cultural representations and signifying practices*. London: Sage.

Hanks, W. F. (1996). *Language and communicative practices*. Boulder, CO: Westview Press.

Hornberger, N. (2000). Multilingual literacies, literacy practices, and the continua of biliteracy. In M. Martin-Jones & K. Jones (Eds.), *Multilingual literacies: Reading and writing different worlds* (pp. 353–368). Amsterdam: John Benjamins.

Hymes, D. H. (1972). Models of the interaction of language and social life. In J. Gumperz & D. Hymes (Eds.), *Directions in sociolinguistics: The ethnography of communication* (pp. 35–71). New York: Holt, Rinehart, & Winston.

Leik, J.,& Altena, S. (1993). *Oral language for daily use*. Grand Rapids, MI: McGraw-Hill.

Levinson, B. U. (Ed.). (2000). *Schooling the symbolic animal: Social and cultural dimensions of education*. Lanham, MD: Rowman & Littlefield.

Lindfors, J. (1987). *Children's language and learning* (2nd ed.). Englewood Cliffs, NJ: Prentice Hall.

Martin-Jones, M. & Jones, K. (Eds.). (2000). *Multilingual literacies: Reading and writing different worlds*. Amsterdam: John Benjamins.

McNaughton, S. (2002). *Meeting of minds*. Wellington, New Zealand: Learning Media.

Miller, P. (1996). Instantiating culture through discourse practices: Some personal reflections on socialization and how to study it. In R. Jessor, A. Colby, & R.

Shweder (Eds.), *Ethnography and human development* (pp. 183–204). Chicago: University of Chicago Press.
Miller, P., & Goodnow, J. J. (1995). Cultural practices: Toward an integration of culture and development. In J. J. Goodnow, P. J. Miller, & F. Kessel (Eds.), *Cultural practices as contexts for development, No. 67, New directions in child development* (pp. 5–16). San Francisco: Jossey-Bass.
Moll, L., & Gonzales, N. (1994). Lessons from research with language minority students. *Journal of Reading Behavior, 26*, 439–461.
New London Group. (1996). A pedagogy of multiliteracies: Designing social futures. *Harvard Educational Review, 61*, 60–92.
Rickford, J. (1999). *African American Vernacular English*. Malden, MA: Blackwell.
Smitherman, G. (2000). *Talkin that talk: Language, culture, and education in African America.* New York: Routledge.
Smitherman, G., & Villanueva, V. (Eds.). (2003). *Language diversity in the classroom*. Carbondale: Southern Illinois University Press.
Street, B. (Ed.). (1993). *Cross-cultural approaches to literacy*. New York: Cambridge University Press.
Thorne, B. (1993). *Gender play: Girls and boys in school.* New Brunswick, NJ: Rutgers University Press.
Volosinov, V. N. (1986). *Marxism and the philosophy of language* (L. Matejka & I. R. Titunik, Trans.). New York: Seminar Press.
Vygotsky, L. S. (1978). *Mind in society*. Cambridge, MA: Harvard University Press.
Williams, R. (1965). *The long revolution*. Harmondsworth, England: Penguin.
Wolfram, W., Adger, C. T., & Christian, D. (1999). *Dialects in schools and communities*. Mahwah, NJ: Lawrence Erlbaum Associates.
Woolard, K. A. (1998). Introduction: Language ideology as a field of inquiry. In B. Schieffelin, K. A.Woolard, & P. V. Kroskrity (Eds.), *Language ideologies: Practice and theory* (pp. 3–50). New York: Oxford University Press.

Part III

LITERACY LEARNING THROUGH HOME AND SCHOOL COLLABORATIONS

"We see possibilities for transformation in schools when teachers understand and calue the cultural practices of every child and family." (Long, Volk, Romero, & Gregory, this volume, p. 204)

All families and communities, including the nonmainstream, use language as well as other symbol systems (mathematics, art, dance, music, engineering, culinary arts, geology, and botany) to construct and express meanings to serve a range of functional purposes they need for their daily lives. Despite this richness and diversity, the *funds of knowledge* (Moll, Amati, Neff, & Gonzàlez, 2005), of families and communities are not universally valued in school settings because they differ from school literacy practices. As a result, economically poor and bilingual children and their parents are often viewed from a deficit perspective and considered illiterate, undereducated, disinterested in education and at risk.

The authors in Part III, *Literacy Learning Through Home and School Collaborations*, challenge the deficit perspective. The chapters that follow illuminate, from different perspectives, the unique ways families and communities are literate and how their literacies reflect their cultural experiences. The authors reveal how young children draw on their home languages, cultures, and communities as rich resources for their personal literacy learning. We learn about the important roles that parents and caregivers play as children's earliest teachers and discover the pivotal roles of other family and community members in the mediation and facilitation of children's continued literacy learning. These works are similar to funds of knowledge research that study household and classroom practices in order "to develop innovations in teaching that draw on the knowledge and skills found in local households" (Moll et al., 2005, p. 72).

The implications of teaching that builds on the knowledge of homes and communities suggest the importance of serious collaborations between families, community members, and school professionals to enhance their learning from and about each other. In this way, they discover each other's strengths to facilitate and support children's literacy development. School professionals are most often hard-working and committed to the literacy learning of their students. As they become knowledgeable about the histories of families and value what their children bring to school, they are able to reject institutional practices that force children into molds that only meet the needs of an industrialized society. They stop thinking of working with families as telling parents and caregivers how to be literate. Rather, they support children to connect their learning in school to the literacy histories of their families, their culture, and their communities. Teachers organize schools and curriculum to respect the challenges and the wonderings of their young learners.

CRITICAL ISSUES RELATED TO LITERACY LEARNING THROUGH HOME AND SCHOOL COLLABORATIONS

- Families and communities are rich in funds of knowledge that influence and affect literacy learning.
- Parents and caregivers are children's earliest teachers.
- Home languages and cultures are rich resources for children's literacy learning.
- The curriculum and all members of the school community benefit from true collaborations between home and school.
- Literacy learning is a social process.

REFERENCE

Moll, L., Amati, C., Neff, D., & Gonzàlez, N. (2005). Funds of knowledge for teaching: Using a qualitative approach to connect homes and classrooms. In N. Gonzàlez, L. Moll, & C. Amanti (Eds.), *Funds of knowledge: Theorizing practices in households and classrooms* (pp. 71–87). Mahwah, NJ: Lawrence Erlbaum Associates.

Chapter 12

Bridging the Worlds of Home and School: Keeping Children's Identities Whole in the Classroom

Kathryn F. Whitmore

Last Day of Mexico, by Teresita

It was almost to go to trouble to California in 1999. That was my very, very, very sad day because it was almost to go. We went to church after that. Me, my dad, my mom, my brother Pablo too went to my grandfather house to say, "Goodbye," and tell him that we were going to California. My mom could not come with us because the house wasn't ready then and the animals—who would take care of them? Long time ago, my gramma take care of the animals but she die. In Mexico we plant mango, lemons, flower, corns, watermelon (sandia), melon, and beans. That is why mom could not come with us. She had to take care of the plants too.

My dad tell my grandfather if he thinks it's right to do because we didn't know nothing. And my dad said "Imagine if we would be lost. How would they get home? They don't know how to read, not even write in Spanish." In Mexico we didn't know how to write and read in Spanish. The teachers were very mean. If you didn't know how to read, they hit you. I think I know how I didn't learn there. The teacher was not responsible for helping you. They hit me many times. One time my sister defend me.

My grandfather answer, "I guess you are right. I think you should take them."

My mom was crying and sad because we were leaving her and we never separate from her since we were little. Then we went home. We were almost ready.

> I was going to give my necklace to my sister Adelina but my dad tell me to take it, so I did.
>
> My sister give me her watch instead so I could remember her.
>
> Then we went to my aunt house and my uncle house too to say goodbye. They said to take care by myself and take care of my brother Pablo and we need to be careful when we want to cross the road. We need to look first if the car it come a little far away so we can cross the road, and we said, "Thank you, Aunt and Uncle."
>
> Then we went back home so we got our bag and went to the river call El Rio Grande. When we got there then I said, "Goodbye, Mom, and don't forget that I love you."
>
> She said, "I would not forget that you love me, and I love you, Teresita."
>
> Then we hug each other and crying.
>
> My dad said, "Let go because the boat driver want to go."
>
> Then I said again, "Goodbye, Mom." Then I got in the boat crying. When we cross the river I was still crying.
>
> I stop crying when we got out the boat to go to California. That was my very sad day.

In 12 years of working with families in a diverse elementary school I have learned how essential the world of a child outside of school is to the child in school. Teresita's story, shared first with her much loved English as a second language (ESL) teacher and then with me, is evidence that Teresita felt safe enough to put her "very sad day" into written words that could be shared at school, responded to, and cherished over time. Her story reveals the importance of early literacy educators coming to know their students from a cultural, social, community, and family perspective that enables children's whole identities to exist in the classroom. It reveals fundamental aspects of Teresita's identity as a Latina immigrant who is learning in a second language in a new community far from her home.

THE SETTING

In 1994–1995, I familiarized myself with Parker Elementary School by conducting ethnographic observations in every classroom and household interviews with families that attend the school from three distinct neighborhoods. Teresita is a member of a community of Latin American immigrant families. These families live in a trailer-park neighborhood a short bus ride from the school building. Analysis of this first year of data led me to conceptualize family and teacher inquiry groups that have grown from two moms regularly attending the original group to the latest groups that serve as many as 50 children and their families each day of the week. Teresita's family participated in *Escuela Familia* (School Family).

Twelve years of family initiatives have established a school community that views its diversity as a resource. Recent initiatives include resources to reduce class size; buses to transport families to school events; a lending library of parenting books and games; child care during parent–teacher conferences; and materials and time for household visits. In short, we consider providing anything that will make it easier for families to enter the school and feel comfortable—to develop what Moll and colleagues describe as *confianza*, or mutual trust, "which is re-established or confirmed with each exchange and leads to the development of long-term relationships" (Gonzalez, et al., 1993, p. 3). Teresita's family's participation in a family inquiry group called *Escuela Familia* facilitated her willingness to share her immigration story.

THEORETICAL FRAME

The intent of the family initiatives at Parker is to bridge children's identities in their households and neighborhoods with their classrooms and school. Rather than changing the families so they fit school, we intend to change school in ways that support families' comfortable and productive positions as active members of the school community. This objective operationalizes what Auerbach (1989) refers to as a social-contextual perspective on family literacy. In the social-contextual view, literacy is assumed to exist in students' homes. Even more critical, "cultural differences are perceived as strengths and resources that can bridge the gap between home and school" (p. 176). Auerbach's view of family literacy meshes smoothly with a transactional view of early literacy development (Whitmore, Martens, Goodman, & Owocki, 2004), which recognizes that although children find individual paths to literacy as they invent written language, particularly in social settings like process-oriented literacy classrooms, "no child...can be viewed as independent of her sociocultural identity, her political status, or her linguistic heritage. [The] transactive perspective on teaching early literacy means socializing children into versions of the world that are limited and expanded according to issues of power and access" (p. 318).

Decades of research have challenged previous low expectations for children growing up in marginalized communities and confirm that all families are literate. Seminal ethnographies and language studies revealed images of real families in varied cultures using language and literacy for multiple and functional purposes. Heath (1983), Philips (1983), Taylor (1983), Wells (1986), and Taylor and Dorsey-Gaines (1988) spent years in homes, schools, and communities, documenting families as active members of print-rich communities who intentionally attend to oral and written language to accomplish the activities of life. This body of research directs early literacy educators to assume young children come from literate communities and to discover what particular literacy exists in each child's home. It challenges us to reconceptualize school literacy accordingly.

The images of families in these seminal studies prompted other researchers to document family literacy in a wide variety of settings. McCaleb (1994), Gonzales, et al. (1993), and Vasquez, Pease-Alvarez and Shannon (1994), among many others, revealed the effective language socialization practices of parents and children at home that are likely invisible at school. Adding more recently to the research base, Blackledge (2000) found Bangladeshi families engaged in a wide range of literacy practices that were not recognized at school, and Rogers (2003) documented that schooled literacy, "defined by de-contextualized skills, individual mastery, practice of skills, and evaluation through external authorities" (p. 152), led her informants to believe they were not literate. Consistently, the research reveals that although family literacy is tied to real purposes and contexts and is meaningful to its users, it typically does not fit within the narrow definition of literacy that exists in school. Scott and Marcus (2001), who differentiate between unidirectional and bidirectional relationships between home and school, indicate that a unidirectional model "operates from the position that when teachers do not understand the cultural capital of students in their classrooms (e.g. the language, values, home environment, or learning styles of the students), they fail to capitalize on the strengths of the acquired modalities that are brought from home" (p. 85).

On the other hand, the abundance of knowledge and experiences that exist in children's homes can inspire culturally relevant and responsive, authentic literacy curriculum for children in school. We know that some children learn to read while hanging out at a local drinking establishment where the first set of print they interact with is found on cases of beer (Norton-Meier, 2005), or by studying Pokemon (Vasquez, 2003). Gillanders and Jimenez (2004) reported that four low-income, Mexican immigrant families promoted formal and informal literacy support and bilingualism at home. These behaviors, paired with the school's use of Spanish, elevated the metalinguistic benefits these kindergartners experienced and contributed to their high levels of emergent literacy. When teachers see their students as members of literate communities, they revalue the children and their families validating and extending their existing literacy via culturally responsive early literacy curriculum.

Family literacy programs that fit within the social-contextual frame serve as mediators between disparate communities as diagramed in Figure 12.1. Vygotskian scholar, Luis Moll says:

> Humans use cultural signs and tools (e.g. speech, literacy, mathematics) to mediate their interactions with each other and with their surroundings...a major role of schooling is to create social contexts (zones of proximal development) for mastery of and conscious awareness in the use of these cultural tools. (1990, p. 11–12)

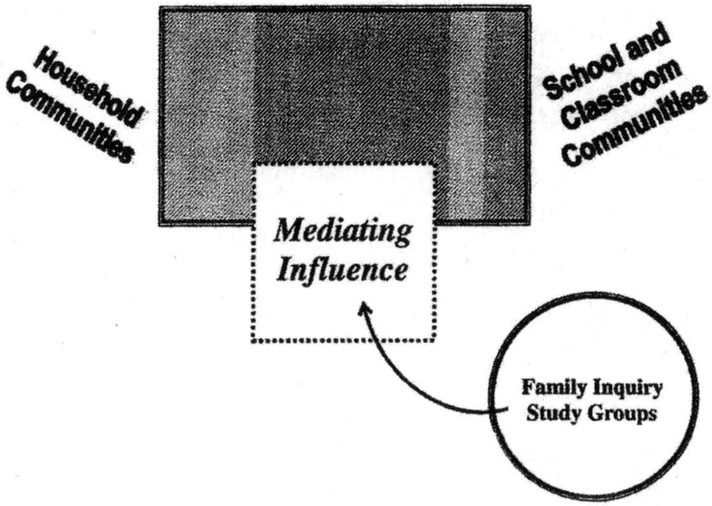

Figure 12.1. Family inquiry groups as mediators in the relationship between home and school.

Escuela Familia intends to understand the cultural signs and tools of the children's household communities and to exploit those tools for literacy learning in their classroom communities.

Two particular theoretical constructs that are consistent with a transactional view of early literacy development and a social-contextual view of family literacy are enacted in *Escuela Familia* to mediate household–school relationships: *funds of knowledge,* and *multiple sign systems*. The remainder of the chapter illustrates how these concepts enable children's whole identities to flourish at school.

FUNDS OF KNOWLEDGE

Researchers, group facilitators, and classroom teachers at Parker strive to come to know what knowledge exists in the households of the children in the school. *Funds of knowledge*, a concept developed and disseminated by the Community Literacy Project (Gonzales et al., 1993) occur in all communities regardless of demographic differences, especially in "the diverse social networks that interconnect households with their social environments and facilitate the sharing or exchange of resources, including knowledge, skills, and labor essential for the household's functioning, if not their well being" (Moll, Tapia & Whitmore, 1993, p. 140). In other words, funds of knowledge refers to the knowledge and skills that families use to live in their communities. Funds of knowledge evolve in families via historical and contemporary occupational, recreational and daily life activities. Immigrant families often experience a disconnect around the funds of knowledge that were valid in their home countries, such as professional work status or an agricultural lifestyle, and are no longer available in their new home, where they are likely to work in a labor job or live in an urban setting.

Woods Glen, where the *Escuela* families live, is a growing Latino community where every household has legitimate funds of knowledge that include highly intellectual uses of oral and written language. The homes are tiny trailers lined up like tin boxes with only a few feet separating them. Each trailer is unique, most are decades old, and all are filled with family stories in the making. Stacey Medd and Karla Brendler (English as a second language and kindergarten teachers, respectively) visit each family regularly, taking interesting reading and writing materials with them to leave for the children. Sometimes they have specific questions to ask or agendas to accomplish, but they also go just to see what's new and to learn more about their students. When we enter families' homes with the intention to learn, rather to teach, we learn amazing and surprising information.

During one visit to the Sanchez family's trailer, it was apparent that someone in the family was assembling dolls; as dolls in various stages of completion were in one corner (see Figure 12.2). Stacey describes the scene:

Figure 12.2. *Quinciñera* dolls made by Rita and Rosa.

> Rosa, a 12 year old, and her talented mother, Rita were the resident experts on making *quinciñera* dolls for the traditional fifteenth birthday parties celebrated by Mexican girls. They had discovered a process in which they could make these beautiful centerpieces economically by using some plastic doll heads, colored paper, and paper towels folded into intricate loops. Together, they communicated the process to Karla and me during an extended visit. Rita and Rosa seemed shy during previous interactions at school, but suddenly their words were flowing easily as they demonstrated their craft. They supported one another while giving precise explanations, and when one forgot a detail, the other chimed in with expertise. Anecdotes were embedded in the list of shared directions, and [caused] verbalized detours to celebrations with family and friends...

The Sanchez family sold the dolls as part of their livelihood. Rita and Rosa used highly intellectual and sophisticated talk to explain making and selling their art.

Later, Rita needed to give a "how to" speech in her classroom. As a shy girl and a novice English speaker, this assignment could have been excruciating for Rita. Given her teachers' awareness of her funds of knowledge, however, Rita was now positioned as someone who "knows something that no one else in the room knows how to do."

The professional literature is full of examples in which literacy curriculum offers children access to meaningful learning that connects to what they already know. McCarty (2002) built academically challenging content for bilingual Navajo learners based on the children's prior knowledge. Reyes (2001) showcased four young girls' dramatic emergence of spontaneous biliteracy in a bilingual primary program that nurtured their linguistic resources. Moll et al. (2005) engaged classroom teachers in mobilizing students' funds of knowledge in the working-class Latino neighborhoods of South Tucson through innovative curriculum development practices.

In the original Community Literacy Project, in order to document funds of knowledge, several researchers conducted multiple-hour interviews on three separate occasions in each household. This was a time-intensive process that classroom teachers cannot accomplish on a regular basis, so we need to find other means to access this information. One way for teachers to identify families' funds of knowledge is to adapt George Ella Lyon's poem, "Where I'm from" (Lyon, 1999). As the original poem is too complex for young children, Stacey composed a brief poem about where she's from and shared it with the *Escuela Familia* children in her ESL classroom. She then invited the children to write their own.

Johan's poem in Figure 12.3 revealed several aspects of his identity, such as proudly claiming himself as Colombian; however, Stacey pursued the potentially rich fund of knowledge about fishing for classroom literacy learning. One day she had the class complete a "backpack dig." When Johan dumped his backpack to research the print within, it included fishing maga-

Figure 12.3. Johan's "where I'm from" poem: I am Johan. I am from fishing. I am from playing baseball. I am from playing tag. I am from Columbia.

zines! Another day, during a household visit, Johan proudly toured her through his new tackle box that he saved his own money to buy. Stacey learned that Johan and his father's relationship was strongly built around fishing trips. Thus, fishing became a clear road into Johan's literacy learning. On their next visit, stationery with fish around the border was included in the literacy materials delivered. Most dramatically, class plans for a real fishing trip with Stacey's father evolved. The curriculum included a day on a river where Johan demonstrated his expertise, attached new English vocabulary to his rich existing Spanish, and built relationships with his classmates and teacher. The fishing trip culminated a few days later with a feast of fish that the children had caught and Stacey's father cooked.

MULTIPLE SIGN SYSTEMS

Leland and Harste (1994) suggest that sign systems, including art, music, mathematics, drama and language are ways of knowing—"potentials by which all humans might mean" (p. 339)—that are overlooked and untapped by school curricula. They say, "In order to be literate, learners need to be able to orchestrate a variety of sign systems to create texts appropriate to the contexts in which they find themselves" (p. 339). Through the process of transmediation, "when meanings formed in one communication system are recast in the context and expression planes of a new sign system" (p. 340), "thinking is pushed and so is language" (p. 344). Research indicates that children's cognitive disposition "is one that sees the connections of all parts of the semiotic world" (Kress, 1997, p. 142) that are less accessible in the typically minimalist, segmented, and verbocentric lessons of school and that "we can no longer treat literacy (or 'language') as the sole, the main, let alone the major means for representation and communication" (Kress, 2003, p. 35). Analysis of data working with English language learners (ELL) in Parker shows that when ELL children initially or simultaneously express what they know and acquire new knowledge through sign systems other than oral and written language, their oral and written language emerges more easily and profoundly (Medd & Whitmore, 2001). Therefore, the family inquiry programs at Parker embed oral and written language in art, music, and movement experiences.

For example, during its first year, the *Escuela Familia* families engaged in a relatively big project we called Family Trees. It began with Karla sitting on the floor of her classroom with about eight children examining the cover of *In My Family/En Mi Familia*, by Carmen Lomas Garza (1996). The children's moms were seated on kindergarten chairs in a semicircle around the group.

"Each picture is a family story," Karla said to the children. "So let's take a look."

She showed the group a page and read its subtitle, "Ah, 'Empanadas.'" The adults and children, who had been really quiet and still before this point, exclaimed, "Ah, empanadas!" They heard a word amid the English that they recognize and their attention was piqued.

"Yum," Karla said appreciatively, "We've been to your house [for empanadas]!"

Johan's mom, Cristina called out, "It's from my country!" and everyone laughed.

For several pages, Karla read the story in English, Stacey read the same in Spanish, and together they facilitated a brief discussion. Suddenly Cristina burst out with her own story sparked by an illustration. Notice that although Cristina's English was developing and her grammar was not conventional, her message came through clearly. She effectively used code switching to support her meaning construction.

"In my country is the dancing is in the street. Yeah, every family in the New Year and in the Christmas every people is in your neighborhood is in the night every the dancing and the *musica* is *salsa*. Every different music every people families outside. Or maybe in the one house every the neighbors and then my house they eat."

Everyone's attention was on Cristina. Stacey and Karla smiled and nodded, absorbed. "Empanadas?" Stacey asked hopefully.

"We have firecrackers," Johan added.

Cristina said, "The party is in the family."

"So every neighborhood?" Stacey asked.

"No, no only in the family is my gra- gra- grandma? *No, como se dice—suegra?*"

"Mother-in-law," provided Stacey.

"My mother-in-law, yeah, every the weekend, the Saturday, every the family in the house is eat *empanada, pero* is very big your family, yeah?"

"Only for special days or is that every week?"

"No every week or two week. *Si.* Your family is very together."

"So a lot of people come together."

"Yeah," Cristina said, "My country, *tambien* is *tamales*. Yeah. Yeah, *pero*, the people is very happy, very happy, in the neighbor, yeah *muy bonito*."

"They know each other."

"Yeah, they see the neighbors, in my country, yeah you go to your work it's 'good morning' or 'bye.' You always in the work. Oh yes, yeah. Very the neighbor. Always one people, two people in the house, no house only, no. Grandma or my everyone people, one, two in the house, not only the house."

Karla found a page in *In My Family/En Mi Familia* that illustrated Cristina's description.

"Yeah, it's OK," she agreed. "The picture, is OK, is OK. I remember that my family. This is my family and my husband."

Karla looked at Johan and said, "So this is like your family. So you have a family story kind of like this."

Books like *In My Family/En Mi Familia* were read before making family trees to demonstrate what family stories are—simple retellings of everyday and special events in the life of a family. Next, each family was provided with a tree branch cemented into a coffee can and marked with their family name. A wide variety of collage materials were offered as inspiration for families to create three dimensional objects to hang on their trees. Construction paper, magazines, newspapers, markers, crayons, string, yarn, pipe cleaners, sticks, small fluffs of yarn, and other craft items were available. The families' task was to decorate their trees with items to represent their family's particular stories, rituals, and regular or special events. Johan's family added a drawing of a house to represent a construction project, a tiny bingo board, and colorful fluffy balls of yarn taped to a string to represent the hanging lights at street fiestas in Colombia, a drawing of a birthday cake, and numerous others (see Figure 12.4).

During the family tree activity, Stacey, Karla, and I listened in and took detailed notes. We didn't know which of these artifacts would hold the

Figure 12.4. Family tree by Johan and Diana's family.

power of a future literacy curriculum. By the end of the activity, we learned that construction, holidays, dance, gardening and photography were just some of the funds of knowledge in the group—each table of family members generated equally important, diverse, and interesting domains.

Once the artifacts were hung and the art materials cleared, the group gathered to share the objects hanging on their trees. This conversation prompted more storytelling. The collection of colorful family trees was placed in the school media center where the whole school community enjoyed and learned from them. But *Escuela Familia*'s work with the family trees had only begun.

We used storyboarding to support children's composition process by inviting families to write books without putting pencil to paper. Each *Escuela* student selected an artifact from their tree to develop into a family story book. First, the children sketched the story on Post-Its. Next, their families helped them develop sound effects to add to their oral telling of the story. Each family audio-recorded their children's oral Spanish storytelling while they looked at the storyboard and made the sound effects. We transcribed the Spanish oral texts, translated them into English, and returned the books to the families for illustrating at an Escuela meeting. In effect, the children had composed a piece of written language without actually writing. All of the nonlanguage support from the symbol systems of construction, art, and sound enabled the families to compose elegant stories that revealed story development knowledge, first and second language development, and significant information about the families. The Parker media center houses the collection of bilingual books on tape, complete with bar codes. Now anyone in the school, including the authors, can check out a bilingual story.

KEEPING CHILDREN'S IDENTITIES WHOLE

Although maintaining positive relationships between home and school is obviously a two-way street requiring the active good intentions of teachers and families, it is the school that has the onus of responsibility for shifting relationships with families toward the positive. "Sadly, many children's literacies are threatened, rather than valued and expanded, in school settings...[but teachers can] interrupt this process by embracing a sociocultural pedagogy that values all children's literacies" (Owocki & Goodman, 2002, p. 25). The activities shared in this chapter use the power of funds of knowledge and multiple sign systems to enact a sociocultural pedagogy, thereby inviting who children are when *out of* school to be bridges to their literacy experiences *in* school.

REFERENCES

Auerbach, E.R. (1989). Towards a social-contextual approach to family literacy. *Harvard Educational Review, 59*(2), 165–181.

Blackledge, A. (2000). *Literacy, power and social justice*. Staffordshire, UK: Trentham Books.

Garza, C .L. (1996). *In my family/En mi familia*. San Francisco, CA: Children's Book Press.

Gillanders, C., & Jimenez, R. T. (2004). Reaching for success: A close-up of Mexican immigrant parents in the USA who foster literacy success for their kindergarten children. *Journal of Early Childhood Literacy, 4*(3), 243–269.

Gonzalez, N., Moll, L. C., & Amanti, C. (2005). *Funds of knowledge: Theorizing practices in households and classrooms*. Mahwah, NJ: Lawrence Erlbaum Associates.

Gonzales, N., Moll., L. C., Floyd-Tenery, M., Rivera, A., Rendon, P., Gonzales, R., & Amanti, C. (1993). *Teacher research on funds of knowledge: Learning from households*. Washington, DC: Report to the National Center for Research on Cultural Diversity and Second Language Learning.

Heath, S. B. (1983). *Ways with words*. New York: Cambridge University Press.

Kress, G. (1997). *Before writing: Rethinking the paths to Literacy*. London: Routledge.

Kress, G. (2003). *Literacy in the new media age*. London: Routledge.

Leland, C., & Harste, J. (1994). Multiple ways of knowing: Curriculum in a new key. *Language Arts, 71*, pp. 337–345.

Lyon, G. E. (1999). *Where I'm from*. Spring, TX: Absey & Co.

McCaleb, S. (1994). *Building communities of learners*. New York: St. Martin's Press.

McCarty, T.L. (2002). *A place to be Navajo.* Mahwah, NJ: Lawrence Erlbaum Associates.

Medd, S., & Whitmore, K. F. (2001). What's in your backpack?: Exchanging funds of language knowledge in an ESL classroom. In P. G. Smith (Ed.), *Talking classrooms* (pp. 42–56). Newark, DE: International Reading Association.

Moll, L. C. (Ed.). (1990). *Vygotsky and education.* Cambridge, England: Cambridge University Press.

Moll, L. C., Tapia, J., & Whitmore, K. F. (1993). Living knowledge: The social distribution of cultural resources in households and classrooms. In G. Salomon (Ed.), *Distributed cognitions* (pp. 139–163). New York: Cambridge University Press.

Norton-Meier, L. (2005). A thrice learned lesson from the literate life of a five-year-old. *Language Arts, 82*(5), 286–295.

Owocki, G. & Goodman, Y. (2002*). Kidwatching: Documenting children's literacy development*. Portsmouth, NH: Heinemann.

Philips, S. U. (1983). *The invisible culture.* White Plains, NY: Longman.

Reyes, M. de la L. (2001). Unleashing possibilities: Biliteracy in the primary grades. In M. de la Luz Reyes & John J. Halcon (Eds.), *The best for our children* (pp. 96–121). New York: Teachers College Press.

Rogers, R. (2003). *A critical discourse analysis of family literacy practices.* Mahwah, NJ: Lawrence Erlbaum Associates.

Scott, J. C., & Marcus, C. D. (2001). Emergent literacy: Home-school connections. In J. L. Harris, A. G. Kamhi, & K. E. Pollock (Eds.), *Literacy in African American communities* (pp.). Mahwah, NJ: Lawrence Erlbaum Associates.

Taylor, D. (1983). *Family literacy.* Portsmouth, NH: Heinemann.

Taylor, D., & Dorsey-Gaines, C. (1988). *Growing up literate.* Portsmouth, NH: Heinemann.

Vasquez, V. (2003). What Pokemon can teach us about learning and literacy. *Language Arts, 81*(2), 118–125.

Vasquez, O. A., Pease-Alvarez, L., & Shannon, S. M. (1994). *Pushing boundaries.* New York: Cambridge University Press.

Wells, G. (1986). *The meaning makers.* Portsmouth, NH: Heinemann.

Whitmore, K. F., Martens, P., Goodman, Y. M., & Owocki, G. (2004). Critical lessons from the transactional perspective on early literacy research. *Journal of Early Childhood Literacy, 4*(3), 291–325.

Chapter 13

No Gain in Blame: Fostering Collaborations Between Home and School

Heather Sample Gosse and Linda M. Phillips

Some praise at morning what they blame at night;

But always think the last opinion right. (Pope, 1711, p. 26)

In his 1711 *Essay on Criticism*, Alexander Pope turned to the art of writing as an effective way to mirror life. His words demonstrate the fickleness evident in opinion and allude to the willingness to base views on an incomplete understanding of the situation at hand. Our purpose is to argue that broad-based collaborations between families and teachers are essential to children's literacy development and that these collaborations are hindered by ill-conceived negative opinions on both sides. We summarize the important role of families in children's literacy development and reveal how the potential for blame arises. We then draw on our longitudinal, cross-sectional control group research extending across 6 years of the *Learning Together* family literacy program to illustrate aspects of successful collaboration between families and teachers. We make the case that ongoing collaborations are supported when educators understand critical facts about home and school, families, teachers and the educational environment. These understandings help to break the barrier of blame and unlock promising new courses of action.

FAMILIES: CONTRIBUTIONS AND CONFLICTS

Children are socialized into literacy, and this socialization begins with the family (Paratore, 2001). Research has demonstrated that families positively influence their children's learning by providing supportive home environments characterized by opportunities to use literacy and adult modeling of literacy practices (Rodriguez-Brown & Meehan, 1998). Early literacy experiences within families have a critical impact on children's knowledge of written registers, vocabulary, print, phonological awareness, and letter–sound relationships, and on their reading attitude and motivation (Purcell-Gates, 2000). Specific experiences with functions, forms, and contexts of literacy events coupled with language interactions in the home prepare children for the language demands of text comprehension (Snow, Barnes, Chandler, Goodman, & Hemphill, 1991).

Not all literacy activities practiced in homes, however, are congruent with literacy activities encountered in school (Sénéchal & LeFevre, 2002). Although literacy events and interactions are present in one form or another in most families, the types of events shared may have little influence on children's school success. It is equally true that the kinds of literacy practiced in classrooms may have little meaning for those children or their families (Morrow & Young, 1997). When home literacy and school literacy are disconnected, a high potential for blame is an unfortunate result. Families are blamed by teachers when their children's socialization differs from that expected at school, and teachers are in turn blamed by families for being judgmental and unresponsive to their children's needs. Both sides may get locked into an unproductive blame cycle. Based on our research, we maintain that collaboration can break this cycle. Successful family literacy programs provide particularly relevant examples of such collaboration.

LEARNING TOGETHER: COLLABORATIVE EXAMPLE AND FIRST STEP

The 13-week *Learning Together: Read and Write with Your Child* program is an example of a collaboratively developed family literacy program. The program, by our partners The Centre for Family Literacy, includes eight units with sessions for adult, child, and joint adult and child components. The units build on what the parents want to learn and focus on creative play, developing language for literacy, games used to give parents alternative ways to interact with children, beginning with books, early reading, writing and drawing, environmental print walks, question and answer for parents, and end-of-course celebration.

All of the 183 urban and rural families participating in our study are of low income and educational backgrounds and have children ages 3 to 5 plus years considered to be at risk for school achievement. Forty-seven percent of the family literacy participants are single. Sixty-nine percent are Caucasian, 13% are Aboriginal, and the remainder are Chinese, Kurdish, Jamaican, Spanish, and South African (Phillips & Sample Gosse, 2005). We have completed extensive interviews to discover these participants' views and experiences with their children's education.

In the *Learning Together* program, a genuine effort is made to interweave culturally, linguistically, personally, and socially appropriate information for different audiences within a common element. For example, in one unit, "early reading," the parent program includes discussing the stages of children's early reading, learning how reading and talking together helps children to learn to read, and discussing the importance of "kidwatching" (Goodman, 1985). This collaborative sharing of ideas, interests, and goals maximizes the potential for family literacy success.

Although an important beginning, family literacy programs such as *Learning Together* should be only the first step toward ongoing collaboration between home and school. As Cairney (1997) clearly states, "The influence of the family does not magically cease at age five" (p. 62). There is a critical need for ongoing collaboration throughout the school years. We can build on the successes of well-designed and executed family literacy programs. Although both families and teachers have roles to play, it is incumbent on the educational community to take the lead given the greater power that educators have within our school systems.

ONGOING COLLABORATION: UNDERSTANDINGS AND ACTIONS

To fully embrace their leadership role in collaborating with families, educators need to increase their understanding of the relationship between home and school, of families, and of teachers and the larger educational environment. Our experiences researching the *Learning Together* program taught us how these understandings help break the barrier of blame and unlock promising new courses of action.

Understanding the Relationship Between Home and School

Undoubtedly many families believe that literacy development starts at school age and yet many teachers expect children to start school with knowledge of the alphabet, numbers, colors, environmental words, and the ability to print their names. Rather than blame the families for lack of interest in their children and the teachers for unrealistic expectations, we must seek greater clarity about the basis of the differences in school achievement of children from varying home backgrounds. Focusing on the two extremes of "educational inadequacy explanations," which view the discrepancies as resulting from the failure of schools to develop student strengths and abilities, and "deficit driven explanations," which blame families for being incapable of creating an environment of support necessary for school success (Cairney, 1997), is unproductive. Instead, educators can acknowledge that the different relationships families have with the curriculum result in a gap between homes and school that is, in part, responsible for differential school performance. This explanation allows for a middle ground: a place where neither families nor teachers are singled out for blame, and where collaboration for the ultimate benefit of the children moves forward under the assumption that change, adjustments, and learning are required of all parties.

With this understanding in place, both sides can work together to plan joint programs to overcome the gap. In our research, we have identified ways to work collaboratively with families to address school literacy skills while respecting their backgrounds and home literacies. We ask the families what they want to learn and make their requests a focal aspect of the program. We highlight the goals that parents and educators have in common, such as a search for a better life for the children and ourselves, and we acknowledge different ways that families show that they care about their children's reading and writing. These discussions with teachers demonstrate that there are many literacy practices in the home even though children come to school without the print concepts that are considered essential for success with reading. We encourage teachers to inquire about and to build on these home literacy practices in their classrooms, and we teach parents the expectations for their children when they arrive at school so that they may better prepare their children at home for successful school experiences. Teachers and parents learn together, and the central focus of both is to enhance the children's school success.

Consider the case of Lori. She is 29 with three children and grew up in several foster homes in a large prairie city in Western Canada. She left school after she became involved in drugs and was pregnant at an early age. Lori made it clear to the teacher that she wanted to know how to teach her children their ABCs. She confided that she would say the alphabet and sing the song but her children "never could tell which one from which one." The *Learning Together* staff respected and accommodated Lori's interest, and together they created a learning focus meaningful to everyone involved.

Lori's example brings up another important point about negotiating the gap. Parental views of literacy were frequently perceived by teachers to be narrow with a focus on learning the alphabet and identifying words. Teachers were encouraged to accept the parents' view as a starting point while building a broader view of reading as the construction of meaning. Another strategy was to work with teachers to assist parents to develop a range of strategic behaviors for sharing text with their children. Teachers were encouraged to see how parents and children would respond to a model of effective literacy learning, rather than reminders of what they could not accomplish.

Understanding the Families

Educators must recognize that as Gadsen (2000) writes, "There is no appropriate, prototypical model of family structure" and that social, cultural, and linguistic variability predominates (Sample Gosse & Phillips, 2006). They must also go beyond the bare facts of the situation and carefully contemplate the influence on children's education.

The number of one-parent families has been increasing. Many of these families are under significant financial and emotional stress (Brodkin, 2002) and consequently have less time available to spend with their children and to participate in home-school activities. The demographic characteristics of the families participating in our study confirm the complex lives of modern families. Just as other researchers have documented strong family commitments to children, despite modern challenges to family life, we have found that the families participating in our study care deeply and profoundly about their children and persevere in their efforts to help them even though they face difficult life circumstances (Phillips & Sample Gosse, 2005).

Educators must be open to acknowledging the universal parental dream that their children enjoy successful school experiences even when families do not present themselves in traditional, middle-class ways. At the risk of sounding like a cliché, the first step is to listen to the families. Parents are often able to clearly articulate what they believe they need to learn in order to help their children, and these beliefs are personally powerful because they are based on the parents' own experiences (Phillips & Sample Gosse, 2005). Mutual understandings are developed through strong interpersonal relationships. Families and teachers each must accept responsibility for developing a positive relationship that keeps the child at the center (Churchill, 2003). Treating parents as a collective group obscures differences that must be considered if productive collaborations are to be developed. We have learned that in addition to what is "typical" of families with certain cultural, linguistic, and social backgrounds, there is always variability within the groups in terms of beliefs about children's learning.

Success is uncertain at times in parent–teacher collaborations. In our experience, teachers may think that parents are irresponsible about, or indifferent to, participation in literacy programs when they fail to show up or are consistently late. The truth may include challenges, including struggles for food, shelter, issues of family violence, substance abuse, health concerns, transportation problems, family breakdown, and financial difficulties. Parents need to feel respected and valued in order to confide their situations to teachers. Teachers have to respond sensitively to an already embarrassing situation for parents and attempt, where possible, to find appropriate services and ways to help. Staff in The Centre for Family Literacy made ongoing attempts to prepare for and provide appropriate program times and service information to parents.

Any initiatives developed to encourage home-school collaborations must consider the time and personal contact needed to develop the interpersonal relationships that make the difference for individual families. Based on our research, many personal contacts are needed before families feel comfortable to reveal their issues and concerns. It is critical, where possible, that the same person continue to develop and foster rapport with the families so that the contact person marks special occasions in the children's and parents' lives with a card and makes frequent calls and visits with the families an ongoing and essential feature of the collaborative initiative.

Strong relationships between teachers and parents result in the development of a common language and mutual awareness of the needs of children. Wesley and Buysse (2003) observed that "parents do not use the vocabulary that has become second nature to educators about parents being their child's 'first teachers,' the process of 'critical thinking,' or the terminology of 'readiness' or 'competence'" (p. 370). Teachers' exclusive use of such terms may serve to embarrass, intimidate, and alienate parents. For example, based on our research, we found that it was meaningless in many cases to tell parents that their child was learning disabled (LD) or exhibited evidence of autism spectrum disorder (ASD). Moreover, many parents assumed that the school would deal with "the problem". In the context of collaborations based on strong relationships, however, participants find mutually acceptable and ultimately more meaningful ways of describing their observations and concerns. We encouraged teachers to be patient and empathetic and to speak candidly at the parents' level of expertise about their child. In addition, teachers were enlisted to educate the parents on how to advocate for and to find support groups such as the Society for the Learning Disabled, the Autism Society, Homework without Tears, and High Special Needs Groups. Teachers were encouraged to respect all of the questions the parents asked, and in some cases, to ask questions for parents that they either did not think about or did not know to ask, and to counsel aggressive parents to be respectful of and professional toward teachers.

Homework is frequently a sore point between teachers and parents. Some immigrant and single parents work at least two jobs to make ends meet. Other parents are unable to help their children for language or literacy reasons, and still others are simply dismissive about homework as work that should have been completed in school. When the children arrive at school without completed homework, the parents are likely to be dismissed by teachers as irresponsible. Teachers should instead ask what purpose is served by providing suggestions to families that, although perhaps justifiable as "good educational practice," do not meet either the families' own expressed needs or their capacity to respond. We found in our research that the teachers' negative perceptions were not confirmed. Teachers worked to ensure that homework was designed to create an opportunity for parents and children to work together, thus demonstrating to the children the value their parents placed on schooling. Some schools have responded to the life circumstances of families by creating after-school homework programs. Parents have been assisted in developing ways to carve out a special time for homework. We agree with Bruckman and Blanton (2003) that one way for teachers to respond to the unique situations of families is to offer parents many different options for involvement in their children's schooling. We add the importance of involving families in the process of determining the available options.

Understanding the Teachers

In addition to developing our understanding of the views held and challenges faced by families and taking action to overcome the challenges, we must acknowledge certain realities about today's teachers. The diversity seen in the families of students is not yet represented in the teaching force. The majority of teachers continue to be White, middle-class, and female (Graue & Brown, 2003). The lack of diversity among teachers may result in perceived value differences that challenge their ability to relate to their students and the students' families. Teachers may expect parents to conform to institutional norms of appropriate parent behavior based on middle-class, two-parent homes (Lasky, 2000). They may rate children as less competent academically and hold lower expectations for their future success when they believe the education-related values of parents differ from their own values (Hauser-Cram, Sirin, & Stipek, 2003).

Based on our research, we noted early on that some parents felt sidelined by teachers and began to turn away from the program. These parents reluctantly told us that the teachers preferred the parents who were more like them, that is, White and better dressed. We observed and discussed the situation with the teachers. We suggested starting with having each parent tell a story about his or her child, and we developed follow-up ideas for a more inviting and engaging program.

The importance of recruiting more diverse prospective teachers notwithstanding, lack of diversity in the current teaching force does not have to be a barrier to collaboration. In our research, we have teachers who have empathy for their students. They think nothing of reading to children during recess and lunch breaks because they see a sparkle in the children's eyes and know that the families have placed their hope and trust in them to "teach their children to read." One teacher, for example, who gave her lunch and break time to read and work with a little boy in Grade 1 was hurt when she asked the parent to read to him at home and the parent responded, "That's your job, not mine. I work at the cleaners, I don't ask you to do my job." The teacher's rejection lasted for several weeks. The little boy was unaware of the incident and innocently assumed that he would stay with his teacher to read, so the teacher did not give up. She started to encourage the child to read to his mother and to get her to read to him. The mother never apologized to the teacher, but appeared at the next parent-teacher night and expressed delight at her son's progress. The teacher's unfailing interest in the little boy bridged the gap with the parent.

Teacher preparation and professional development programs may encourage the development of this type of empathy. Prospective and practicing teachers may be guided, through a process of reflection, on how their views toward education and home-school relations are shaped by their past experience, their privilege, and their need to establish professional authority with the ultimate goal of allowing them to identify the constraining effects of their assumptions (Hauser-Cram et al., 2003). Teacher education programs also support more productive home–school collaborations by emphasizing content related to social, gender, language, and cultural influences on parenting and teaching and by working to expose their students to varied experiences with families (Graue & Brown, 2003). The importance of this work should not be underestimated. When teacher education programs fail to challenge the set beliefs, images, and expectations of family involvement held by prospective teachers, most of them will fall back on what they know and "parents start with one strike against them" (Graue & Brown, 2003, p. 731).

Understanding the Educational Environment

Teachers and families are embedded in the educational environment of their schools, districts, and boards. This environment influences how they feel about education and about each other and therefore affects the potential for collaboration. In a telling study, Wesley and Buysse (2003) examined beliefs and expectations about school readiness among parents and professionals. Although parents and educators shared a common concern with the overall development of children, principals and kindergarten teachers referred to great contrasts in the richness of children's experiences prior to school, referring to "haves" and "have-nots" (p. 362). These educators reported a need to show parents how to teach their children certain skills prior to school entry. The kindergarten teachers held negative views about parents, who they saw as failing to do their job as children's first teachers. The way the professionals in the Wesley and Buysse study blamed the parents is understood in the context of the researchers' description of the stress that the teaching staff and administration were under to obtain strong academic outcomes for all students. The professionals described themselves as at odds with the difference between their personal philosophies of teaching and learning based on developmentally appropriate practices and the province or state and district instructional expectations and pressure to perform. A "push-down" phenomenon was described in which schools were pressured to develop specific academic skills in students in earlier and earlier grades.

Given the increasing influence of outside political pressures on the atmosphere within schools, it is easy to extrapolate from this example the potential for harm to the spirit of cooperation, trust, and patience needed to make collaborations between homes and schools productive. Politicians, administrators, and policymakers blame teachers for students' lower than expected performance. Teachers blame students' difficulties on inadequate prior instruction, parents' lack of interest, or both. Moreover, the added pressure to provide evidence of children's literacy performance at a younger and younger age seems to be setting up a dynamic that will increase the amount of blame directed at the families of young children.

Strong relationships and productive collaborations between home and school can facilitate joint initiatives to influence educational policy. Families and school professionals who find themselves equally bound by the current "straitjacket of accountability" can come together to talk back and push back at the top-down policy influences on their schools (Cummins, 2004). Pressure for children and teachers to perform to district and provincial or state norms has prompted some teachers and parents to challenge the system. For example, it is common in some schools for children to be labeled as learning disabled in reading and writing as early as Grades 1 and 2. In some of these schools, high-referral teachers recommend children to special education classes on the basis of one district or state standardized test, whereas in others teachers have developed compensatory early literacy programs. In the case of the high-referral teachers, parents react, if they have the resources, by moving their children to another school, and in the case of the latter, teachers explain the situation to parents and solicit their support to assist at home with specific aspects of the alternative program. Although the parents and teachers have not directly challenged the top-down policy, they are working around the system.

CONCLUDING REMARKS

The case we have presented on families and teachers clearly suggests that although both groups are challenged by events somewhat beyond their control, they both, by and large, share a deep commitment to children. Coming to understand each other's views and challenges opens the door for families and teachers to take collaborative action based on this shared commitment.

Cairney (1997) recognized productive home–school collaborations as "simultaneously our greatest challenge, and yet our greatest possibility for breaking down educational inequities characterized by widely differing abilities to use literacy in and out of school" (p. 70). We agree and contend that attending to understanding inequities prior to action provides a way to reduce the blame that characterizes home–school relationships, and allows genuine grass-roots collaborations to develop.

Home–school collaborations are a critical issue in emergent literacy. Early literacy development is a complex phenomenon widely acknowledged to be affected by many aspects of child development, as well as by the gap between home and school perceptions and practices. Although it is easier to do as Pope mused in 1711, "Some praise at morning what they blame at night" (p. 26), than to take on the challenge of collaboration between home and school, it is time for the educators to take the lead in acknowledging that there is no gain in blame.

REFERENCES

Brodkin, A.M. (2002). I'm at daddy's this week. *Early Childhood Today, 17(3)*, 20–22.

Bruckman, M., & Blanton, P. W. (2003). Welfare-to-work single mothers' perspectives on parent involvement in Head Start: Implications for parent–teacher collaboration. *Early Childhood Education Journal, 30*(3), 145–150.

Cairney, T. H. (1997). Acknowledging diversity in home literacy practices: Moving towards partnership with parents. *Early Child Development and Care, 127–128*, 61–73.

Churchhill, S. L. (2003). Goodness-of-fit in early childhood settings. *Early Childhood Education Journal, 31,* 113–118.

Cummins, J. (2004, January). *From literacy to multiliteracies: Designing learning environments for knowledge generation in culturally and linguistically diverse schools.* Presented at the Building Capacity for Diversity in Canadian Schools Lecture Series, Calgary, Alberta.

Gadsden, V. L. (2000). Intergenerational literacy within families. In M. L. Kamil, P. B. Mosenthal, P. D. Pearson, & R. Barr (Eds.), *Handbook of reading research* (Vol. III, pp. 871–887). Mahwah, NJ: Lawrence Erlbaum Associates.

Goodman, Y. (1985). Kidwatching: Observing children in the classroom. In A. Jaggar & M. Smith-Burke (Eds.), *Observing the language learner* (pp. 9–18). Newark, DE & Urbana, IL: IRA & NCTE.

Graue, E., & Brown, C.P. (2003). Preservice teachers' notions of families and schooling. *Teaching and Teacher Education, 19,* 719–735.

Hauser-Cram, P., Sirin, S.R., & Stipek, D. (2003). When teachers' and parents' values differ: Teachers' ratings of academic competence in children from low-income families. *Journal of Educational Psychology, 95,* 813–820.

Lasky, S. (2000). The cultural and emotional politics of teacher-parent interactions. *Teaching and Teacher Education, 16,* 843–860.

Morrow, L., & Young, J. (1997). A collaborative family literacy program: The effects on children's motivation and literacy achievement. *Early Child Development and Care, 127–128,* 13–25.

Paratore, J. R. (2001). *Opening doors, opening opportunities*. Needham Heights, MA: Allyn & Bacon.

Phillips, L. M. & Sample Gosse, H. L. (2005). Family literacy: Listen to what the families have to say. In J. Anderson, M. Kendrick, T. Rogers, & S. Smythe (Eds.). *Critical issues in family, community, and school literacies: Intersections and tensions* (pp. 91–107). Mahwah, NJ: Lawrence Erlbaum Associates.

Pope, A. (1711). *An Essay on Criticism*. London: Lewis. (Facsimile ed., Scolar Press).

Purcell-Gates, V. (2000). Family literacy. In M.L. Kamil, P.B. Mosenthal, P.D. Pearson, & R. Barr (Eds.), *Handbook of reading research* (Vol. III, pp. 853–870). Mahwah, NJ: Lawrence Erlbaum Associates.

Rodriguez-Brown, F. V., & Meehan, M. A. (1998). Family literacy and adult education: Project FLAME. In Smith, M.C. (Ed). *Literacy for the twenty-first century: Research, policy, practices, and the national adult literacy survey* (pp. 175–193). Westport, CT: Praeger.

Sample Gosse, H. L., & Phillips, L. M. (2006). Family literacy in Canada: Foundation to a literate society. In A. McKeough, L. Phillips, V. Timmons, & J. Lupart (Eds.), *Understanding literacy development: A global view* (pp. 113–135). Mahwah, NJ: Lawrence Erlbaum Associates.

Sénéchal, M., & LeFevre, J. (2002). Parental involvement in the development of children's reading skill: A five-year longitudinal study. *Child Development, 73*(2), 445–460.

Snow, C. E., Barnes, W. S., Chandler, J., Goodman, I. F., & Hemphill, L. (1991). *Unfulfilled expectations: Home and school influences on literacy*. Cambridge, MA: Harvard University Press.

Wesley, P. W., & Buysse, V. (2003). Making meaning of school readiness in schools and communities. *Early Childhood Research Quarterly, 18,* 351–375.

Chapter 14

Invisible Mediators of Literacy: Learning in Multicultural Communities

Susi Long, Dinah Volk, Mary Eunice Romero-Little, and Eve Gregory

> It is evident that the families with whom we were working…are active members of a print community in which literacy is used for a wide variety of social, technical, and aesthetic purposes, for a wide variety of audiences, and in a wide variety of situations…no one can deny that these are literate homes. (Taylor & Dorsey-Gaines, 1988, p. 20)

Eighteen years ago, Denny Taylor and Catherine Dorsey-Gaines wrote about families who were typically viewed as lacking literate experiences or as illiterate. Their work and the work of others (Heath, 1983; Moll & Greenberg, 1990) had an incredible impact on educators' perspectives about ways that families in marginalized communities use language and literacy richly, effectively, and efficiently when the prevailing paradigm was to view those families from a deficit perspective. This prompted work that further illuminated literacy resources not typically recognized or valued in schools (Haight, 2003, and Valdés, 1996, to name two). However, deficit paradigms continue to exist as assumptions are made about children, families, and communities based on limited understandings about the use and support of language and literacy in their lives.

To counter that deficit view, we believe that more stories need to be told. In this chapter, we share such stories by focusing on mediators of literacy learning beyond teachers and parents across diverse cultural settings. Based on the belief that we have much to learn from the skillful ways that other teachers in children's lives support learning, we describe three studies: (a) Dinah Volk's look at supportive interactions among Puerto Rican siblings at home, (b) Susi Long's investigation of Mexican American peer interactions at school, and (c) Mary Eunice Romero's study of learning in a Cochiti Pueblo community. Our work is grounded in a commitment to long-term observational research that looks closely at day-to-day interactions embracing an ethnographic stance that considers cultural context basic to understanding phenomena.

IDEAS THAT GUIDE OUR WORK

We believe that learning is a sociocultural process, that learners come to think in new ways through opportunities to interact meaningfully with more knowledgeable others (Vygotsky, 1978). Extensions of Vygotskian thought help us move beyond the notion that learner and more-knowledgeable-other constitute a fixed relationship. Engaged in purposeful interactions, learners move seamlessly in and out of roles of apprentice and expert (Rogoff, 1990). Zones of proximal development are created and recreated by learners who are also teachers, as they engage one another in going beyond prior understandings (Lindfors, 1999).

Our work uses the concept of *syncretism* to describe the creative process through which people reinvent culture as they draw on diverse resources from prior experiences (Gregory, Long, & Volk, 2004). This builds on other investigations of ways that children appropriate practices from multiple contexts as resources for learning (Gutiérrez, Baquedano-López, Tejeda & Rivera, 1999; Solsken, Willett, & Wilson-Keenan, 2000). Some of these studies are rooted in the work of Bahktin (1981) and use his term *hybridity* to refer to the blending of different voices. We use the term *syncretism* because it suggests not just a blending of old practices but the creation of new ways of teaching and learning.

A critical stance guides our research as we consider the damage done by deficit views that attribute the lack of school success for children of color, children whose home language is other than English, and children from low socioeconomic communities to deficits in families and cultures. A hierarchy is created that privileges middle-class literacy practices and devalues or ignores others. Challenging this status quo, we draw from studies that highlight rich cultural practices in diverse communities (Gregory & Williams, 2000; Moll & Greenberg, 1990) and from work that suggests using that knowledge to transform pedagogy (Hull & Schultz, 2002; Nieto, 1999). We see possibilities for transformation in schools when teachers understand and value the cultural practices of every child and family.

WHAT CAN WE LEARN FROM THE OTHER TEACHERS IN CHILDREN'S LIVES?

Mediating Networks for Literacy Learning: The Role of Puerto Rican Siblings (Dinah Volk)

Cross-cultural research confirms that older siblings play an important role in the care and education of children in most cultures (Zukow, 1989). Described as cultural and linguistic mediators, older siblings often introduce younger ones to valued knowledge and skills, syncretizing resources from varied settings within the familiar context of the home. In Latino families (Valdés, 1996), sibling caretaking and teaching are typically valued aspects of family life. The data I present here describes sibling teaching in the home of 5-year-old Julializ Torres, one of three bilingual, Puerto Rican kindergartners participating in a broader study about children's literacy lives (Volk & de Acosta, 2001). Julializ, like the others, was embedded in a network of people that mediated her developing literacy in her bilingual kindergarten, home, and community.

To understand the children's literacy lives, I used an ethnographic approach to study literacy as a cultural practice. The analysis was multilayered, investigating teaching strategies that supported literacy interactions within broader social contexts. The aspects of literacy that were the focus of each strategy were identified (oral language development, concepts of print, word identification, word analysis, comprehension) and patterns of use were analyzed.

Participant observation took place during one academic year in the children's kindergarten, their homes, churches, and Sunday schools. I audiotaped twice monthly between January and June in the classroom and homes and conducted semistructured interviews with the teacher, parents, and children. The parents also completed network maps charting the relationships that mediated their child's developing literacy.

The Network of Support

Julializ's school and home were located in a working class neighborhood with a substantial Puerto Rican population in a large Midwestern city. She lived with her mother, brothers Francisco, 9, and Fernando, 12, and a "church brother and a sister." Her cousins, Zoila, 6, and Hilary, 3, were raised with Julializ, "*como hermanitas*" [like sisters]. Julializ was learning to read in Spanish in school. She understood concepts of print and was putting her energy into word identification, word analysis, and comprehension. Sra. Torres, Julializ's mother, reported that she was teaching Julializ to read in Spanish using a phonics primer she studied as a child in Puerto Rico.

Julializ also read English library books and used workbooks that her mother purchased. Sra. Torres and Julializ's uncle, often read to the three girls and the family read the Bible in Spanish daily with everyone taking turns.

Constructing Literacy With Siblings

I selected the following examples to illustrate one type of interaction that occurred regularly in all three homes: deliberate instruction when children read texts with sibling assistance. The children also engaged with texts in play and in interactions with adult family members characterized by both direct instruction and instruction embedded in ongoing activities.

In the example that follows, Francisco, a struggling student, helped Julializ by emphasizing concepts of print as he said each word for Julializ to repeat.

Francisco:	One day a pig and a dog met a frog //on a log.//[1]
Sra Torres:	//Pero papi suave.// [But slowly dear.]
Julializ:	One.
Francisco:	Day.
Julializ:	Day.
Francisco:	A.
Julializ:	A.
Francisco:	Dog. I mean a fro- I mean a pig.
Julializ:	A pig.

Critical of this method of merely providing text, Sra. Torres prompted Francisco to go slowly and attend to word meaning. "*Enseñale la palabra nene*" [Teach her the word boy], she said, "*si no, no aprende*" [if not, she doesn't learn.] She then asked Julializ if she had understood the story, modeling a comprehension question. Francisco followed with his own comprehension question, checking her understanding. Julializ responded by retelling the story.

In the next example Julializ read a book with Fernando, a confident, biliterate student. In contrast to Francisco, he focused on comprehension by providing translations of the English words and directing Julializ's attention to a picture. With his help, Julializ read several words together on her own, participating more actively and competently than when she was reading with Francisco. Fernando appeared to have more accurately gauged her level of competence and the assistance she needed.

---

[1]Transcription conventions include: empty parentheses ( ) for unclear speech; double slashes // // for overlapping speech; translations in square brackets.

Fernando:	...We.
Julializ:	We. //Are.//
Fernando:	//Went.// Went.
Julializ:	Went. To. The. Zoo.
Sra Torres:	Mhum.
Julializ:	It. Whhhas.... A.
Fernando:	Grande. [Big.]
Julializ:	Big. Park. Www//www//...With.
Fernando:	Mucha. [A lot.]
Julializ:	A lot....
Fernando:	Mhmh. Of.
Julializ:	Of.
Fernando:	Diferente. En inglés. [Different. In English.]
Julializ:	Different animals.
Fernando:	Mhum....
Julializ:	The lllions wwwear....
Fernando:	((points to picture)) ¿Qué son éstos?... [What are these?...]
Julializ:	Cubs.

In a third example, Zoila, a confident English reader, helped Julializ read a list of English words by providing scaffolding for word analysis that drew on their shared knowledge of Spanish and English letter sounds. For groups of words with the same vowel, Zoila provided the Spanish vowel sounds as cues for troublesome English ones. For example, Julializ was able to read the word *to* after Zoila cued the English O sound in *to* using the sound of U in Spanish. Zoila then cued the English O in *not* using the Spanish A, and Julializ was able to read that word too.

Julializ and the other children in this study were "people rich," with substantial funds of knowledge (Moll & Greenberg, 1990) relevant to literacy and shared through mediating networks. Julializ's siblings were skillful mediators who often provided bilingual assistance within her zone of proximal development. The aspects of literacy they emphasized seemed influenced by their differing abilities to gauge the level of assistance needed, their age, their literacy competencies in both languages, and the assistance *they* received. Overall, these interactions were co-constructed syncretically, as children re-created literacy, drawing on educational and religious texts in Spanish and English, from home and school contexts, from the U.S. mainland and Puerto Rico.

Scaffolding Literacy Learning: Mexican-American Kindergartners and Peers (Susi Long)

In 1995, I completed a study of an American child in Iceland that helped me understand a range of strategies used by the child and peers to support learning in a new cultural setting (Long, 1998). Returning to the United States, I wondered about children who were learning English as a new language. How did they create practices with peers in support of their own learning? I initiated a study that looked at Mexican-American kindergartners and their peers. Data were collected weekly from September through March. Data sources included field notes, video and audio tape during informal and formal activities at school, including interviews with the children in English and Spanish. Conversations with the children's mothers at home provided further data. Data were analyzed and triangulated by the primary researcher, the teacher, and the graduate assistant working in the classroom.

The three primary participants—Marcial, Martita, Juan—lived in the same low socioeconomic community and were 5 years old when they entered the school district's English as a second language (ESL) kindergarten. In their class of 23 children, there were 16 nonnative English speakers representing five different language backgrounds. Martita, Juan, and Marcial began the year as monolingual Spanish speakers. Findings highlight strategies used by the children and their peers to scaffold literacy learning. They drew syncretically from diverse funds of cultural knowledge to make sense of new experiences and participate in literacy events.

Strategies Used to Support Literacy Learning

Providing Demonstrations Through Side-By-Side Reading. A strong pattern that emerged was the support children provided and received as they drew on demonstrations from multiple contexts to read books during free choice periods. For example, one morning Marcial sat on the floor with an English book reading the pictures aloud in Spanish. Kiesha, a monolingual English-speaking peer, joined him. Moving her book between them, she began reading in English. Martita and Juan, playing nearby, stopped to watch. Later, Martita and Juan sat together, holding a book between them while Juan read pictures aloud in Spanish. To participate in this literacy event, it seems likely that Juan blended strategies learned from demonstrations across contexts—Marcial's picture reading in Spanish, Kiesha's side-by-side reading in English, and demonstrations of reading behaviors by the teacher at school and by family members using Spanish at home.

Translating and Clarifying. Often, the bilingual Spanish/English-speaking children in the class provided support for Juan, Martita, and Marcial by translating and clarifying. An example occurred in September when the teaching assistant, a native Spanish speaker, read an English picture book to a group that included Marcial, who spoke a few English words, and Maya, a bilingual Spanish/English speaker. The teaching assistant, speaking English, asked Marcial to describe an illustration:

Assistant:	Tell me what you see here (pointing to the illustration).
Marcial:	(Looks closely at the illustration).
Assistant:	What do you see here?
Marcial:	(Looks at the illustration, but says nothing).
Maya:	¿Qué ve usted aquí? What do you see? (translating the teaching assistant's question into Spanish for Marcial)
Assistant:	Tell me about the picture. (prompting Marcial in English)
Maya:	He is looking. (explaining Marcial's behavior to the assistant)
Assistant:	Marcial, what do you see here?
Marcial:	Hay un chico y un perro. [There's a boy and a dog]
Maya:	He sees a boy and a dog. (translating for the assistant)

An expert mediator, sensitive to the needs of both Marcial and the teaching assistant, Maya provided support for both by translating the teaching assistant's question into Spanish, explaining Marcial's behavior, and translating Marcial's words into English. In a true blending of culture and language Maya created practices that allowed Marcial and the teaching assistant to interact successfully.

Enacting Cultural Roles Through Sociodramatic Play. Free activity time provided opportunities for the children to engage in sociodramatic play in ways that allowed them to practice strategies that were central to literacy learning in their classroom. Through play, they drew on multiple experiences to teach and learn. By spring of that school year, Martita was observed taking on the role of teacher when playing school. In the example that follows, she led a group of children reading the sentence, "This tiger lives at the zig-zag zoo":

Martita:	Okay, like this (pointing to the words). This tiger.
Other Children:	(Reading with Martita) This tiger (they stop at the word "lives," because they don't recognize it).
Martita:	Something. Say "something." Skip it (instructing them to use the word,"something" as a place marker, to skip the word and read on, a strategy learned from the teacher). This tiger *something* at the zigzag—This tiger l-l-l-l-l- (focusing on the beginning consonant in "lives," another classroom strategy).

Teacher:	(Joining them) What makes sense? What can we do?
Martita:	Stretch it out.
Children:	L-l-l-l –iv
Juan:	Lives!
Martita:	(Reading) This tiger lives at the zigzag zoo!

The opportunity to play sociodramatically created a place where it was safe to risk active participation. In this instance, it allowed Martita to merge prior knowledge about interactions with text (strategies demonstrated frequently by the classroom teacher) with her growing English competence. The result was a syncretic blending of experience that supported literacy learning and provided a window for the teacher into Martita's knowledge.

Celebrating Multilingual Abilities. Foundational to the success of every strategy used by the children was a teacher who honored children for their multilingual abilities. In turn, the children celebrated that ability in one another. One of many examples occurred one day when the class was reading the Morning Message. Juan raised his hand and identified the word *October*. Juan's friend Rocio said, "He is learning a lot of English…He knows a lot of Spanish too!"

Syncretizing language and experience, Juan, Martita, Marcial, and their peers supported each other's participation in literacy events while deepening the learning potential for everyone. In a context created by a sensitive teacher, they often appropriated and extended strategies demonstrated by others. In addition to those mentioned here, they used demonstration and gesture; altered tone of voice; celebrated approximations in Spanish and English; expected success; and used predictable texts and other supportive artifacts. Given opportunities for purposeful interaction in an environment where they felt valued for using knowledge from multiple worlds, they drew on that knowledge. Moving fluidly between the roles of expert and novice, they expertly engaged one another in going beyond (Lindfors, 1999).

Teaching Literacy in Pueblo Societies: A World of "Visible" Meditators (Mary Eunice Romero)

This 3-year ethnographic study (Romero, 2003) examines how one Pueblo community perpetuates their way of life and important values and practices. In Cochiti Pueblo societies, adults take on roles and responsibilities crucial to perpetuating the community's life and ways of knowing. Consequently, the children must be well prepared to assume these critical roles and responsibilities in adulthood. For Pueblo children, learning the language and knowledge they need for literacy in the Pueblo world requires continual linguistic and social interactions with many highly visible mediators. This process begins well before they enter the doors of mainstream schools and extends into adulthood.

Today approximately 700 Cochiti people reside in the small Keres community located 35 miles southwest of Santa Fe. Non-Indian accounts hold that the Cochiti people have resided in the area for over 1,000 years (Preucel, 2000), whereas the Cochiti themselves trace their agrarian and communal existence in the area to time immemorial (Sando, 1992). At its heart, this study examined *how* Cochiti children come to know or learn to become Kuchite-me' [Cochiti]. Research methods included open-ended interviews and home and community participant observations. Two generations of Cochitis, 13 grandparents (56 to 73 years) and 19 young parents (21 to 47 years), were interviewed to obtain an understanding of key values and beliefs guiding the socialization of their children. Observations focused on the socialization practices and behaviors in which Cochiti adults engage with children.

A World of Visible Mediators

The world of Cochiti children is full of daily interactions with a myriad of visible mediators or teachers who pass on to them important beliefs, values, principles, and practices. In Cochiti families, parents, grandparents, and siblings are the central mediators in child socialization. Grandparents spend extended periods of time with their grandchildren. Young grandsons accompany their grandfathers to the practice house[2] where men and boys gather to compose traditional native songs. Young girls frequently accompany their grandmothers and mothers to familial and communal social activities. In the wider community, children come to know a third group of mediators, the secular and traditional leadership, including clan and cultural society members. These leaders are responsible for the cultural and spiritual guidance, social welfare, safety, and harmony of the community.

Ways of Teaching and Learning. In this subsection, I briefly consider how children learn the Cochiti ways. For purposes of this discussion they are described separately, but in reality they are often interrelated and collectively comprise a unique learning context for children and adults alike.

In these complex oral Pueblo societies, the religious and social life of the people revolve around a rich ceremonial calendar permeated with communal activities in which there are numerous opportunities for Cochiti children to participate. As a result, they are visible and significant participants in the community's traditional and social life, as we see in the

[2]A communal building for social and ceremonial activities.

vignette that follows. In this vignette, a young Cochiti boy is deeply immersed in *learning through participation* in a winter buffalo dance: It is a cool winter morning. People sit in the plaza wrapped warmly in blankets waiting for the buffalo dance to begin. High-pitched melodies along with white puffs of cold air come from the north end of the plaza. Singers are in Plains Indian regalia customary dress for this dance. In front of the choir of men are 10 children dressed accordingly, singing the traditional buffalo songs. Two male and two female buffalo dancers and a "hunter"[3] enter the plaza. The drummers begin a rhythmic beat and the dancing begins. A 4-year-old child, dressed as a buffalo dancer, watches. Before long, he raises his feet high in the air, mimicking the adult dancers. He looks down at his feet as if instructing them how to move. He glances back up at the adult dancers and follows their motions.

From infancy, children are exposed to interaction in which *teaching by doing* plays a crucial role in their learning. For example, Pueblo bread making is a refined and multifaceted mediated process in Cochiti homes. Usually two or more women work together to make the bread. Infants are often positioned near the activity, where they may watch the bread makers at work. When they are older and able to hold and manipulate objects, they are given a small piece of dough to handle and are praised for their attempts at rolling out a ball of dough. When children are adept enough to manipulate dough purposely, usually around 3 years of age, they are positioned next to someone who models the action for them and praises the child for being a "good helper." If the child does not attempt the task, one of the adults or an older sibling will assist. At 4 and 5 years of age, children are expected to participate without much coaxing. At each stage, guidance, praise, and encouragement are given continuously.

A prevalent form of learning found in the Cochiti context is *learning through engaged observation*, which takes place when the learner is an active participant in the activity even though he or she may be only watching and listening to others. As a young mother explained:

> It's so funny because I remember when he started going with his dad to [the] practice [house]...he would get his little drum and he would walk like an old man and sit on a little stool and start beating his drum...He picked up a lot just by going with his dad and seeing the older men.

The previous snapshot also illustrates another powerful form of mediated learning, *teaching through example of role modeling*. Cochiti children learn proper social behavior and discourse by observing and listening to

---

[3]The hunter dresses in a buckskin shirt and leggings and carries a leather sheath across his back; he and the buffalo dancers represent the traditional hunting excursions conducted years back.

adults. Boys watch and listen to their fathers, grandfathers, and/or uncles in home interactions and in leadership roles. Girls observe their mother, grandmothers, and other females performing their respective roles in the home and community. A nonnative man visiting a Cochiti family asked their 5-year-old son, "What do you want to be when you grow up?" The boy responded in Keres, "A leader." The visitor expected the boy to respond with a common mainstream occupation (i.e., fireman or policeman), but the boy, who has witnessed both his father and grandfather in traditional leadership roles, responded that he aspired to be like them.

Starting early in their lives, Pueblo children are provided with many rich and meaningful opportunities to acquire the literacy—the cultural symbols and intellectual traditions (Benjamin, Pecos, & Romero, 1997)—vital for the perpetuation of their cultural worlds and for developing strong individual and communal identities. Ultimately, this may contribute to their successes in schools when mainstream teachers and others understand and respect the varied ways of learning and the multifaceted talents and wisdoms that children bring from their homes and communities.

WHAT MIGHT THIS MEAN FOR CLASSROOM TEACHERS?

In 1988, Taylor and Dorsey-Gaines wrote about a child whose home-based knowledge was all but invisible to the school-based educators in his worlds. Today, the dilemma continues to exist. In 2002, Lisa Delpit wrote: "Teachers seldom know much about the children's lives and communities outside of the classroom and either don't know how to or aren't willing to connect instruction to issues that matter to students, their families and their communities" (p. 41). We share our stories in hopes that they will prompt educators to learn from the networks of support in homes, communities, and among peers in school—the invisible teachers in children's lives—and the strategies used by those teachers to scaffold learning. The children in our studies were supported by mediators who (a) provided opportunities for active apprenticeship in contexts that were purposeful and valued by the learner and the community, (b) honored the time necessary for learners to observe, interact, and experiment, and (c) valued the expertise of learners, celebrating the knowledge and strategies they used to syncretize learning across experiences.

Understanding the skill and sensitivity of those who play integral roles in children's lives, educators can continue to vigorously challenge the deficit perspective that relegates the same children and their families to the margins year after year, and limits teaching and learning possibilities for all students. When too many children continue to be left behind, the need to seek such understanding is great. We believe that creating classrooms grounded in these convictions has the potential to make a difference not only in schooling but in society.

REFERENCES

Bakhtin, M.M. (1981). *The dialogic imagination: Four essays*. Austin, TX: University of Texas Press.

Benjamin, R., Pecos, R., & Romero, M. E. (1997). Language revitalization efforts in the Pueblo de Cochiti: Becoming "literate" in an oral society. In N. H. Hornberger (Ed.), *Indigenous literacies in the Americas: Language planning from the bottom up* (pp. 115–136). New York: Mouton de Gruyter.

Delpit, L. (2002). *The skin that we speak: Thoughts on language and culture in the classroom*. New York: New Press.

Gregory, E., Long, S., & Volk, D. (2004). *Many pathways to literacy: Young children learning with siblings, peers, grandparents, and communities*. London: Routledge Falmer.

Gregory, E., & Williams, A. (2000). *City literacies: Learning to read across generations and cultures*. London: Routledge.

Gutiérrez, K.D., Baquedano-López, P., Tejeda, C., & Rivera, A. (1999, April). *Hybridity as a tool for understanding literacy learning: Building on a syncretic approach.* Paper presented at the meeting of the American Educational Research Association, Montreal, Canada.

Haight, W. (2003). *African American children at church*. Cambridge, UK: Cambridge University Press.

Heath, S. B. (1983). *Ways with words: language, life, and work in communities and classrooms*. Cambridge: Cambridge University Press.

Hull, G., & Schultz, K. (Eds.). (2002). *School's out: Bridging out-of-school literacies with classroom practice*. New York: Teachers College Press.

Lindfors, J. (1999). *Children's inquiry*. New York: Teachers College Press.

Long, S. (1998). Learning to get along: Language and literacy development in a new cultural setting. *Research in the Teaching of English*, *33*(1), 8–47.

Moll, L. C., & Greenberg, J. B. (1990). Creating zones of possibilities: Combining social contexts for instruction. In L. C. Moll (Ed.), *Vygotsky and education: Instructional implications and applications of socio-historical psychology.* (pp. 319–348). Cambridge: Cambridge University Press.

Nieto, S. (1999). *The light in their eyes: Creating multicultural learning communities*. New York: Teachers College Press.

Preucel, R. W. (2000). Living on the mesa: Hanat Kotyiti, a post-revolt Cochiti community in the northern Rio Grande. *Expedition*, *42*, 8–17.

Rogoff, B. (1990). *Apprenticeship in thinking: Cognitive development in social contexts*. Oxford: Oxford University Press.

Romero, M. E. (2003). *Perpetuating the Cochiti way of life: Language socialization and language shift in a Pueblo community*. Unpublished doctoral dissertation, University of California at Berkeley.

Sando, J. S. (1992). *Pueblo nations: Eight centuries of Pueblo Indian history*. Santa Fe, NM: Clear Light Publishers.

Solsken, J. Willet, J., & Wilson-Keenan, J. (2000). Cultivating hybrid texts in multicultural classrooms: Promise and challenge. *Research in the Teaching of English*, *35*(2), 179–212.

Taylor, D., & Dorsey-Gaines, C. (1988). *Growing up literate: Learning from inner-city families.* Portsmouth, NH: Heinemann.

Valdés, G. (1996). *Con respeto: Bridging the distance between culturally diverse families and schools*. New York: Teachers College Press.

Volk, D. & de Acosta, M. (2001). "Many differing ladders, many ways to climb": Literacy events in the bilingual classroom, homes, and community of three Puerto Rican kindergartners. *Journal of Early Childhood Literacy*, *1*, 193–224.

Vygotsky, L. (1978). *Mind in society*. Cambridge, MA: Harvard University Press.

Zukow, P. G. (Ed.). (1989). *Sibling interactions across cultures: Theoretical and methodological issues*. New York: Springer-Verlag.

Part **IV**

CULTURAL AND POLITICAL PERSPECTIVES ON EARLY LITERACY

Because children's literature has the potential to play such a key role in an education that is multicultural and focused on social justice, all children should have access to culturally authentic literature.... [W]e must hold fast to our belief that literature and democracy are intertwined and that the thoughtful use of literature can enhance education for a democratic way of life.... The debates about cultural authenticity in children's literature matter because they foster the dialogue that is essential to democracy. (Short & Fox, this volume, pp. 232–233)

The political contexts in which schools are situated greatly impact what happens in schools and, at the same time, frame the responses of educational professionals, educational and test publishers, the public, the parents with children in the school and the children themselves. In this historical period, teachers and children who are being asked to set aside enriched curricular experiences that enhance literacy learning and replace them with specific lessons that represent narrowly conceived notions of accountability and standardization (Dyson, this volume, chap. 11). Many educators, especially in public school settings, have admonished teachers not to be political. In response, some school personnel have negated the importance of professionals understanding the influences that ideology has on educational policies that impact what happens daily in classrooms to the lives of young children and their families.

All the chapters in this volume represent issues that relate to the political nature of schooling and home and school relations. However, the authors in Part 4, Political Perspectives on Early Literacy, challenge us to become critically conscious about democracy, social justice, and the rights of teachers and children. The authors pose problems and raise questions that involve us in thinking politically. Each chapter explores ideological issues from various perspectives providing readers with different lenses through which to view a variety of critical issues. The authors have concerns about what criteria should be considered to choose literature for children; ways for teachers to engage young children in reading and responding to serious issues presented in literature and other print media; how to provide support for preservice and in-service teachers to engage in self-reflection as they develop a critical consciousness; and how governments form pedagogical practices and goals regarding literacy teaching and how such practices and goals influence children's biliteracy.

The authors make clear that curriculum and pedagogy in schools, especially for the youngest children, must go beyond simplistic notions that focus on decontextualized skills devoid of literacy as a cultural construct. The chapters document that how literacy is taught and defined by law influences learners' views about literacy—what it is, what it does and whom it benefits. It is time to put to rest the old adage: "First children learn to read and then they read to learn."

Rather, in every engagement young children have with literacy in school, in their homes and in their communities, children are learning literacy, learning through literacy, and learning about literacy (Halliday, (1979). Each child comes to school influenced by their unique history of literacy learning that begins at birth influenced by family members as children's initial teachers. Schools and teachers are in the position to support children's literacy learning or to disrupt or thwart it based on how the literacy curriculum is organized and how the world of the children's literacy is valued and respected.

Children learn best as they are immersed in literacy experiences enriched by knowledgeable teachers who know about and value the literacy histories of the children, their culture, and their communities, who know how to organize classroom environments that invite children to become literate, and who know how to use provocative and engaging children's literature and other materials that draw children into being inventive and becoming literate. The purposes of their engagements in literacy are to engage their minds in their own personal imagination and to find ways to make the world a better place for all.

Ferriero (2003) unequivocally states the political and ideological nature of the work of early literacy educators:

> Literacy is neither a luxury nor an obligation: it is a right. A right of boys and girls who will become free men and women (at least that's what we want), citizens of a world in which linguistic and cultural differences will be considered a wealth and not a defect. Different languages and different systems of writ-

ing are part of our cultural patrimony. Culture diversity is as important as biodiversity: if we destroy it, we will not be able to recreate it. (p. 34)

CRITICAL ISSUES RELATED TO "CULTURAL AND POLITICAL PERSPECTIVES ON EARLY LITERACY"

- Understanding children's early literacy learning with an international perspective supports organizing classrooms that honor social justice and democracy.
- Teachers need to reframe the language of schooling in response to governmental mandates and controls.
- A diversity of research methodology is necessary to develop the richest insights and understandings of literacy learning.
- The power of literature and instructional material written for children impacts their views of themselves as learners, as readers, and as members of the human community.
- Literacy learning in social contexts establishes the social conventions for literacy learning.

REFERENCES

Ferriero, E. (2003) *Past and present of the verbs to read and to write.* Toronto: Douglas & McIntyre

Halliday, M. A. K. (1979). Three aspects of children's language development: Learning language, learning through language, learning about language. In Y. M. Goodman, M. M. Haussler, & D. S. Strickland (Eds.), *Oral and written language development research: Impact on the schools* (pp. 7–19). Proceedings from the 1979 and 1980 IMPACT Conferences. Newark, DE, & Urbana, IL: International Reading Association & National Council of Teachers of English.

Chapter **15**

Debates About Cultural Authenticity in Literature for Young Children

Kathy G. Short and Dana L. Fox

Cultural authenticity in children's literature is one of those contentious issues that continuously resurface, always eliciting strong emotions and a wide range of perspectives. Authors, illustrators, editors, publishers, educators, librarians, theorists, and researchers have different points of view that they feel strongly about, based on their sociocultural experiences and philosophical perspectives. Their arguments about cultural authenticity are not just academic; the voices in these debates are passionate and strong, reflecting deeply held beliefs at the heart of each person's work in creating or using books with young children.

We became involved with debates about cultural authenticity as editors of *The New Advocate*, a professional journal for those involved with young people and their literature. We found the complexity and the intensity of the debates to be provocative; however, too often the debates seemed to swirl back to dichotomies and simplistic outsider/insider distinctions. To gain a greater understanding of these complex issues, we conducted a critical review of the essays and research published on cultural authenticity. Our goals were to examine the past and current debates, discover patterns and themes in the literature, suggest possible directions for future research, and explore implications for the use of culturally authentic literature in classrooms (Fox & Short, 2003).

In this chapter, we relate our major findings about the complexity of cultural authenticity in children's literature and explore implications for research and instruction in early literacy. We first discuss the difficult task of defining cultural authenticity, particularly within the sociopolitical context of multicultural education. Next, we describe the methodology for our critical review. Using the themes that we found most prevalent in the professional literature, we organize the remainder of the chapter around eight major questions that explore the complicated issues. Finally, we suggest implications for research and pedagogy in early literacy.

DEFINING CULTURAL AUTHENTICITY IN CHILDREN'S LITERATURE

Most authors and educators discuss the complexity of cultural authenticity rather than define it. Many seem to agree with Bishop (2003) that cultural authenticity cannot be defined but "you know it when you see it," as an insider reading a book about your own culture. Howard (1991) says that we have to pay attention to what the book does to the reader, arguing that we know a book is "true" because we feel it, deep down, saying "Yes, that's how it is." The reader's sense of truth in how a specific cultural experience is represented within a book, particularly when the reader is an insider to the culture portrayed in that book, is probably the most common understanding of cultural authenticity. For example, Guevara (2003), an illustrator, believes that an authentic book is one in which there is a sense of aliveness, a feeling that something true from the culture exists in that book. For her, authenticity is determined by whether or not a sense of connection is created between an author and a reader through a book.

Howard (1991) maintains that an authentic book is one in which a universality of experience permeates a story that is set within the particularity of characters and setting. The universal and specific come together to create a book in which "readers from the culture will know that it is true, will identify, and be affirmed, and readers from another culture will feel that it is true, will identify, and learn something of value about both similarities and differences among us" (p. 92). Given that each reading of a book is a unique transaction that results in different interpretations (Rosenblatt, 1938), and given the range of experiences within any cultural group, this definition indicates why there are so many debates about the authenticity of a particular book.

Even though there are always differences within a cultural group, Mo and Shen (2003) argue that cultural authenticity can be defined as whether or not a book reflects those values, facts, and attitudes that members of a culture as a whole consider worthy of acceptance or belief. Similarly, Bishop (2003) proposes that cultural authenticity is the extent to which a book reflects the worldview of a specific cultural group and the authenticating details of language and everyday life for members of that group. She notes that although there will be no one image of life within a specific cultural context, there are themes, textual features, and underlying ideologies for each cultural group that can be used to determine authenticity.

THE SOCIOPOLITICAL NATURE OF MULTICULTURAL EDUCATION

Central to these debates are definitions of culture and multicultural education. Culture and multiculturalism are sometimes defined superficially as awareness and appreciation of the traditions, artifacts, and ways of life of particular ethnic groups, specifically people of color. At a deeper level, culture can be understood as all the ways in which people live and think in the world. Geertz (1973) defines culture as "the shared patterns that set the tone, character, and quality of people's lives" (p. 216). These patterns include race, ethnicity, gender, social class, language, religion, age, sexual orientation, nationality, geographical regions, and so on. Most social scientists define culture as primarily consisting of the symbolic, ideational, and intangible aspects of society; the values, symbols, interpretations, and perspectives that distinguish one group of people from another (Banks, 2001). Cultures are considered dynamic, complex, and changing and so are viewed as wholes, rather than as composed of discrete parts.

Multiculturalism is often viewed as a curriculum reform movement that involves changing the curriculum to include more content and children's books about ethnic groups, women, and other cultural groups. This view limits multicultural education to lessons on human relations and sensitivity training, along with units on ethnic festivals, foods, folklore, and fashions (Nieto, 2002). Cai (1998) points out that this practice conflicts with the goals of multicultural education, which have never been just to appreciate cultural differences, but to transform society and reform education in order to ensure greater voice, power, equity, and social justice for marginalized cultures. Both Banks (2001) and Nieto (2002) argue that the goals and purposes of multicultural education have always been to challenge and reject racism and discrimination and to affirm pluralism, particularly for individuals and groups considered outside the cultural mainstream of society. Cai (1998) points out, therefore, that issues of inequality, discrimination, and oppression cannot be excluded from multiculturalism without losing its fundamental sociopolitical basis, particularly in work with young children as they form cultural perspectives and attitudes toward themselves and others.

These understandings provide an important backdrop for the controversies about children's literature and cultural authenticity. Multiculturalism and cultural authenticity are often dismissed as "political correctness," a movement characterized by the popular press as suppressing statements (or books) deemed offensive to women, African Americans, or other groups (Taxel, 1997). Lasky (1996), a children's author, takes this perspective, viewing cultural authenticity as political correctness, a fanaticism that has led to "self-styled militias of cultural diversity" that dictate who can create books about specific cultural groups. Rochman (1993) asserts that concerns about authenticity have sometimes led to "politically correct bullies" who use pretentious jargon to preach mindless conformity.

Some educators consider these concerns about political correctness to be a backlash against the goals of multiculturalism. Taxel (1997) argues that cries of political correctness ignore the history of racist representations in children's books and the lack of equal access to publishing for authors of color. This lack of access continues, with children's book publishing and the academic study of children's literature remaining overwhelmingly in the control of Whites. Bishop (2003) believes that political correctness has been used to denigrate those who raise questions about the cultural content of children's books and to question White privilege.

Although multicultural literature is typically defined as books about specific cultural groups, either people of color or people who are members of groups considered to be outside of the dominant sociopolitical culture, Bishop (2003) argues that the definition of multicultural literature has more to do with its ultimate purpose than with its literary characteristics. Multicultural literature can be seen as a pedagogical construct that has the goal of challenging the existing canon by including literature from a variety of cultural groups. Debates about multicultural literature, and therefore about cultural authenticity, are not so much about the nature of the literature itself, but about the function of literature in schools and in the lives of readers. If *multicultural literature* is a pedagogical term rather than a literary term, then the issues of cultural authenticity take on significance related to the role of literature in young children's lives, specifically in the potential power of literature to change their views of the world.

These understandings about multicultural education indicate that debates about cultural authenticity are not just ivory tower bickering. As Cai (1998) points out, different definitions reflect different stances and courses of actions that change what happens in classrooms and in children's lives.

METHODOLOGY FOR REVIEWING THE PROFESSIONAL LITERATURE

Given these definitions of culture and cultural authenticity, we searched the professional literature for articles and book chapters on cultural authenticity published over 10 years (1993–2003). Because cultural authenticity has been debated so vigorously, we discovered that many authors extensively referenced others' writing about these issues. We narrowed our search by identifying those works and/or voices that were referenced multiple times. The 20 pieces selected for more in-depth analysis included published manuscripts that had been widely referenced as well as several recent chapters that represented the current research of scholars who had been referenced previously within multiple articles. We selected only those whose major focus was cultural authenticity in children's literature.

We read the selected works to derive the themes and patterns in the issues raised about cultural authenticity. Through our reading, extensive discussion, and writing together, we identified eight major questions related to the central issues cutting across the pieces and also identified the varied perspectives related to each question.

THE COMPLEXITY OF DEBATES ABOUT CULTURAL AUTHENTICITY

Each person who has written about cultural authenticity adds another layer of complexity. These layers relate to their differing roles within the field and to their differing sociopolitical experiences and beliefs as members of a range of cultural groups. The following eight interrelated questions about cultural authenticity reflect the key debates in the field.

Can Outsiders Write Authentically About Another Culture?

The outside/insider distinction is probably the most frequently, and endlessly, debated issue. The question is often asked and answered from oppositional positions, with both sides vehemently arguing their perspective. Some children's authors see this question as a form of censorship and an attempt to restrict an author's freedom to write (Lasky, 1996). From this perspective, cultural authenticity seems to be a personal attack on an author's ability as a writer.

Other authors and educators argue that the question reflects larger issues of power structures and a history of negative misrepresentations of people of color in children's literature (Bishop, 2003; Harris, 1996; Woodson, 1998). They believe that this question ignores the historical context of racist stereotypes and misrepresentations of African Americans by White authors in children's books and the desire of African Americans to have African American children see themselves more positively portrayed within literature.

The majority argues that this question is simplistic, setting up a dichotomy that overlooks the broader sociopolitical issues. Woodson (1998) points out that this question is typically asked by Whites to authors of color. Another issue is that publishers often limit authors of color to writing only books about their own specific ethnic group. Some authors of color state that they are viewed as representative of their racial identity and not allowed to assume multiple perspectives, whereas White authors are seen as the norm (Harris, 1996; Rochman, 1993).

A further issue is the cultural complexity of those who create children's books. Speaking from a biracial perspective, Guevara (2003) argues against definitions that establish rigid boundaries based on appearances and experience. She believes that valuing the complexity in what is "true" makes literature and life rich and varied.

Does an Author Have a Social Responsibility and, If So, How Does That Responsibility Relate to Authorial Freedom?

Some children's authors see authenticity in opposition to authorial freedom—the freedom of authors to use their creative imaginations and literary skills to tell a powerful story. They believe this freedom is at the heart of great literature and is endangered by the call for cultural authenticity (Lasky, 1996). Taxel (1997), however, argues that this debate is really about social responsibility and that authors have both a social and artistic responsibility to be thoughtful and cautious when they write about characters, plots, and themes related to specific cultural groups, whether they are insiders or outsiders to that culture. Rosenblatt (1938) maintains that social responsibility is not in opposition to freedom because although authors need freedom to determine their own writing, their work has social origins and effects that also need to be examined and critiqued.

Another related issue is whether authors have a social responsibility to provide multicultural characters that are role models. Harris (1996) argues that these stories should provide role models who either inspire readers or correct stereotypes. Rochman (1993) notes, however, that stories can be too reverential and need to provide a complex picture of individuals showing both their faults and courage.

Some educators argue that the real issue is the contrast of authorial freedom with authorial arrogance, the belief that authors should be able to write without subjecting their work to critical scrutiny (Harris, 1996; Taxel, 1997). Authorial arrogance can be viewed as White privilege, resulting from Whites being socialized into a racialized society that gives them particular privileges and status that are not available to people of color and that are not acknowledged but simply taken for granted as the way life is for everyone (Bishop, 2003). Without critical scrutiny, White authors are often unable to transcend their positions of privilege when writing books about people from marginalized cultures and so continue subtle forms of racism, even when the more blatant racism and misrepresentations of the past have been eliminated from their writing. Educators argue that this cultural arrogance is based in the implicit assumption by many members of mainstream society that what they value is universally valued by other cultures (Nodelman, 1988).

Another aspect of authorial arrogance is identified as the assumption of Whites that they can represent everyone themselves. Seto (1995), an author, sees this arrogance as silencing those who demand the right to represent themselves. Woodson (1998) argues that the issue is not about preventing White people from writing certain stories, but about the rights of people of color to tell their own stories. She believes that focusing on the authorial freedom of White writers keeps Whites in a position of power instead of focusing on the real issues. Bishop (2003) agrees, stating that the real issue is the desire of members of a particular culture to tell their own stories as a way to pass on their culture and that this desire is not the same as restricting the freedom of authors to choose their own topics.

How Does the Criterion of Authenticity Relate to Literary Excellence in Evaluating a Book?

An issue that appears in most of the articles and chapters we reviewed is some variation of the question of what criteria should be used to evaluate children's books, specifically whether cultural authenticity should be a criterion when the book reflects the experiences of a specific cultural group. Although everyone agrees that children's books should be evaluated according to standards of literary excellence, most believe that cultural authenticity should also be an essential criterion for evaluating a book. Some, however, argue that literary excellence should stand alone as the primary criteria for evaluating a book. Aronson (1993), an editor and author, is concerned that authenticity involves only judging a book by the ancestry of the author and so does not reflect the complexity of culture with conflicting values and points of view. He views multiculturalism as the "mess of stories" we all receive and write, and so believes in demanding high standards of artistry rather than trying to assess the author's cultural qualifications. Lasky (1996) agrees that authenticity often leads to prejudging a book based on authorship, instead of allowing a book to stand or fall based on its own literary merits and ability to generate "literary heat" through the artist's craft.

Many educators and authors take the stance that literary excellence and cultural authenticity are not in opposition and are both essential. Cai (1995) notes that a book is always evaluated for both content and writing style and that cultural authenticity focuses on content whereas literary criteria focus on writing. He argues that there is no dichotomy between a good and an authentic story. Thus, the debate is not whether or not cultural authenticity should be part of the criteria for evaluating a book, but the kind of criteria and understandings that should be used, particularly when a book has been written by an outsider.

What Kinds of Experiences Matter for Authors in Writing Culturally Authentic Books?

The question of what counts as experience and the kinds of experiences needed to write with truth as an outsider of a specific culture is often raised. Cai (1995) notes that imagination is needed for a book to have literary excellence but that too much imagination without experience leads to inaccuracies and bias and defeats the purpose of multicultural literature to liberate readers from stereotypes. Other educators and authors agree that specific authors have successfully crossed cultural gaps to write outside their own experiences, but point out that crossing cultural gaps is very difficult and requires extreme diligence by authors to gain the experiences necessary to write authentically within another culture.

There is disagreement, however, on what count as the experiences necessary to cross a cultural gap as an outsider and how direct those experiences must be. Seto (1995) takes the strong position that it is morally wrong for Whites to write about other cultures unless they have direct, personal experiences with that culture that lead to understanding that culture within their hearts. Using the metaphor of sitting around a dinner table, Woodson (1998) argues that an author must experience another's world through personal experiences and/or significant personal relationships in order to write with truth about that world. She is not arguing that authors can only write semiautobiographical novels, but emphasizing that the experiences must be deep and significant. Nikola-Lisa (1998), an author and educator, argues against this perspective, noting the increasing diversity of who sits around our tables and the multiracial nature of communities, families, and individuals. He believes that there are other kinds of experiences beyond personal relationships that count, including negative intercultural experiences and an awareness of one's prejudices.

Most authors who successfully write outside their own culture have had significant in-depth experiences within that culture over many years and have engaged in careful and thorough research (Cai, 1995). Moreillon (1999) provides insights into the strategies she used as an author writing a children's book outside her culture, including consulting a range of information sources, asking for responses to her text from an insider who also had expertise in the study of that culture, and hiring an insider illustrator for the text. She shares the ways in which readers from a range of cultural backgrounds have responded to her book, reflecting the criteria that authenticity relates to how a book affects readers.

Guevara (2003) believes that all authors and illustrators create from their own experiences, intuition, and research, so there can never be a simplistic scale for evaluating authenticity based on appearance or experience. As an illustrator, she reads a story from the perspective of whether or not the story moves her, whether she experiences the world of the story, instead of whether or not the story is authentic. If she is able to experience the world of the story, she knows she will be able to draw from her own experiences, relationships, and multiple identities to illustrate the book. What she is unable to envision through experience, she researches. If she does not feel a sense of connection, she chooses not to illustrate that text.

Some educators argue that authors should be explicit about the difficulties inherent in writing outside their own culture and should indicate how they have worked to gain the "real" experiences needed to write a particular book (Bishop, 2003). Evaluating authenticity could thus involve an author's note or some other indication of the process by which a book was created. The types of experiences necessary to write a particular book relate to the author's intentions for that book. Bishop (2003) notes that children's books that are multicultural are both specific and universal in that they reflect difference by portraying a culturally specific experience as well as commonality through universal themes. She points out that some authors write generic books that only are based in universal themes and experiences. The intentions of these authors are not to portray a specific cultural experience, so the ethnicity of the characters is interchangeable and only apparent by skin color, not in the character's actions, dialogue, relationships, or ways of thinking. An author who intends to write a generic book does not need the same depth of experience as an author who intends to write a culturally specific book. These generic books can be evaluated on literary criteria, but not for authenticity because a specific cultural experience has not been portrayed.

Yenika-Agbaw (1998) argues that these universal or generic books are problematic because they are based on the assumption that a unitary and homogeneous human nature exists. This focus on universal themes, separate from a specific cultural experience, maintains the superiority of the dominant culture and so marginalizes and excludes oppressed cultures. Her views connect to discussions about cultural arrogance and White privilege in which the dominant worldview is accepted as the "normal" one.

Many educators draw from the framework created by Sims (1982) for examining the distinguishing characteristics of African American books. She identified a category of culturally conscious books that place a child of color within the context of families and neighborhoods, tell the story from that child's perspective, and indicate through text and illustrations that this is a story about a child of color. Her framework is used to argue that authors need to write with cultural consciousness to accurately portray the cultural traditions, behaviors, and language of a specific cultural group while also drawing on human universals (Noll, 1995).

What Are an Author's Intentions for Writing a Particular Book?

An author's motivation for writing a particular book is also relevant when considering authenticity. Bishop (2003) proposes that one question authors ask themselves is *why* they want to write a particular book. Not only does making an author's intentions and ideology explicit influence the criteria for evaluating a book, but this process also engages an author in the critical self-examination necessary to choosing whether or not to write outside one's culture and to clarifying the kind of story the author is really seeking to write. She points out that authors of color often write within their own culture based on their intentions to enhance the self-concept of children of color and to challenge existing stereotypes and dominant culture assumptions, as well as to pass on the central values and stories of their culture to children. Authors writing outside their cultures often focus on intentions of building awareness of cultural differences and improving intercultural relationships. These differing intentions result in different stories for different audiences and different evaluations of authenticity.

Authors who write outside their own culture for monetary gain provide an even more problematic critique of intention. Seto (1995) believes that writers who do not have direct, personal experiences with the culture they are writing about are stealing from other cultures. Similarly, Smolkin and Suina (1997) label these intentions as cultural exploitation where property and possessions are taken from the culture for the financial benefit of the author.

What Are the Criteria Beyond Accuracy for Evaluating the Cultural Authenticity of the Content of a Book?

The criteria that are typically considered in evaluating the content of a book are the accuracy of the details and the lack of stereotyping and misrepresentation. Some educators argue that authors cannot ignore cultural facts, and that both the visible facts of external reality and the invisible facts of internal reality must be accurately represented (Cai, 1995).

Several educators discuss criteria for recognizing culturally offensive images. Noll (1995) raises the issue of historical literature where accurate perspectives must be provided without perpetuating negative images. She points out the need to portray accurately the prevailing views of a particular historical time period while also presenting alternative views.

A further debate concerns whether locating inaccuracies is enough to determine authenticity. Smolkin and Suina (1997) use the term "cultural sensitivity" to get at whether or not a book is sensitive to the concerns of the culture that is portrayed. Cai (1995) refers to this cultural sensitivity as an ethnic perspective, the worldview of a specific cultural group that has been shaped by an ideological difference with the majority view. He believes authors who write outside their own culture often do not take on an ethnic perspective and instead may unconsciously impose their own perspective onto that culture, an attitude of cultural arrogance.

Mo and Shen (2003) agree that authenticity is not just accuracy or the avoidance of stereotyping, but involves the cultural values and practices that are accepted as norms within that social group. They argue that accuracy focuses on cultural facts whereas authenticity focuses on cultural values. Evaluations of accuracy can therefore indicate whether or not the facts in the story believably exist in a culture but not whether those facts actually represent the values held by most of the people in that group. From their perspective, a story can be accurate but not authentic by portraying cultural practices that exist but are not part of the central code of a culture. This central code relates to the range of values acceptable within a social group and so recognizes the conflicts and changes in beliefs within a culture. However, Mo and Shen also argue that there are certain values that are appropriate to all cultures and that authenticity does not provide the right to introduce values that are in violation of basic human rights. They further complicate authenticity by discussing issues involved in value conflicts between the culture from which a story is taken and the culture for whom the book is intended and the need to consider both cultures in determining authenticity.

These same issues of cultural facts and values are relevant to international contexts. Yenika-Agbaw (1998) argues that a postcolonial theoretical perspective is essential to deconstructing colonial ideologies of power that privilege Western cultural practices, challenge the history of colonized groups, and give voice to those that have been marginalized by colonization. She extends issues of domination and unequal power distribution to nations, rather than only to specific cultural groups within a nation.

Illustrations provide the basis for additional criteria for authenticity. Mo and Shen (2003) indicate that authenticity is based on whether the art form serves its purpose in relation to the story, but argue that an authentic art form does not have to be rigidly interpreted as the typical traditional style. They value the creative process that leads to art that is part of the story to create an authentic whole. However, the role of art differs across cultures, and mainstream traditions of graphic experimentation with art elements to enhance meaning can change or confuse meanings for members of particular cultural groups when that experimentation contradicts specific cultural traditions (Smolkin & Suina, 1997).

The use of particular words and phrases from a specific culture within an English-language book is another consideration (Barrera & Quiroa, 2003).

The issue of language centers not so much on accurate translations as on how the words are used, particularly whether the words are added for cultural flavor and result in stereotypes. Instead, these elements have to be used strategically and skillfully with cultural sensitivity to create powerful bilingual images of characters, settings, and themes. Not only must these phrases and words enhance the literary merits of the book, but they must also make the story comprehensible and engaging to both monolingual and bilingual readers without slighting the language or literary experience of either. Barrera and Quiroa argue that the tendency to stay with formulaic and safe uses of Spanish and to translate literally these words in order to cater to the needs of monolingual readers often results in culturally inauthentic texts for bilingual readers and poor literary quality for all readers.

What Is an Insider Perspective on Cultural Authenticity?

Several educators point out that there is no *one* insider perspective that can be used to evaluate cultural authenticity. Smolkin and Suina (1997) document how variations within a culture lead to opposing evaluations of the authenticity of a book by readers from different groups of insiders. Yenika-Agbaw (1998) found that authors who are insiders can inadvertently perpetuate stereotypes of their own culture. In addition to showing how insiders vary in their views of their own culture, she also examines how authors who are outsiders create different types of stereotypes and images, based on their own intentions and ethnic perspectives.

Recognizing the complexity of both insider and outsider perspectives adds another layer to what is considered "truth" about a particular cultural experience. Bishop (2003) argues that because variance always exists within a specific culture, no one set of definitive criteria can ever be created to evaluate books about that culture. However, she also points out that scholars can create a set of criteria that show the range of themes and ideologies at the core of a particular culture through a serious scholarly study of the body of books published by insiders.

So Why Does Cultural Authenticity Matter?

These discussions about cultural authenticity in children's literature can be viewed as ivory tower debates that do not really matter in the lives of young children, parents, and teachers. Cai (1998), however, points out that these definitions determine the actions we take in classrooms and the ways in which children approach the reading of a book. Many educators argue that cultural authenticity matters because all children have the right to see themselves within a book, to find within a book the truth of their own experiences instead of stereotypes and misrepresentations (Harris, 1996; Taxel,

1997). This argument can be extended to assert the right of authors of color to tell the stories that are used within a particular cultural group to pass on their cultural identity to children (Bishop, 2003; Woodson, 1998). Many authors and educators contend that literature is one of the significant ways that children learn about themselves and others and therefore those images should not be distorted ones.

Dudley-Marling (1997) points out that culturally authentic books are more engaging for young children from the culture that is portrayed, as well as a source of intercultural understandings for children from other cultures. In addition, these books provide children with insights into power and to social and political issues while also serving to challenge the monocultural perspective of dominant society that characterizes most schooling. Although Dudley-Marling argues convincingly for the necessity of making a wide range of culturally authentic books available for children, he also points out the dangers of teachers assuming that they should match their perceptions of children's cultural identities with specific books. The teacher's role is to make available authentic texts reflecting diverse cultural and ethnic images and to create a space where students can represent themselves and find themselves represented within books.

One concern is that evaluations of the cultural authenticity of a book not be used to censor books but to engage children in critical readings of these books where they question the meanings embedded in texts from dominant cultural perspectives (Smolkin & Suina, 1997; Yenika-Agbaw, 1998). Cai (1998) points out that because the goal of multicultural education is to work for equity and social justice, children need to be able to tackle issues of cultural difference, equity, and assumptions about race, class, and gender as they read literature. Thus, criteria for evaluating cultural authenticity and raising complex issues are not just issues that those creating or choosing books for children need to consider, but criteria that children themselves need to understand and employ as critical readers. Although some educators believe that critical literacy is not developmentally appropriate for young children, other scholars, such as Vasquez (2004), report that critical literacy promotes a depth of thinking for young children who find these engagements powerful, pleasurable, and hopeful.

The dominant cultural code can be reinforced and sustained throughout the entire process of writing and reading a book when there is no attention to the discourses of power and dominance. Fang, Fu, and Lamme (1999) document the misuse of books about specific cultural groups within classrooms where students are taught to look at culture through categories such as food and holidays that actually reinforce stereotypes and mainstream domination. They argue that children need to learn how to take negotiated and oppositional positions in their interpretations of literature and to analyze the authenticity of a book and the perspective presented to the reader.

WHERE DO WE GO FROM HERE?

Taken as a whole, these discussions about cultural authenticity provide more complex understandings than simply judging whether or not the author is an insider or outsider to the culture in a book. These understandings provide the basis for educators and authors to engage in new conversations about cultural authenticity instead of continuing to repeat the old ones.

Our analysis of these past and current debates about cultural authenticity reveals the strong need for further research to investigate the concept of cultural authenticity as it plays out in practice within the classrooms of young children. There continues to be a dearth of research examining the ways in which teachers and young children think about and respond to these issues as they engage with both culturally authentic and inauthentic literature. In particular, research is needed to identify the strategies of effective teachers who use controversial books with young children in exploring a critical perspective and to identify the ways in which children take on this perspective in their own thinking. This research on effective teaching is needed in order to offer teachers and teacher-educators alternative images and perspectives so that they can avoid "pedagogical arrest" or self-censorship in the use of controversial books, especially in the classrooms of young children. In particular, this research should include an exploration of strategies for teaching young children how to evaluate literature for authenticity.

More research is also needed to investigate young children's responses to culturally authentic and inauthentic literature. The responses of multiple members of a culture to children's books representing that culture need to be examined, as well as whether or not young children respond in different ways to books that reflect or do not reflect their culture in authentic ways. We believe that this research should be based in an understanding of the powerful role that literature can play in an education and a society that are truly multicultural. Stories *do* matter in these troubling times when the constraints of scripted reading programs, mandated high-stakes testing, and monocultural standards often relegate literature and multicultural concerns to the fringes of the classroom life of young children. The recent changes in the publishing of children's literature are also disturbing, particularly the acquisition of publishing companies by huge entertainment conglomerates. This consolidation of control has led to less diversity in what and who are being published.

We must ensure that young children have regular engagements with quality children's books that are culturally authentic and accurate. Because children's literature has the potential to play such a key role in an education that is multicultural and focused on social justice, all children should have access to culturally authentic literature. Above all, we must hold fast to our belief that literature and democracy are intertwined and that the thoughtful use of literature can enhance education for a democratic way of life (Rosenblatt, 1938). Democracy highlights the value of individual beliefs within the context of considering the consequences those values may have for others and of maintaining an open mind to other points of view. The debates about cultural authenticity in children's literature matter because they foster the dialogue that is essential to democracy.

REFERENCES

Aronson, M. (1995). A mess of stories. *Horn Book Magazine, 71*(2), 163–168.

Banks, J. (2001). *Cultural diversity and education* (4th ed.). Boston: Allyn and Bacon.

Barrera, R., & Quiroa, R. (2003). The use of Spanish in Latino children's literature in English: What makes for cultural authenticity? In D.,L. Fox & K. G. Short (Eds.), *Stories matter: The complexity of cultural authenticity in children's literature* (pp. 247–265). Urbana, IL: National Council of Teachers of English.

Bishop, R. S. (2003). Reframing the debate about cultural authenticity. In D. L. Fox & K. G. Short (Eds.), *Stories matter: The complexity of cultural authenticity in children's literature* (pp. 25–37). Urbana, IL: National Council of Teachers of English.

Cai, M. (1995). Can we fly across cultural gaps on the wings of imagination? Ethnicity, experience, and cultural authenticity. *The New Advocate, 8*(1), 1–16.

Cai, M. (1998). Multiple definitions of multicultural literature: Is the debate really just "ivory tower" bickering? *The New Advocate, 11*(4), 311–324.

Dudley-Marling, C. (1997). "I'm not from Pakistan": Multicultural literature and the problem of representation. *The New Advocate*, 10(2), 123–134.

Fang, Z., Fu, D., & Lamme, L. L. (1999). The trivialization and misuse of multicultural literature: Issues of representation and communication. *The New Advocate, 12*(2), 259–276.

Fox, D. L., & Short, K. G. (Eds.). (2003). *Stories matter: The complexity of cultural authenticity in children's literature*. Urbana, IL: National Council of Teachers of English.

Geertz, C. (1973). *The interpretation of cultures*. New York: Basic Books.

Guevara, S. (2003). Authentic enough: Am I? Are you? Interpreting culture for children's literature. In D. L. Fox & K. G. Short (Eds.), *Stories matter: The complexity of cultural authenticity in children's literature* (pp. 50–60). Urbana, IL: National Council of Teachers of English.

Harris, V. (1996). Continuing dilemmas, debates, and delights in multicultural literature. *The New Advocate, 9*(2), 107–122.

Howard, E. F. (1991). Authentic multicultural literature for children: An author's perspective. In M. Lindgren (Ed.), *Cultural substance in literature for children and young adults* (pp. 91–99). Fort Atkinson, WI: Highsmith.

Lasky, K. (1996). To Stingo with love: An author's perspective on writing outside one's culture. *The New Advocate, 9*(1), 1–7.

Mo, W., & Shen, W. (2003). Accuracy is not enough: The role of cultural values in the authenticity of picture books. In D. L. Fox & K. G. Short (Eds.), *Stories matter: The complexity of cultural authenticity in children's literature* (pp. 198–212). Urbana, IL: National Council of Teachers of English.

Moreillon, J. (1999). The candle and the mirror: One author's journey as an outsider. *The New Advocate, 12*(2), 127–139.

Nieto, S. (2002). *Language, culture, and teaching*. Mahwah, NJ: Lawrence Erlbaum Associates.

Nikola-Lisa, W. (1998). "Around my table" is not always enough. *Horn Book Magazine, 74*(3), 315–318.

Nodelman, P. (1988). Cultural arrogance and realism in Judy Blume's *Superfudge. Children's Literature in Education, 19*(4), 230–241.

Noll, E. (1995). Accuracy and authenticity in American Indian children's literature: The social responsibility of authors and illustrators. *The New Advocate, 8*(1), 29–43.

Rochman, H. (1993). *Against borders: Promoting books for a multicultural world.* Chicago: American Library Association.

Rosenblatt, L. (1938). *Literature as exploration*. Chicago: Modern Language Association.

Seto, T. (1995). Multiculturalism is not Halloween. *Horn Book Magazine, 71*(2), 169–174.

Sims (1982). *Shadow and substance: Afro-American experience in contemporary children's fiction.* Urbana, IL: National Council of Teachers of English.

Smolkin, L., & Suina, J. (1997). Artistic triumph or multicultural failure? Multiple perspectives on a "multicultural" award-winning book. *The New Advocate, 10*(4), 307–322.

Taxel, J. (1997). Multicultural literature and the politics of reaction. *Teachers College Record, 98*(3), 417–448.

Vasquez, V. (2004). *Negotiating critical literacies with young children.* Mahwah, NJ: Lawrence Erlbaum Associates.

Woodson, J. (1998). Who can tell my story? *Horn Book Magazine, 74*(1), 34–38.

Yenika-Agbaw, V. (1998). Images of West Africa in children's books: Replacing old stereotypes with new ones? *The New Advocate, 11*(3), 203–218.

Chapter **16**

War and Peas in the 21st Century: Young Children Responding Critically to Picture Story Texts

Janet Evans

> *This book makes me think about the war in Iraq and all the wars in the world, for example the Gulf Wars 1 and 2 and the World Wars 1 and 2 . I wish all the wars would stop so the world would be a happy place and everybody would be friends. Peace not war. (Imran, 6.0 years)*
>
> *The moral of this story is about good and bad. Peace is where you're all working together and no one is bad, it's about friendship and kindness. The fat king is saying, "Not peace again." The lion king is saying, "Peace not peas." (Matthew, 5.9 years)*
>
> *I wish World War 2 never happened. My granddad told me about WW 2. I wish all wars would stop and everybody would be happy and safe. (Adam, 6.2 years)*

These statements, made after reading and talking about Michael Foreman's book *War and Peas* (1974/2002), clearly indicate how responding to books in a socially critical manner stimulates deep and powerful thoughts and emotions in young children. Other responses emanating from group conversations in a school in the United Kingdom included equally thought-provoking statements and clearly indicated that the book had acted as a catalyst, stimulating the children to think and communicate their ideas in relation to what was happening in the wider world in a socially perceptive, critical manner.

Six children were first introduced to the book *War and Peas* when they were 5 years old, in their first year in school. On three separate sessions over a 14-month period spanning two academic years we worked collaboratively, using the book as a stimulus for reader response and to relate to things that concerned the children; things that were happening in the world both nationally and internationally. I was amazed to find how aware of social and political world issues these children were when they were enabled to talk freely and express their thoughts and ideas.

RESPONDING CRITICALLY TO TEXTS

The increasing number of picture story texts that touch on social, moral, political, and environmental issues means that children can be introduced to difficult, sometimes sensitive subjects through this genre. For example, a text set of books on bullying, loneliness, old age and dying, or war and conflict enables children to read, discuss, and respond to issues such as these in depth. The concept of reader response, initially studied by Louise Rosenblatt (1938, 1978) has become an effective vehicle for recognizing, exposing, and critically analyzing many of the implicit and explicit messages found in picture story texts. The notion that there is only one single, predetermined meaning of a text has long since been challenged. In enabling children to respond to texts in a critical manner, we encourage them to identify the stance that the author is taking, and in so doing we help them to realize that any text is, in taking a particular stance, positioning them. We need to help children to realize that there is no single correct meaning of a text. In looking at multiple and critical readings of texts, Anstey and Bull (2000) note that "texts are ideological sites representing particular views of the world and associated attitudes and values" (p. 207). They point out that meanings in texts are not fixed and are constructed differently according to who is reading and responding to them.

In agreement with this view, Kempe (1993) is of the opinion that although there is no one way in which to interpret texts, some responses are nevertheless more highly valued than others. Luke and Freebody (1997) state that literacy is never neutral, that all texts contain particular views along with associated attitudes and values. They feel that children should be encouraged to question the beliefs and ideologies that are embedded in texts while at the same time questioning their own beliefs and viewpoints. This notion of critical literacy is considered by McLaughlin and DeVoogd (2004a), who clearly state that "critical literacy is not a teaching method but a way of thinking and a way of being that challenges texts and life as we know it" (p. 150). They propose four principles of critical literacy, which include questioning the power relationships between a reader and a text. They state that critical literacy:

- Focuses on issues of power and promotes reflection, transformation, and action.
- Focuses on a problem and its complexity.
- Focuses on strategies that are dynamic and adapt to the concepts in which they are used.
- Disrupts the commonplace by examining it from multiple perspectives (McLaughlin and DeVoogd, 2004b).

Vasquez (2001) constructed a critical curriculum with young children around their questions about their everyday life, issues of social justice, and classroom conversations around critical questions. In some work done with kindergarten children, Vasquez used books and other texts to promote socially and critically aware youngsters who are capable of offering insightful points of view and of making suggestions for altering the status quo by taking thoughtful social action when appropriate. This work, done in collaboration with colleagues, highlights examples of how children can be encouraged to negotiate critical literacy. These include: comparing and contrasting everyday texts such as newspapers, posters, greetings cards, and advertisements with texts written especially for children; focusing on social issues by bringing real-world events into the classroom; using children's books and the themes they cover to discuss social issues; and critically analyzing curricular, social issues texts. Vasquez points out that although the use of books and associated texts creates opportunities for critical conversations, the important point is to encourage children to take social action in relation to the problems they are considering. They need to see that their actions make a difference (Vasquez et al., 2003).

WAR AND PEAS AS A CRITICAL TEXT: PERSPECTIVES FROM THE AUTHOR

War and Peas, initially published in 1974, is a powerful, thought-provoking, polysemic picture book that resonates with many contemporary political situations being experienced world wide. It is about two kings and two armies. One king, the lion king, is poor and his land is so barren that his starving subjects are unable to dig it to plant seeds. He decides to travel to the neighboring land, which is extremely fertile with plenty of food, to ask the ruling rich king if he would help them. As he approaches the land with his Minister of Food, they are seized for trespassing and after they ask for help the extremely fat, rich king accuses them of begging and trying to steal. They manage to escape and travel back to their own land, pursued by the fat king's soldiers, intent on making war. These soldiers are so fat that they get stuck in the ground with all their weapons and supplies of food. The lion king and his civilian army bombard the opposition with peas. Ultimately the battle is won and the fat king surrenders. Finally the lion king suggests that there should be peace. It is evident from the fat king's initial retort that he has misunderstood what was said, as he pleads for peas not to be mentioned ever again (due to the flatulent results of their digestion). Upon hearing the proposal for peace a second time, the fat king asks for the recipe for peace, showing that he has no idea what is being suggested—his main concern being food and his own well-being.

Michael Foreman, unaware of the book's indisputable relevance to a time almost 30 years in the future, created a commanding allegory of war and conflict, selfishness, greed, wealth, and poverty at the beginning of the 21st century. Both the text and the illustrations are full of satirical humor and yet are so serious in their underlying, fundamental meanings that most readers are given cause to think and talk about the deeper issues being alluded to.

Reading and writing are constructed differently in different social, historical, political, and cultural contexts, and it is interesting to note that Foreman's book was first published in the mid seventies, at a time of relative peace but with a growing awareness of the possibility for international conflict and its repercussions. When asked what made him write this book initially and what were the influences on his writing and illustrations, Michael Foreman, a self-professed "Ban the Bomb-er," (Foreman, personal telephone interview, 2003), mentioned the menace of war through the Cuban missile crisis; the repercussions of America pulling out of Vietnam; the "flower power" movement; and, the poignant peace songs of Joan Baez. He also talked of his growing awareness that, even in the 1970s, we were steadily destroying our environment. Foreman (2001), sharing the influences on some of his books, writes:

> After the war my teenage years were lived under a nuclear cloud. The Cold War threatened instant and mass destruction. So when I came to do my first book, aged 21, at the height of the Cold War, I was not going to do a book about fairy tale princesses and furry animals. My first book, *The General* (1961), was an anti-war book, as was the second, *The Two Giants* (1967), to be followed by *Moose* (1971) and *War and Peas* (1974). To do books showing the folly of war seemed natural to me. What surprised me was that I could find no other picture books dealing with this subject. (p. 97)

War and Peas was republished in 2002, prior to the war in Iraq, but at a time of huge political change and heightened threats of international terrorism as a result of the terrorist attacks on the Twin Towers in New York on September 11, 2000. When asked whether the decision to republish was done because of the book's strong message accentuating the futility of war, Foreman (personal telephone interview, 2003) stated that it was totally unlinked and purely coincidental despite the strong connections. Clearly this book would have been read and considered differently in 1974 compared with how it is read and considered at the beginning of the 21st century. Foreman's autobiographical notes (2001) relating to the origins of his books undoubtedly alert us to the fact that books are written from a particular stance, in his case an anti-war, pro-peace stance.

RESPONDING TO *WAR AND PEAS*: CRITICAL LITERACY IN THE CLASSROOM

I chose Foreman's book, as part of a text set of books on war and conflict, to allow me to reflect on the children's responses to picture books dealing with interpersonal relationships, conflict, war, and world environmental issues. It proved to be the perfect choice! My previous investigations had shown how working with picture books and providing opportunities for inquiry-based reader response help children develop meanings and understandings about the immediate world in which they live and about the international world further afield (Evans, 1998a; Short, 1997). I wanted to examine how children, if given the opportunity to think about and discuss the embedded social issues in certain picture story texts, can become critical, reflective thinkers with discriminating minds.

In using this book with young children I was replicating work I did with older children at the same time. The responses of the 10- and 11-year-olds were sophisticated; the students showed the capacity to make connections between the events in the book and complex social and political world issues, along with personal experiences relevant to them in their own local environment. At the time the research was being done, the media coverage of the terrorist attack on the Twin Towers in New York was still fresh, even though it had happened over 9 months previously. It was strongly influencing the way the students related to the issues being raised in *War and Peas*. Their conversations spontaneously moved beyond the traditional curriculum as they pondered important world issues raised through the book: issues such as: conflict and war—Osama Bin Laden and the situation in Afghanistan; winners and losers—competitive sports such as football (an important talking point in Liverpool!); poverty and world hunger; the need to share food and wealth more fairly, as seen through the absurdity of food mountains in rich, developed countries and finally, the destruction of the world environment. In responding critically to texts the children were starting to ask complicated questions, as Comber (2001) states:

> "When teachers and students are engaged in critical literacy, they will be asking complicated questions about language and power, about people and lifestyle, about morality and ethics, about who is advantaged by the way things are and who is disadvantaged" (p. 271).

The first session, spread over two full days, was toward the end of their first year in school when they were all 5 years old. The other two sessions were in their second school year when some had just turned 6. The class teacher chose children who were willing to converse and offer opinions.

The group consisted of four boys and two girls; however, one girl left school at the end of the first year, leaving a group of just five children. My experience of using books focusing on important issues to stimulate critical conversations about things that matter to children has always been revealing and informative (Evans, 1998b, 2005). Although I had hopes about how they would respond, the resulting critical responses, conversations. and ensuing literacy activities were more thought-provoking than I imagined for such young children.

Before reading the book, I told the children that the story was about two kings and two armies, that it was called *War and Peas* and was written and illustrated by Michael Foreman. I wrote the title so they could see the way it was spelled but they were not shown the book cover. I then asked the children to draw a picture of what they thought the story would be about and what they thought might happen. As expected at this early stage, prior to listening to the story they all drew pictures of fighting (see Figures 16.1).

Before reading the book, I also asked them to predict what they thought the story would be about, what might happen to the two kings and the armies, and how they thought the story might end. Their individual predictions, tape-recorded and transcribed away from the other group members,

Figure 16.1. Two kings are fighting and one of the knights got shot and a man is falling from a parachute (Imran, 5.4 years).

showed that the book title itself had stimulated thought—even before any collaborative discussion had taken place.

Imran, 5.4 years, predicted:

> I think the good army wants peace and the bad army wants war. There is a good army and a bad army because the bad army always wants war and the good army always wants peace. Some armies always, always, always want war and some armies want peace because they want to come alive in heaven and hell (because) bad armies don't know they're going to go to hell and good armies will be sent to heaven if they're good.

Adam, 5.6 years, commented:

> The baddy king shot the goody king and the goody canon shot the baddy army truck. Nothing else happens- grass grows and the trees and flowers grow in the story. It finishes with war—the king fighting the king, and the army fighting the army. That's all.

They shared their predictions with each other and compared their differing ideas, and then I read the book. The book reading took over an hour! The children kept relating back to their illustrations and predictions of what they thought the book would be about. Illustrations have a crucial role to play in enabling children to gain meaning from books and, apart from wordless texts, they work in partnership with print in picture books. Alongside the words, illustrations provide a starting point from which the reader gets meaning and to which the reader gives meaning (Evans, 1998a).

Once the book had been read the children each wrote a summary in their own writing (see Figure 16.2). Some of these summaries were clear and unambiguous, and when made into individual books along with the children's illustrations they provided explicit records of their written and illustrative responses to Foreman's text.

During the second block of work, nine months later, we returned to the same book. In this session the children re-read and reflected on Foreman's book in relation to their changing views of contemporary world issues. The children each chose a favorite part to draw, then wrote a second story summary having reread their first one. Each child had moved on in maturity since the first block of work. Matthew's detailed drawing (see Figure 16.3) shows his emerging talent, whereas Imran's written summary (see Figure 16.4) clearly shows his developing ability to express his ideas in writing.

> The elephant spat peas out of its trunk because the bad team were shooting peas back. The lion is just running away so the peas don't hit him on his back. The fat king was saying, "Stop that elephant firing peas."(Matthew, 5.9 years)

The story was abilts wury pand Peas
it was abot ane muls anay pepl
and the amems. Wan
and robuot Llyenn wun and the
fat kink Lost and it suves
the fat King riyt.
bcuaes he was Men

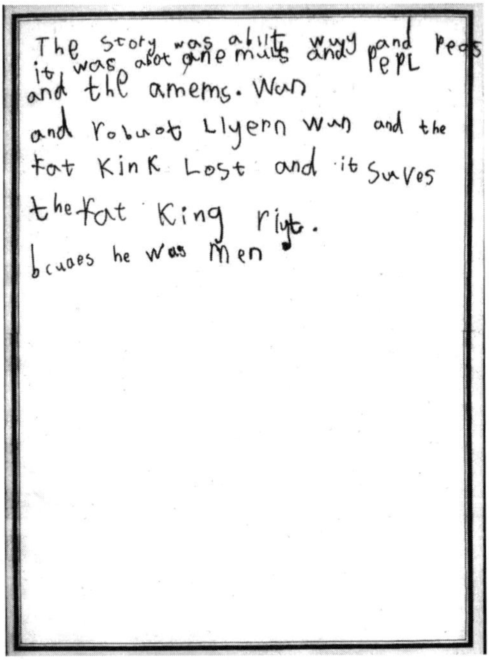

Figure 16.2. Imran's emergent writing: "The story was about war and peace, it was about animals and people and the animals won and robot lion won and the fat king lost and it serves the fat king right because he

Figure 16.3. Matthew's drawing.

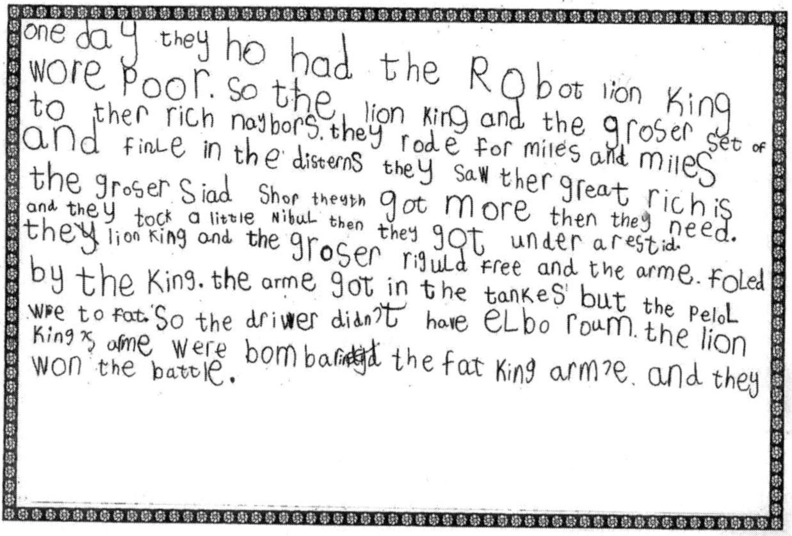

Figure 16.4. Imran's written summary.

> One day they who had the robot lion king were poor. So the lion king and the grocer set off to their rich neighbours. They rode for miles and miles and finally in the distance they saw the great riches. The grocer said, "Surely they've got more than they need" and they took a little nibble then they got under arrest (arrested). The lion king and the grocer wriggled free and the army (was) followed by the king. The army got in the tanks but the people were too fat so the driver didn't have elbow room. The lion king's army were bombarding the fat king's army and they won the battle. (Imran, 6.0 years)

The children concluded this second block of work by placing each of their story summaries into a group book which they entitled *Peas and Peace—Friendship and War.* They found it fascinating to look at the progress they had made since writing the individual books only 9 months earlier.

MOVING FROM THE TEXT TO THE WORLD: THE CHILDREN AS CRITICAL LITERACY USERS

In the third full-day session I saw a real change in the children's responses. This final session, which was 3 months after the second session, showed the children's willingness to share and discuss ideas collaboratively in response to the text.

Their responses and activities at the start of the project—talking, reading, illustrating, and writing—were very much related to the content of the book. During the first two sessions I had recorded and transcribed the children's oral responses, whilst their written responses to the text (Hornsby & Wing

Jan, 2001), had been made into individual books followed by the group book. The initial work was absorbing and showed a real involvement on the part of the children; however, in group discussion 12 months later their discussions moved quickly from the story's theme to their own thoughts, experiences, and perceptions of what was happening in the world. As young children they were experiencing intense media coverage of the war in Iraq; *War and Peas* became a real catalyst for discussing extremely pressing, complex issues. Anstey and Bull (2000) state that the difference between ordinary book-response classrooms and classrooms where responses are critically perceptive, relating to relevant social issues, is that "in the former the individual experiences of students are being interrogated, in the latter the texts are being interrogated" (p. 207). These 6-year-olds had certainly moved away from the text and yet were still using the issues emanating from the text as the impetus for their conversations involving world issues.

During this final session I asked the children if the book made them think about anything that was happening at that moment in the world around them. It was like opening the flood gates—their responses were astounding:

Janet:	What does this book make you think about?
Imran:	It makes me think about the war in Iraq and all the wars in the world e.g. the Gulf Wars 1 and 2 and the World Wars 1 and 2 . I wish all the wars would stop so the world would be a happy place and everybody would be friends. Peace not war.
Matthew:	It makes me think that everyone should be friends and no wars.
Libby:	I want all the wars to stop because people die and get hurt.

(all five children talked simultaneously about people dying in wars)

Janet:	How do people die in wars?
Imran:	They get shot and weapons go in them—knocking their heads off and bombs shoot their legs off. They get hurt and they die and the kings and queens get hurt and might even die and I don't want that to happen. If the prime ministers and the king and queen and the MP's die there will be no one in charge of all the kingdoms of the United Kingdom and the world.
Oliver:	What are MP's
Imran:	The MP's make the Prime Minister they vote for the Prime Minister.

Matthew:	The United Kingdom of America is next to us. It's over the Pacific Ocean, that's the biggest ocean.
Imran:	No, the Pacific Ocean isn't the biggest, the Atlantic Ocean is the biggest.
Adam:	I wish World War 2 never happened. My granddad told me about WW 2. I wish all wars would stop and everybody would be happy and safe.
Matthew:	What was that man's name in Iraq?
Imran:	Saddam Hussein
Matthew:	He has lots of nasty weapons.
Imran:	Yea—weapons of mass destruction. He has weapons of mass destruction. The government says he has weapons of mass destruction. Saddam Hussein has moved from the Arabic countries and he might even be here in England. England is controlling Iraq and they can't find him. I don't get it. I just don't get it.
Matthew:	He might even be here in school!
Oliver:	I wish all the war wouldn't be. Why do we have wars?
Imran:	Arguments start small and get bigger and bigger such as chopping fingers off and they get bigger and bigger. ...*pause*...they said Iraq would become World War 3 because we had loads of people on our team—China, America, Italy, France. Half of our team didn't want war so just England and America did it.
Janet:	Do you think wars teach us anything?
Imran:	The war teaches us that we should be friends.
Oliver:	Friendship and respect.
Matthew:	I think there should be friendship all over the world. Everyone is just dying to get rid of Saddam Hussein and nobody got him.
Libby:	It teaches us not to do it but it doesn't, we keep having wars. The wars don't stop.
Janet:	So how could we stop wars?
Imran:	We could make a list of things to do to stop wars—like a recipe to stop war.
Janet:	What is war anyway?
All together:	Fighting and killing
Janet:	So what is the opposite of war?
Oliver:	Peace.
Janet:	What is peace?

Matthew:	Not fighting.
Libby:	Friendship and no killing, peace and quiet.
Imran:	We could have a recipe for peace.
Janet:	What would be in a recipe for peace?
Libby:	Friendship.
Oliver:	Respect.
Matthew:	Wildlife—be nice to them even the bad, scary animals.
Adam:	Love and hearts, and being nice to people.
Janet:	What would we do with all of these things?
Oliver:	Put them altogether and boil them hard so they are stuck together like biscuits.
Matthew:	Put them in the fridge. Open the fridge up and it makes peace and quiet and it looks like a love heart.
Imran:	What about a piece of paper? (he refers to the other way of writing peace)
Janet:	Ah good point, there are two ways of writing peace—piece and peace. (I write the two words and briefly explain how they sound the same but are spelled and used differently.) What would you do with the peace biscuits?
Oliver:	Give the peace biscuits to your enemies to make them friends.
Imran:	But what happens if the enemies make war biscuits and give them to us and start fighting? It will go all wrong? We will try to stop fighting but it won't be any use.

TAKING ACTION: REDESIGNING A RECIPE FOR PEACE

The children's responses to the text and subsequent discussions had shown an intensity of thought and an elevated level of understanding that were remarkable. Their understanding about the war in Iraq, who caused it, and what the repercussions would be to civilians and soldiers alike was very thought-provoking. They were evidently exposed to media coverage of the conflict and had been influenced by discussions about winners and losers: discussions that led them to make suggestions as to what they could do to stop war and conflict.

The children decided to accept Imran's suggestion to eliminate the conflict between nations by writing a "recipe for peace" which could be sent to politicians to encourage them to stop the war. This was a perfect example of Vasquez's entreaty that children must take action and do something in relation to the critical issues they were considering, (Vasquez, 2003). It also related to Comber and Nixon's work on children as textual producers capable of rewriting and redesigning their own texts in relation to critical issues (Comber & Nixon, 2005). They began to compose immediately after a shared writing which focused their attention on what textual elements should be included in a recipe, for example, title, ingredients, bullet points, method written in sequential order, and so on. The results, showing a strong sense of audience, were enlightening and humbling and through their simplicity indicated that the children understood what was needed to convince powerful people to change their minds (see Figure 16.5).

CHILDREN'S REFLECTIONS ON THE PROJECT

To ascertain what the children thought about the project, I returned to school shortly after the third session to ask them to reflect on what they thought they had learned from reading and talking about the book and from completing the writing, illustrating, and bookmaking. The children's

Transcription of Oliver's Recipe

<u>Recipe for Peace</u>

Ingredients

- No war
- Friendship
- Respect
- Sharing
- Love

What you do

1. Put the ingredients into a mixing bowl
2. Then mix the ingredients up
3. Make into a heart shape
4. Put it into the fridge.
5. Put icing (on it).
6. Then Serve to enemies to make them stop fighting.

Figure 16.5. Oliver's recipe.

oral responses showed that the whole project had provided food for thought in many diverse ways:

- If you be nasty other people fight. If you be nice other people be nice to you.
- To be nice—not to be horrible 'cos if you're horrible God will punish you.
- Not to be mean, share and be nice and kind to people.
- It is good to have your own books to read when you get older.

The children went beyond the ideas on the page. The book had provided the stimulus enabling them to make critical responses related to international social and political issues in their everyday world that they heard about from the media. Their conversations were complex. They laid bare the thoughts of young children, socially and politically aware of what was going on in the world around them, and able to comment on these events in a perceptive and critical manner. The children were also more than capable of making suggestions to remedy the existing situation by planning a recipe for peace to send to politicians—George Bush, Tony Blair, and Saddam Hussein, among others, to start to create social justice (Edelsky, 2000).

The children were given the chance to express their points of view in a non-threatening, open manner. They were at ease with expressing a viewpoint and expected their ideas to be listened and responded to. We need to ask ourselves: When do children get the chance to talk about "big issues" in normal school circumstances? The opportunity to respond reflectively to texts and to issues in general should be an integral part of a child's education. However it takes time and teachers themselves don't always feel at ease with the subject matter, that is, allowing free rein to children's responses in relation to "difficult" subjects such as war and conflict, drugs, abuse, sex, racism, bullying, and so on. Providing the opportunity for children to engage in this kind of critically reflective discussion in response to texts is a far more effective assessment of whether and to what extent they have understood issues being considered than any formally written test. For this reason alone, this kind of critical literacy should be integrated into the elementary curriculum with young children (Vasquez, 2001).

CONCLUSIONS

Critical literacy should start with young children and build up over time. Educators need to start with issues that are relevant to the children and move on from there, encouraging children to question the assumptions and ideologies that are embedded in texts as well as their own assumptions and preconceived ideas. In relation to appropriately challenging texts, thought-provoking questions may be asked, such as:

Whose voice is being heard/not heard?

Whose point of view is being represented/not represented?

Who is being advantaged/disadvantaged?

Who is present/absent in this text?

Text-related questions of this kind provide children with the opportunity to talk about and analyze social and political situations that seem to value certain groups of people above others.

Using picture story texts as a way of addressing "big issues" should not be seen as the only way of addressing critical literacy. Other texts, for example, news reports, posters, advertisements, and so on, can also be used to help children realize that texts are never neutral and that they are constructed for particular reasons and for particular audiences. As Vasquez et al. (2003) state, talking about books " is not about literature study circle per se but about using books differently in combination with other texts to create spaces for critical literacy" (p. 6).

One child's thoughts summed up the project: "I've learned that when you read a book you can learn a lot more about the world around you if you look at it and its issues more closely."

CHILDREN'S LITERATURE REFERENCES

Foreman, M., & Charter, J. (1961). *The general.* London: Routledge/Dutton.
Foreman, M. (1967). *The two giants*. London: Brockhampton/Pantheon.
Foreman, M. (1971). *Moose.* London: Hamish Hamilton/Pantheon.
Foreman, M. (2002). *War and peas.* London: Anderson Press. (Original work published 1974)

REFERENCES

Anstey, M., & Bull, G. (2000). *Reading the visual: Written and illustrated children's literature.* London: Harcourt.
Comber, B. (2001). Critical literacies and local action: Teacher knowledge and a "new" research agenda. In B. Comber & A. Simpson (Eds.), *Negotiating critical literacies in classrooms* (pp. 271–282). Mahwah, NJ: Lawrence Erlbaum Associates.
Comber, B., & Nixon, H. (2005). Children reread and rewrite their local neighbourhoods: Critical literacies and identity work. In J. Evans (Ed.), *Literacy moves on: Using popular culture, new technologies and critical literacy in the elementary classroom* (pp. 127–148). Portsmouth, NH: Heinemann.
Edelsky, C. (2000). *Making justice our project*. Urbana, IL: National Council of Teachers of English.
Evans, J. (1998a). Introduction: Responding to illustrations in picture books. In J. Evans (Ed.), *What's in the picture: Responding to illustrations in picture books* (pp. xiii-xviii). London: Paul Chapman.

Evans, J. (1998b). "Real boys don't go to dance classes": Challenging gender stereotypes. In J. Evans (Ed.), *What's in the picture: Responding to illustrations in picture books* (pp. 96–114). London: Paul Chapman.

Evans, J. (2005). Beanie babies: An opportunity to promote literacy development, or an insidious money-spinner for the business tycoon. In J. Evans (Ed), *Literacy moves on: Using popular culture, new technologies and critical literacy in the elementary classroom* (pp. 106–126). Portsmouth, NH: Heinemann.

Foreman, M. (2001). Flesh on the bones. In F. Collins & J. Graham (Eds.), *Historical fiction for children: Capturing the past* (pp. 97–101). London: David Fulton.

Hornsby, D. & Wing Jan, L. (2001). Writing as a response to literature. In J. Evans (Ed.), *Writing in the elementary classroom: A reconsideration* (pp. 71–93). Portsmouth, NH: Heinemann.

Kempe, A. (1993). No single meaning: Empowering students to construct socially critical readings of the text. In H. Fehring & P. Green (Eds.), *Critical literacy: A collection of articles from the Australian Literacy Educators' Association* (pp. 40–57). Newark, DE: International Reading Association & Australian Literacy Educators' Association.

Luke, A., & Freebody, P. (1997). Shaping the social practices of reading. In S. Muspratt, A. Luke, & P. Freebody (Eds.), *Constructing critical literacies: Teaching and learning textual practice* (pp. 185–225). Cresskill, NJ: Hampton Press.

McLaughlin, M., & DeVoogd, G. (2004a). *Critical literacy: Enhancing students' comprehension of text.* New York: Scholastic.

McLaughlin, M., & DeVoogd, G. (2004b). Critical literacy as comprehension: Expanding reader response. *Journal of Adolescent and Adult Literacy, 48*(1), 52–82.

Rosenblatt, L. (1938). *Literature as exploration.* New York: Modern Language Association.

Rosenblatt, L. (1978). *The reader the text the poem: The transactional theory of the literacy work.* Carbondale, IL: Southern Illinois University.

Short, K. (1997). *Literature as a way of knowing.* York, ME: Stenhouse.

Vasquez, V. (2001). Constructing a critical curriculum with young children. In B. Comber & A. Simpson (Eds.), *Negotiating critical literacies in classroom* (pp. 55–66). Mahwah, NJ: Lawrence Erlbaum Associates.

Vasquez, V. (2003). Setting the context: A critical take on using books in the classroom. In V. Vasquez, with M. Muise, S. Adamson, L. Heffernan, D. Chiola-Nikai, & J. Shear (Eds.), *Getting beyond "I like the book": Creating space for critical literacy in K–6 classrooms* (pp. 1–17). Newark, DE: International Reading Association.

Vasquez, V., with Muise, M., Adamson, S., Hefferman, L., Chiola-Nakai, D., & Shear, J. (2003). *Getting beyond "I like the book": Creating space for critical literacy in K6 classrooms.* Newark, DE: International Reading Association.

Chapter 17

Learning to be Culturally Responsive: Lessons From a Beginning Teacher

Richard J. Meyer

We have explained educational failure without being able to show how to reverse it. The losers are not only the children, but our social science. (Cazden, 1986, p. 447)

Sylvia is a new teacher who completed her teacher education program and secured a first-grade teaching position at a diverse school in a medium-sized southwestern U.S. city. Although some scholars argue that *educational failure* is a "manufactured crisis" (Allington, 2002; Berliner & Biddle, 1995), Sylvia is quite willing to assume responsibility for the failures of her first-grade students. Her student-teaching and first year of teaching, chronicled in this chapter, are beleaguered with predictable stressors such as classroom management, learning the curriculum of her school, learning about the culture and ethos within her building, and overcoming the isolation that many new teachers feel. Beneath those issues lie some foundational pieces of teaching and learning with which Sylvia did not connect during her teacher education program. As she begins to face those issues—issues of culture and identity—she starts to sense that she not only could explain educational failure but she could contribute to making her students winners.

STUDYING SYLVIA'S TEACHING AND LEARNING

Near the conclusion of a reading methods course I taught in the fall of 1999, I invited students to stay in touch with me through their student-teaching semester so that I might understand the influences that the course had on their subsequent teaching practices. None did. Partway through the semester, I contacted them and asked if any would be willing to have me visit their student-teaching site to observe them teaching reading. Sylvia (pseudonym) is one of five students who agreed to let me study their teaching of reading and writing through student-teaching and into their first 2 years of teaching.

I observed and took field notes in Sylvia's classroom three times during her student-teaching semester. During her first year of teaching, I observed her teaching of reading almost weekly; I observed once a month during her second year of teaching. Following each observation, I interviewed Sylvia about teaching strategies, issues, and problems that she identified. I also interviewed Sylvia in depth about teaching reading and writing (Spradley, 1979) for 1½ hours twice (once each year) during her first 2 years of teaching. Sylvia attended monthly study-group meetings at which she and four other new teachers gathered for 3 hours to discuss the teaching of reading, although other issues often dominated our meetings. Study-group meetings were also audiotaped, transcribed, and analyzed (Glaser & Strauss, 1967; Spradley, 1980). I kept a teaching journal during the semester of the methods course and a researcher's journal (Bogdan & Biklen, 1982) during the years that the new teachers were in schools.

SYLVIA IN THE TWO-SEMESTER PROFESSIONAL DEVELOPMENT PROGRAM

Sylvia's preservice teacher education program was two semesters long. Each semester, methods coursework was taken alongside student-teaching. During her first semester, Sylvia took four methods courses (including reading) and was at her student-teaching site 2 days each week. During the second semester, she took two methods courses and was at the student-teaching site 4 days each week. For 3 consecutive weeks near the end of her second semester, she solo taught for 5 days per week (and methods courses were suspended). Sylvia struggled to balance her coursework and days at her student-teaching site with keeping her part-time job. She often arrived at the reading methods class tired and struggled to stay awake during some class sessions. Her pierced tongue-stud made a sound as the lead-colored ball affixed to it hit her front teeth. She slumped in her chair and listened to her colleagues in the class as they struggled to understand the reading process and miscue analysis, and worked with case studies. Sylvia always handed her assignments in on time; they demonstrated a high level of understanding of the content.

Over 75% of the students at Sylvia's host school are on free or reduced lunch, a figure included to suggest the high poverty rate of the school's children. About 65% of the children are Hispanic; 2% are American Indian; 1% are African American; and about 30% are Caucasian. Sylvia studied culturally responsive (Au, 1993) and relevant (Ladson-Billings, 1994) pedagogy through readings, discussions, and presentations during the reading methods course. She also read about, wrote about, and responded to the idea of community or family funds of knowledge (Moll, Amanti, Neff, & Gonzalez, 1992). "Where," she asked in a writing assignment, "are the examples that we can go and look at?" I referred her to some of the teachers I taught in a graduate course, but she does not accept the invitation.

During her second semester in the professional development program, I visited Sylvia at her student-teaching site. She was professionally dressed and did not have a stud in her tongue. Sylvia told me that she was miserable during her student-teaching. Her unhappiness continued into her first year of teaching in her own first-grade classroom; she found that her feelings were directly related to her identity as a Hispanic woman and the fact that she had not paid significant attention to her Hispanic self.

IDENTITY ISSUES

Knowing about Sylvia's family life and upbringing helps to paint the portrait (Lawrence-Lightfoot & Davis, 1997) of the teacher that her students experience in her classroom. That portrait is also the stuff she draws on in her ways with children and her thinking about relationships that are foundational to teaching and learning.

Sylvia's mother is from a northern European country and came to the United States having learned some English in her home country. She learned to speak, read, and write English fluently upon arriving in the United States. She did not learn Spanish, even though she fell in love with and married a man whose first language is Spanish. He, too, speaks, reads, and writes fluently in English, the language in which they fell in love. Sylvia's father grew up in a Spanish-speaking family in the southwestern United States. Sylvia attended many family functions and listened as her father, grandparents, aunts, uncles, and cousins—all of whom she saw very regularly—spoke Spanish. Sylvia preferred speaking English with and to her mom, only playing with her Spanish-speaking relatives at her mother's insistence.

Sylvia's northern European roots are manifested in her light skin color. She married a Hispanic man during the summer prior to her first year of teaching and reported that many of her students and their families thought she was a Caucasian woman who acquired her husband's Hispanic surname. Listening to her students at her first teaching job, she realized that she understands Spanish and even risked speaking it increasingly. She encouraged parents to speak to her in Spanish if they felt that would allow them to articulate more effectively their concerns, thoughts, and responses about their children's learning. When it came time for conferences with families, she wasn't sure she would understand every word they say or that she could respond in Spanish, so she invited her father to be part of the conferences for linguistic support. This impressed her students and their families and also made her Hispanic roots public.

STUDENT-TEACHING WOUNDS

Understanding Sylvia's first year of teaching demands stepping back to her student-teaching placement. Her cooperating teacher, Ms. Stringer, is a Caucasian woman; she uses the *Four Blocks* program to teach reading and writing to her first grade students because that is the program adopted by the school. Ms. Stringer does not respond to the children in her class through culturally responsive lenses, but Sylvia does not recognize that this is a problem. The children in Ms. Stringer's class are compliant, following the rules, and perform as they are told when Ms. Stringer teaches; however, when Sylvia teaches, lessons typically become unruly and disorganized. Sylvia carefully plans each of her lessons, yet as she lives them out, her face loses its color, her eyes do not focus on the children, and she almost robotically proceeds through her plans paying little attention to the children.

Sylvia suggests to me that her cooperating teacher isn't "nice to the children." I ask Sylvia if she (Sylvia) is nice to the children. "I can't be," she says. "It's not my classroom. I have to do what she tells me to do. I want to learn to do this [teach]." I ask Sylvia if she wants to change her student-teaching placement. "No, I have to do this. I have to do this here." Sylvia feels what many of the Hispanic children in the class are feeling: She feels like an outsider (Valdés, 1996).

SYLVIA'S FIRST YEAR AT LA MESITA ELEMENTARY SCHOOL

Sylvia's first job as a new teacher is at La Mesita Elementary School (LMES), which closely resembles where she student-taught. Eighty-two percent of the LMES children receive free or reduced lunch. She has one Caucasian child, one African American child, one American Indian child, and the rest of her class members are Hispanic, with about half reporting that their home language is Spanish. LMES is growing, with over 700 students. The school is consistently on the district's list of low-performing schools, and the teachers are regularly reminded of this by the principal.

LMES also uses the *Four Blocks* reading program. At the beginning of the year, Sylvia is very strict with the children and uses as much teacher power as she can muster to keep them quiet and busy. Failure to comply results in being separated from the group until Sylvia decides they may return. She has control, but she feels unsure of the overall direction of her teaching and describes her teaching as chaotic. The chaos does not seem apparent during my visits. She has the day timed almost to the minute as she leads her students from activity to activity. She maintains a very teacher-centered classroom and demands student obedience and compliance.

Sylvia is confused about what to do with all the information about home and community life that her students volunteer to her in the tiny open spaces of time around the official curriculum. At a study session in October of her first year of teaching, Sylvia discusses what she is learning about her students:

> I sent this note home and so his [student's grandmother] ended up calling me and said, "Well about three days ago, V—'s mom, in essence, was doing all these drugs in a hotel room with the kids and left the kids in there... So, we're in the process of trying to get custody and the reason why he was probably starting acting rude like three days ago is cuz he was left in the hotel room before." [Pause, her eyes fill with tears and the group is silent]

Monica, another teacher in the study group, suggests that Sylvia listen to V—when he talks about things that scare him. Monica suggests asking, "What scared you, do you know? What scared you, babe?" Still, Sylvia's knowledge of their lives begins to overwhelm her when a girl comes to school and announces that her baby brother died. Sylvia's aunt had died the previous evening and Sylvia only came to school to prepare for a substitute teacher so she, Sylvia, could attend the funeral. Sylvia breaks down crying as she organizes for the sub and listens to her student discuss her dead brother. Later in the month at a study-group meeting, Sylvia expresses deep concern about how to balance her emotionality, their emotional needs, and the pressure for academic performance.

PLATICAS: FROM FATIGUE TO COMMUNITY THROUGH TALK

Just after winter break of her first year, Sylvia is exhausted because of the tension between content (curriculum) and her growing awareness of her students' lives. One day in January as the children gather on the rug to start their day, a child tells a story about something that happened at home. Exasperated at having another home story hanging in the air, Sylvia asks, "OK, what else?" There is silence. The children don't know what she means because these stories usually seem more bothersome than interesting to their teacher. She asks again, "Who else wants to tell what happened at home?" Sylvia's cultural consciousness and competence are finally coming into play.

In the Hispanic culture, stories about lived experiences are very important on a few different levels. *Platicas* (Guerra, 1998) are almost like coffee klatches, where groups sit and tell stories of their families and the neighborhood. It's not quite gossiping because of the negative connotation of gossiping, but more like informing each other as a way of staying connected, although sometimes judgments are implied. Sylvia, as she asks the children "What else?," is essentially inviting into her classroom a cultural norm of the

Hispanic neighborhood. On the following days, the children arrive, hang up backpacks, and sit huddled together around the chair where Sylvia sits in one corner of the room. "Who has something?" she asks. Someone tells about a puppy that got away. Someone else tells that it was run over. Someone else explains that their cousin saw it first and ran home to tell her aunt, who knew the owner. Many of the social connections of the neighborhood are now legitimate within the classroom as the children and their teacher engage in a sociocultural practice they know well. Gradually, the children focus more on their *Four Blocks* work and they also treat each other in a more neighborly way; further, some of their teacher's stress dissipates.

CONSEJOS: A COMMUNITY AS A STORY COLLECTIVE

One day Sylvia adds another facet of Hispanic culture to her classroom. Rather spontaneously, during a *Four Blocks* lesson, she tells a very brief story about one of the children in the class. "Oh, we all know that your work is always neat," she says to one child. "Yours is just so neat. You are the neat one." Later, she adds, "I want everyone to be like his. Neat neat neat." Many Hispanic families, indeed many families of many different cultural groups, tell stories about individuals within their families. The use of story "to influence behaviors and attitudes" is referred to as *consejos* (Valdés, 1996, p. 125). These stories preserve family history, teach beliefs and values, and position family members in certain ways. Sylvia begins to tell stories of her students to them, just as some of their families do when they are at family gatherings. "My first graders," she explains to them, "are neat and careful." When she does this, sometimes some of the children glance at each other and nod their heads in agreement. This is as much like being at their aunt's house as being at school, because their unique characteristics are recognized and become part of the official funds of knowledge (Moll et al., 1992) of the classroom.

SYLVIA MAKES *FOUR BLOCKS* WORK

Sylvia takes no risks in using the reading portions of the program. She does as the program and the advisers from the district office and within the school building suggest. Together, the children all look at the same text for the guided reading piece, following a student as he or she reads or via choral reading. They are allowed to choose a book for silent reading from a plastic tub of books that are leveled. Sylvia remains true to the recommended time periods for each of the three reading blocks. Throughout the reading blocks, she uses *consejos* to talk about how the children are doing, who is doing what they were known for, and who is surprising her. She laughs at silly things she does and reminds the children to focus on the words, be neat, and always think hard about what they were doing. Although she knows that her students are at very different points in their reading development (from those beginning to respond to print to children who can read quite sustained and complex texts), she delivers these three blocks as they are described in the guides for teachers.

In the writing part of *Four Blocks*, Sylvia departs from the program, allowing children to write in journals, compose stories, publish books, make posters, and do other activities. She allows the students to approximate spellings on first drafts, consult with each other about ideas, and share their writing daily in small groups or at an author's chair. At the end of her first year of teaching, Sylvia's students perform above average on tests that she is required to administer, showing higher than average growth from the beginning of the year.

Sylvia asks to move to second grade with her class and her principal allows her to do this. After reading Fraser and Skolnick (1994) over the summer, Sylvia cultivates the writing block so that it looks like a writers' workshop. She focuses on having them write for meaning and encourages them to expand their writing, draw pictures to go with it, and rely on each other for ideas and the spelling of words. Near the end of the year she begins to question her teaching of reading and asks me for suggestions for summer reading.

IMPLICATIONS FOR METHODS COURSE TEACHING

My purpose in following Sylvia from student-teaching through her second year as a teacher was to study the influences of my reading methods course on her subsequent practice. Learning the impact that Sylvia's consciousness of and responsiveness to her own and her students' roots had on her creating a classroom that was a familiar and safe place for children to learn led me to revise my reading methods course.

Autobiography

Sylvia drew on the cultural and linguistic similarities between herself and her students to make her classroom what she wanted it to be. Therein lies one important change I've made in my teaching of the reading methods course. Although the first assignment in the course was a literacy autobiography (Meyer, 1996), I've changed that from recollections to a more systematic study of language, social contexts, and cultures as important elements of understanding self. The preservice teachers now interview family members and other significant individuals from their early literacy lives, working like anthropologists to uncover artifacts of their pasts (including memories, photos, books, writing, worksheets, workbooks, projects, movies, and more). In class, we work to put the artifacts into historical, cultural, linguistic, gender, familial, and other contexts. I challenge students to discuss ways in which politics and economics factor into their identity by asking questions such as, "What would it have been like if you were rich? African American? Caucasian? Spanish speaking at home?" It is within the contrasts of their stories that students get a sense of positions and roles that they assumed. I then work to have them understand how these positions are socially constructed within and around them. It is when we move to the next assignment that came out of this study that students begin to understand the relationships between identity and teaching.

Contexts for Literacy Learning

During the Contexts for Literacy Learning assignment, students spend one full day of their student-teaching as participant observers at their school sites. I teach them how to take and analyze field notes, using the factors that emerged in their autobiographies as tentative categories or themes to consider. They look at gender, language, culture, power, position, politics, the arts, and economics as they study the many contexts in which children learn to read. They note who sits where (drawing maps and diagrams), who gets to talk, whose needs seem to be getting met (or not), and the differences between the genders in classroom discourse. They also interview a family of a student, make a home visit, and map the community (including nearest library, busy streets, and more).

In class, they use maps of the classroom to analyze how space is used and analyze who benefits from the use of space. They discuss ways in which their own lived experiences resonate with or are different from what they are seeing. They also interview their cooperating teacher about her or his childhood, teaching experiences, and understanding of language, culture, and literacy. This assignment takes weeks and I have them do small parts for each class session.

On the due date, they share their findings along side of their literacy autobiographies. It's at this point that many of them see the connections. Some cry as they realize that the pain they felt in school was not only real, it is being relived by some of the children and perpetuated by some of the teachers in the classrooms in which they are student-teaching. I draw them back to the reading process, reading pedagogy, and assessment, and as the stories continue, the evidence emerges as almost irrefutable: Lived experiences, language, culture, economics, religion, color, and more are part of learning to read.

Enhancement Project

As I watched Sylvia's students feel safe, fall in love with her, respond to her cultural with-it-ness (Kounin, 1970), and comply with her pedagogical demands as rooted in the *Four Blocks* reading program, I realized the need to increasingly build into the reading methods course strategies for new teachers to use within mandated programs. One requirement of the course continues to be the study of the classroom reading program. Now it also involves enhancing the program through inquiry questions that arise from the study of the program. For example, a question I posed to a *Four Blocks* student-teacher was, "If some of the kids already know the words for the phonics part of the program, if they can spell them, read them, and write them, how can you justify the child spending their time doing this activity?" Thus, enhancing the program by meeting individual needs might become an enhancement project to which the student commits for the rest of the semester (with the cooperating teacher's approval).

Choosing Cooperating Teachers

Having been at my new university for 3 years, I've established professional relationships with teachers via graduate courses and other venues. I now (some semesters) hand pick the cooperating teachers I want my students to work with. Instead of university-based supervisors, the cooperating teachers agree to join a series of seminars entitled *Teacher as Teacher Educator* in which they work on a case study of their student-teacher. The cooperating teachers are paid twice: the university supervisor's salary for attending the seminars and also their cooperating teacher stipend for the time they have the students in their classrooms. The seminars for cooperating teachers include literature on teacher education, observation, evaluation, communication, mentoring, and some information on reading instruction as recommended by national organizations.

A Three-Semester Program

A big change occurred in our program when a state law passed requiring that new elementary teachers have two reading courses, rather than just one. This makes it virtually impossible to finish our teacher education program in two semesters. Additionally, as the analysis from this study unfolded, I began insisting that student-teaching not occur while students are still taking methods courses. The serendipitous law and the push by some faculty and myself for a longer, more reflective program resulted in a three-semester program during which our students are at different placements each semester.

Mentoring

This research project has multiple layers of mentoring, all of which influenced Sylvia in a variety of ways. Sylvia was verbose during the study-group sessions, in formal interviews, and when we met informally following my observations of her teaching. She took her colleague's suggestions seriously, as when Monica suggested she listen to her students. There is no way to compare Sylvia's first 2 years of teaching to what those years *might* have been had she not been in the study. The study group and her relationship with me outside of the group were places for her to be honest, to celebrate, to think, to disagree, to grow, to talk, and to weep in the silent support that embraced her when we didn't know what to say. Real mentoring is about sustained relationships, forums in which a teacher is safe to ask, answer, laugh, and cry; and it is a thought collective in which there are few known answers.

BECOMING WINNERS

The Cazden quote at the head of this chapter refers to winners and losers. Spending 2 years with beginning teachers has led me to think that such an orientation is too dichotomous to be useful in serving teachers and their students. Sylvia and her students are winners in some senses. They learn in a respectful environment that is responsive to some of their cultural realities, making school a familiar (rather than strange) place. But Sylvia's reading program doesn't respond to the individuality of her students' needs. They don't read books and discuss them in *platicas*, and much of their time in school remains teacher-centered and does not provide opportunities for the children to make choices. Sylvia is becoming responsive to the differences in reading that she sees in her students as she begins to see them as individuals with literacy identities, just as she saw them as having cultural identities and responded to that.

In the present *No Child Left Behind* climate, as teachers and children are being forced to be homogeneous in curriculum and performance, Sylvia's lived experiences serve as a call for individuality, uniqueness, and a commitment to the complexities of teaching and learning reading in diverse settings. Her case is a call for methods courses that consider the whole teacher and the implications and possibilities of that wholeness for unique and effective practice.

REFERENCES

Allington, R. (Ed.). (2002). *Big brother and the national reading curriculum: How ideology trumped evidence*. Portsmouth, NH: Heinemann.

Au, K. (1993). *Literacy instruction in multicultural settings.* Fort Worth, TX: Harcourt Brace Janovich.

Berliner, D. C., & Biddle, B. J. (1995). *The manufactured crisis: Myths, fraud, and the attack on America's public schools*. Reading, MA: Addison-Wesley.

Bogdan, R., & Biklen, S. (1982). *Qualitative research for education: An introduction to theory and methods*. Boston: Allyn and Bacon.

Cazden, C. (1986). Classroom discourse. In M. Wittrock (Ed.), *Handbook of research on teaching* (3rd ed., pp. 432–462). New York: Macmillan.

Fraser, J., & Skolnick, D. (1994). *On their way: Celebrating second graders as they read and write.* Portsmouth, NH: Heinemann.

Glaser, B., & Strauss, A. (1967). *The discovery of grounded theory*. Chicago: Aldine.

Guerra, J. (1998). *Close to home: Oral and literate practices in a transnational Mexicano community.* New York: Teachers College Press.

Kounin, J. (1970). *Discipline and group management in classrooms.* New York: Holt, Rinehart & Winston.

Ladson-Billings, G. (1994). *The dreamkeepers: Successful teachers of African American children*. San Francisco: Jossey-Bass.

Lawrence-Lightfoot, S., & Davis, J. D. (1997). *The art and science of portraiture.* Hoboken, NJ: Wiley.

Meyer, R. (1996). Literacy autobiographies. In K. Whitmore & Y. Goodman (Eds.), *Practicing what we preach: Voices of teacher educators* (pp. 129–130). York, ME: Stenhouse.

Moll, L., Amanti, C., Neff, D., & Gonzalez, N. (1992). Funds of knowledge for teaching: Using a qualitative approach to connect homes and classrooms. *Theory into Practice*, *XXXI*(2), 132–141.

Spradley, J. (1979). *The ethnographic interview.* New York: Holt Rinehart & Winston.

Spradley, J. (1980). *Participant observation*. New York: Holt Rinehart and Winston.

Valdés, G. (1996). *Con respeto: Bridging the distance between culturally diverse families and schools.* New York: Teachers College Press.

Chapter 18

Critical Issues in Early Foreign Language Literacy Instruction: Taiwan Experience

Yueh-Nu Hung

In Taiwan, learning English is not just a national trend; it is a national craze. In the national curriculum guide released in 2000 by the Ministry of Education, English class was, for the first time, mandated in the fifth and sixth grades. Starting in 2005, English teaching was extended to the third and fourth grades. Studies show that 71% of children in Taipei, the capital city, and 60% to 70% in Taiwan have been learning English outside the school system at cram schools or private language institutes (Chen, 1995; Wu, 1998). The entry into the World Trade Organization, the talk of globalization, and the trend of knowledge economy are among the forces that push the people of Taiwan to have their children learn English at a very early age.

At a time when the importance of English is nationally recognized in Taiwan, I want to discuss how language policies, curriculum structure, and teaching practice affect children's learning of English as a foreign language (EFL) and comment on the practice of English literacy teaching and what changes will construct a more balanced and wholesome elementary EFL curriculum for children in Taiwan. I first provide a brief account of English education in Taiwan, followed by discussions of the critical issues in Taiwanese children's learning of EFL literacy. After that, I discuss theories and review research findings that are particularly enlightening in solving our problems. Finally, I suggest policy and curriculum modifications.

WHAT WE ARE DOING AND THE CRITICAL ISSUES

Unlike the situation in some neighboring Asian countries that were once ruled by English-speaking people, English is a foreign language in Taiwan. Most people in Taiwan learn English at school. Before 2001, English was taught as a school subject from the 7th to the 12th grades in secondary school and in the freshman year of college, although some local governments, private schools, and experimental programs taught English at the elementary level. Starting in the 2001 school year, as a part of the "Nine-Year Integrated Curriculum" educational reform, English began to be taught in the fifth and sixth grades. According to a later modification to the curriculum guide, elementary English education was extended to the third and fourth grades starting in 2005.

The national curriculum guide, compiled by the Ministry of Education, states that the goals of teaching English at the elementary level are to help students (a) develop basic English communication abilities, (b) develop interests and methods of learning English, and (c) learn about their native culture and customs and those of the target language (Ministry of Education, 2000). However, only one to two class periods (40 to 80 minutes) per week are allotted to English teaching, and a range of issues I explore next is influential in Taiwanese children's EFL literacy learning.

Political Issues

One political issue that directly impacts elementary English education is the lack of a consistent and clear English language policy. Such a policy will guide us to make appropriate decisions, including the age at which children will start learning English at school, how much time is assigned for English class in a week, what English abilities are to be emphasized, what types of teaching methods and materials are most helpful, and what qualifications teachers should have. Instead, our English education policies are constantly altered by sudden demands, manipulated by legislators, and influenced by political considerations.

Another political issue that shapes the teaching of English at the elementary school level is the competition between the central and the local governments and among different local governments as well. When the Ministry of Education mandated English in the fifth and sixth grades, several county and city governments decided to start English teaching in the fourth, third, second, and even first grades. This divisive competition caused many problems. Parents complain that English lessons are not offered for younger children as they are in other cities and countries; legislators press local governments to extend English education to a lower grade; school administrators are busy meeting the sudden demands for a larger number of elementary English teachers.

Sociocultural Issues

Several sociocultural issues are influential and unique to the Taiwanese scene. The first issue has to do with how English was taught in the past in Taiwan. Most young parents in Taiwan who are now in their 30s and 40s started learning English as a school subject in the seventh grade. English education at that time emphasized reading and writing, simply because senior high school and college entrance exams were paper-and-pencil exams and oral English was not tested. As a result, a lot of these students who are now young parents are very hesitant English speakers. Recognizing the deficiency of reading-and-writing-only English teaching, many of these parents stress the importance of being able to speak English. This history of English education in the past contributes to the belief that oral English training should be the core of beginning English instruction.

The other important sociocultural issue is related to a deep-rooted Chinese cultural value for education. A Chinese saying goes, "Hoping the son to become a dragon; hoping the daughter to become a phoenix," which means that parents want their son to be the best of men and their daughter the best of women. This ardent concern for children's education in the Chinese culture traces back to some centuries ago when civil exams were the threshold for fame and wealth. Studying hard was the key to passing civil exams in the past just like excelling in school today is the key to better educational opportunities. Parents want their children to "win at the start point" in the long race of schooling, and therefore send their children to learn English in private language institutes before it begins to be offered in school. This results in great individual English proficiency differences among elementary school students. Since most schools do not have enough administration and personnel support to provide grouping-by-ability English instruction, teachers are facing a difficult challenge of teaching students of vastly different English backgrounds.

Linguistic Issues

A pedagogical issue concerns the role and function of phonics in EFL reading instruction. Elementary English teaching materials that involve phonics instruction abound in Taiwan. Phonics is used to teach both pronunciation and reading. The problem is that these children do not speak English yet. Even if they are able to sound out words using regular phonics rules, they do not understand the meanings. It will be a tragedy if the student's interest and motivation for learning English wither because classroom instruction emphasizes memorizing phonics rules and words (some of which are nonwords) that are not connected to children's lives. Children will lose interest, and an early start in English learning will only mean an early end to their motivation and effort.

WHAT OTHER PEOPLE SAY

There is considerable research on children's second-language learning, but less on young children's second-language literacy acquisition (Tabors & Snow, 2002). I would argue that there is even less research on children's foreign language literacy learning. There's a genuine need for more longitudinal and classroom-based research to record and analyze children's foreign language literacy experiences and development. In what follows, I briefly review research and theories concerned with three issues: emergent literacy, age factor in second/foreign language acquisition, and the place of phonics in second/foreign language literacy learning.

Emergent Literacy

Studies by Clay (1966) and Y. Goodman (1984, 1996) have shown that young children have already started the journey of becoming literate before schooling starts. Children observe the print and literacy practices in the environment, and begin to understand what written language is and approximate reading and writing in their daily lives. The classroom implication of emergent literacy research is that children born into literate societies are not blank sheets to be filled when entering school. Teachers need to be aware of this research and support their children's emerging literacy.

Although English is a foreign language in Taiwan, English print is rich and highly visible in the environment. I have argued that it's next to impossible to find a household without Chinese print (Hung, 2002), and I would also argue that the same goes for English print. Moreover, with the government's efforts to promote bilingual environmental print in Chinese and English, children encounter English in their daily lives. Many children already have some understandings of the English writing system when entering the first grade. It would be a shame if these beginning understandings of English literacy are denied and ignored in elementary schools.

Age Factor in Second/Foreign Language Acquisition

Generally, younger children have shorter attention spans and their cognitive skills are less mature, whereas older learners are better at memorizing vocabulary and analyzing grammar and rules. Is starting young in the learning of a second/foreign language really better? Research results in this aspect are mixed. On the one hand, there are studies claiming that the critical period hypothesis applies to second-language acquisition. For example, Patkowski (1980) found in his study that age is very important in achieving native-like proficiency in a second language. Johnson and Newport's study (1989) also found that there is a strong relationship between starting young and achievement in learning a second language. On the other hand, there are also studies claiming that an early start does not necessarily result in a higher second-language achievement. For example, Snow and Hoefnagel-Höhle's study (1978) found that in the three age groups of their English-speaking subjects who were learning Dutch as a second language in Holland, adolescents were more successful than children and adults. In Genesee's study (1987), English-speaking Canadian students who started learning French at a later age (around seventh and eighth grade) did better than those who started in the first grade.

The question of whether starting early is better is researched and well discussed in Taiwan. Based on the discussions of scores of researchers (Cao, Wu, & Xie, 1994; Liu, 2002; Yu, 2003; Zhou, 1989), there seems to be a consensus among Taiwanese scholars that an early start does not guarantee a higher English achievement in the long run. However, parents do not accept such professional advice. They want their children to start early in order to win the race of schooling. Communication with parents on the age factor is necessary.

The Place of Phonics in Second/Foreign Language Literacy Learning

Phonics is the set of relationships between the sound system and the written system in the alphabetic language of an individual (K. Goodman, 1993, 1996). The teaching of phonics in reading an alphabetic language is naturally required and linguistically legitimate because it is how the written system works. According to the position statement of the International Reading Association (1997), 98% of teachers in the United States teach phonics. The statement also stresses that the most effective way to teach phonics is having phonics lessons embedded in the meaningful context of literacy events.

Children in Taiwan generally do not have an oral English background when they start learning to read and write English. This means phonics is abstract and challenging for them because they need to learn the sound system of English, the spelling system of English, and the relations between the two simultaneously. This is why Liu (2002) also says that phonics plays two roles in Taiwan: to teach pronunciation and to teach reading. I once questioned a linguistics professor who was compiling phonics textbooks for the elementary English course in Taiwan by saying that even if students were able to sound out a regular word, they still didn't know the meaning. She replied that being able to sound out was good enough. I would argue that this kind of learning experience is meaningless for children. In the context of second foreign language learning, rich, authentic and meaningful learning experiences are the key to literacy development (Hudelson, 1994).

HELPING TAIWANESE CHILDRE LEARN TO READ AND WRITE ENGLISH

After discussing the critical issues in early EFL literacy instruction in Taiwan and related research and theories, I now discuss what actions to take to help Taiwanese children learn to read and write English as a foreign language.

A Consistent and Clear Language Policy

There are many types and forms of bilingual and second/foreign language programs used in different parts of the world. Many of them are effective and successful for foreign language learning (for a comprehensive review, see Baker, 2001). If the Taiwanese government makes it a national educational goal for people to become proficient in both oral and written English, then educators need to work together to design a comprehensive and balanced English language policy.

To start learning at an earlier age doesn't necessarily guarantee a higher achievement. Now in Taiwan many counties and cities have their children begin English education in the first grade for only one or two class periods (40 or 80 minutes) per week. Many teachers have complained that there isn't much they are able to teach during such limited class time. It has been argued that such a "drip feed" program is not effective for second/foreign language, even if it lasts for many years (Lightbown & Spada, 1999). I believe that with the same amount of time and expenditure for English class, English instruction would be more effective if the instruction were postponed until the fifth grade and offered for at least 3 or 4 hours per week. The time has come for educational policymakers to draw up an English education blueprint that guides the design of programs and classroom practice.

The Four Aspects of Language Equally Emphasized

There is no denying that language is culture and language learning is cultural learning. However, for many foreign language learners, one major motivation for learning a foreign language is utilitarian. Moreover, the 21st century of knowledge economy makes accessing information written in English more important for non-English-speaking populations than ever before. English literacy should be at least equally emphasized in Taiwan's elementary EFL curriculum. As mentioned earlier, many Taiwanese parents consider oral skills as the core of English learning. Dai (2002) is not exaggerating when he writes that an English program that stresses oral language and ignores written language can't prepare students for future occupational and academic reading and writing needs.

Songs, dances, and games can be easily incorporated into the curriculum and are a fun way for children to learn English, but they should not fill every minute of an English class with no time left for reading and writing activities. English reading and writing learning can be inviting (i.e., not just fun), if students are encouraged and motivated to engage in authentic and meaningful learning experiences. These experiences should equally emphasize reading, writing, listening, and speaking in the elementary curriculum to achieve balanced and effective language learning.

Strengthening Teacher Qualification

English teachers need to be helped and supported to develop professional and linguistic knowledge and expertise in order to help Taiwanese children learn English more effectively. Many of our elementary English teachers may lead a fun class filled with songs, games, and kinesthetic activities, but when it comes to teaching reading and writing, the teachers are aimless. I suggest that English education professional courses like English linguistics, children's language acquisition, children's written language development, and English children's literature be made widely available to those who teach English to young children. Teachers should be competent in making professional instructional judgments based on their training, observations and conversations with students, and the sociocultural environment of the school and the society at large.

Strengthening Elementary English Curriculum

In Taiwan, a large number of textbooks and materials for children's English learning are compiled based on phonics rules from simple to complex. This creates a one-legged elementary English curriculum. In an EFL scenario where children do not speak English yet, phonics is abstract and difficult for them.

I strongly argue that our elementary English curriculum be strengthened to include various English instructional methods and language experiences. Children's emerging English reading and writing experiences should be valued. The communicative approach, as currently endorsed by the Ministry of Education, is effective, and so are language experience, whole language, and other approaches that introduce the students to rich and authentic language activities and experiences. Classroom teachers need to expand on their professional expertise to design their own English literacy lessons, and the national curriculum guide compilers need to provide clear curriculum guidelines to support classroom teachers.

CONCLUSION

Bilingualism and multilingualism are the norm in the world today. Some bi- and multilingual populations learn two or more languages from birth; others acquire a second or third language later in life. In the 21st century of globalization, many countries try hard to increase their competitive edge, and one important key is literacy: literacy in their native languages and in international languages like English. I have discussed the critical issues that shape the teaching and learning of English literacy at the elementary school level. Suggestions are made to call for a more comprehensive and balanced elementary English literacy curriculum. I hope this discussion of the Taiwan experience adds to the understanding of the complex picture of early literacy teaching and learning.

REFERENCES

Baker. C. (2001). *Foundations of bilingual education and bilingualism* (3rd ed.). Clevedon, England: Multilingual Matters Ltd.

Cao, F.-F., Wu, Y.-X., & Xie, Y.-L. (1994). Xiao Xue San Nian Ji Ying Yu Jiao Xue Zhuei Zong Fu Dao Hou Xu Shi Yian Jiao Xue [Teaching English in the third grade: A follow-up supplementary instruction experiment]. *Jiao Yu Yian Jiou Zi Xun, 2,* (3), 111–122.

Chen, C.-M. (1995). Rang ABC Bu Zai Xun: Guo Xiao Kai She Ying Yu Ke Cheng [Effective English learning: English curriculum in elementary school]. *Shi You, 337,* 4–23.

Clay, M. (1966). *Emergent reading behavior.* Doctoral dissertation, University of Auckland, Auckland, New Zealand.

Dai, W.-Y. (2002). Guo Xiao Ying Yu Ke Cheng De Yian Ge Yu Zhan Wang [Teaching English to the primary school students]. *Zhang Deng Jiao Yu, 53,* 32–51.

Genesee, F. (1987). *Learning through two languages: Studies of immersion and bilingual education.* New York: Newbury House.

Goodman, K. S. (1993). *Phonics phacts.* Portsmouth, NH: Heinemann.

Goodman, K. S. (1996). *On reading.* Portsmouth, NH: Heinemann.

Goodman, Y. M. (1984). The development of initial literacy. In H. Goelman, A. Oberg, & F. Smith (Eds.), *Awakening to literacy* (pp. 102–109). Exeter, NH: Heinemann.

Goodman, Y. M. (1996). Roots of literacy. In S. Wilde (Ed.), *Notes from a kidwatcher: Selected writings of Yetta M. Goodman* (pp. 121–147). Portsmouth, NH: Heinemann.

Hudelson, S. (1994). Literacy development of second language children. In F. Genesee (Ed.), *Educating second language children: The whole child, the whole curriculum, the whole community* (pp. 129–158). New York: Cambridge University Press.

Hung, Y.-N. (2002). Yue Du De Li Lun [Reading theories]. In *Proceedings of the Multiple Language Education and Academic Exchange Conference* (pp. 17–35). Taipei: Taipei Municipal Teachers College.

International Reading Association. (1997). *The role of phonics in reading instruction: A position statement of the International Reading Association.* Newark, DE: International Reading Association.

Johnson, J., & Newport, E. (1989). Critical period effects in second language learning: The influence of maturational state on the acquisition of English as a second language. *Cognitive Psychology, 21*(1), 60–99.

Lightbown, P. M., & Spada, N. (1999). *How languages are learned* (rev. ed.). New York: Oxford University Press.

Liu, C.-G. (2002). Qian Tan Phonics Yu Ying Yu Fa Yin [Phonics and English pronunciation]. Ying Wen Gong Chang, *4*, 4.

Ministry of Education. (2000). *Guo Min Zhong Xiao Xue Jiou Nian Yi Guan Ke Cheng Zhan Xing Gang Yao* [1st -9th Grades Curriculum Alignment Temporary Guide]. Taiwan: Author.

Patkowski, M. (1980). The sensitive period for the acquisition of syntax in a second language. *Language Learning, 30*(2), 449–472.

Snow, C., & Hoefnagel-Höhle, M. (1978). The critical period for language acquisition: Evidence from second language learning. *Child Development, 49*(4), 1114–1128.

Tabors, P. O., & Snow, C. E. (2002). Young bilingual children and early literacy development. In S. B. Neuman & D. K. Dicknson (Eds.), *Handbook of early literacy research* (pp. 159–178). New York: Guilford Press.

Wu, H. (1998). Guo Xiao Xiao Yuan ABC: Ying Yu Jiao Xue De Tan Tao Yu Xing Si [English in elementary school: Exploration and reflection on English teaching and learning]. *Shi Shuo, 116,* 6–27.

Yu, M.-C. (2003). On the appropriateness for introducing an early-start English curriculum at the primary grades in Taiwan. *Elementary Education Journal, 10,* 1–43.

Zhou, Z.-T. (1989). *Er Tong Ti Qian Xue Xi Ying Yu Duei Qi Ri Hou Ying Yu Neng Li Ying Xiang Zhi Yian Jiou* [A study of the influence of starting learning English early on later English proficiency]. Taipei: National Science Council.

Chapter **19**

Reading Everybody's Child: Teaching Literacy as a Human Right

Denny Taylor and Bobbie Kabuto

Denny Taylor: This chapter is about the ways in which teachers can use literacy to support children who struggle for their human rights. In an increasingly chaotic world it is a hopeful piece because it is about teachers and recognizes that teachers have knowledge and understandings that can make a difference in the life of everybody's child (Taylor & Yamasaki, 2006). Teachers know about human development. Teachers recognize the importance of children's cultural heritage, the languages they speak and the social groups to which they belong. Teachers' pedagogical practices are informed by their deep understandings of sociolinguistics and psycholinguistics. They are critically conscious of the ways in which the programs they are made to use and the tests that they are forced to give do not reflect the language abilities and life experiences of the children that they teach. In the first section of this chapter I present a rationale for the statements I have just made and I frame my argument with a view of science that counters the view of science promoted by the U.S. federal government in laws that control the ways in which reading and writing are taught. Then, Bobbie Kabuto uses the framework to introduce us to her daughter Emma, to her languages and literacies, and to what happened to Emma when she went to school. Bobbie's ethnographic study provides support for the arguments presented in the first section and deepens our understandings of recognizing how important it is to embrace the language ideologies of young children when they learn to write. In the last section Bobbie and I reflect on Emma's experiences and the important lessons her experiences provide.

EVERYBODY'S CHILD

"Nana, did you know that Humpty Dumpty was an egg?" my granddaughter asked me when she was 3. On the same day that she asked me whether I knew that Humpty Dumpty was an egg, she also said, "Do you know I'm the only one on this page." We were holding hands walking down the stairs and she looked around as she spoke. Then she added, "None of my friends are on this page?" Again she looked around. "This is my page," she said. "What's a page?" I asked. "A page is in a book," she said. While we were eating dinner a few weeks later she sat looking thoughtful and then said, "I can see my pink umbrella in my brain," and then after a pause she added, "but I can't see my brain." "She gets it," I thought, "even if researchers working for the federal government don't."

Every time I visit a family and sit talking with a child, every time I visit a classroom and children talk with me, I experience the same feeling of hopefulness that I do when my granddaughter talks with me. Not just for this child in this place but a hopefulness for humanity. In this time of great catastrophes humanity is not too big an idea for us to be thinking about. Not in any grand sense, just in the sense that humanity is signified by each and every child. *Everybody's child*, that's what this chapter is about. It's about teaching in the cracks for a more just and caring world, about literacy as a human right, literacy for the common good and literacy as the basis of mutual aid. It is filled with hope and possibility as we struggle for democracy in the ways we teach and children learn in an increasingly chaotic and often incomprehensible world.

WORKING WITH CHILDREN WHO LIVE IN AREAS OF EXTREME POVERTY, NATURAL DISASTERS, AND ARMED CONFLICT

I have worked for most of my life with families who live in poverty, families who struggle to survive in a racist society, who are considered minorities, families in which both parents and children have been sexually and physically abused, mothers and fathers who are homeless or in jail, some of whom are addicted to alcohol, heroin, crack, or cocaine. Now my work focuses on children who live in areas of armed conflict or have experienced a social or natural disaster and how teachers respond to mass trauma.

At the time that I write this, the earthquake in Pakistan has just taken place. So many lives have been lost, 73,000 was the last count I heard, and millions of people have been left without shelter to live through a Himalayan winter. The tsunami in Sri Lanka, Indonesia, and Thailand was similarly catastrophic. Here, in the United States, Katrina was quickly followed by Rita, and between them these two hurricanes have devastated Louisiana and Mississippi. In the Gulf Coast region 372,000 thousand children have been evacuated from the communities in which their families used to live.

Hurricane Katrina: Teachers Helping Teachers

In Baton Rouge every child has a story. They are living in shelters and with people in the community who have taken them in. They have no homes and many children have been separated from families and friends. One little boy was in his house when it was crushed by a truck driven by high winds and water. His mother managed to get him to a neighbor's house and together they climbed up to the attic as the water rose behind them. The boy's mom found a piece of Styrofoam and told him to hold it. "Whatever happens don't let it go," she kept telling him as she sat on the roof holding on to him.

On his first day in his new school the boy cries. He doesn't want his mother to leave him. "I want you to make lots of friends," she tells him. As he leaves with his new teacher, the counselor comforts his mother. "I thought I'd lost him," she says.

In schools, teachers welcome every child. Lynne Lay, the principal of Westminister School, invited children to come on Sunday so that "they've been here before" when they arrive on Monday. At her school, supplies have been donated by the community. "Let's go shopping," Lynne says to a little girl. "I need a notebook," the girl says. "I bet you need a red pen too," Lynne replies, and the little girl says, "Yes, I think I do."

"This is the first time people have been kind to me since I left New Orleans," a mother says when she registers her three children in Lynne's school.

At the end of the day, teachers meet and focus on the children, but many of them are suffering, too. "Many members of my family have lost everything," one teacher says. "My house is okay," another says, "but my mother lost hers, my sister's is destroyed, and my brother's house is gone."

A teacher talks about a principal she knows. "All her family are living with her. Her grandmother was killed in the storm and they can't find her body," she says, "but she is still in school."

Teachers' stories are told in passing. They focus on the children. "Healing can begin at school," a teacher says. "It's important that the children feel loved." They talk about children from the shelters who are so exhausted they sleep with their heads on their desks and about the need for pillows. They puzzle over children who are acting out and how they can support them. "I have a child who is somewhere else," a teacher says. They discuss the conditions in the shelters and share stories that the children have told them.

Teachers are helping teachers. At the Kate Middleton Elementary School in Jefferson Parish, across the Mississippi from New Orleans, the teachers talk of respecting children's wishes and of children doing their best to cope (Taylor & Yamasaki, 2005). They know that the first responders in the shelters are so overwhelmed by the sheer enormity of the catastrophe that they have not been able to take care of all the children's basic needs. On October 3, when the school reopens the principal's office is filled with boxes of Red Cross emergency meals, bottles of water, kindergarten mats, and clothes for children. Aretha Williams, the principal has lost her home, but in September, in the midst of devastation caused by Hurricane Katrina, she has met with her teachers every day in the weeks before the school reopened; they discussed ways in which they will support each other and how they will support the children who they hope will find places to stay so they may return to school. Then, on the first day of school when they welcome the children and tell them they love them, they work together to reestablish basic routines and, at the same time, they engage children in creative activities, drawing, writing, reading, singing, and playing. The teachers know that the children need time to catch up with their thoughts and feelings, and that they need time, too.

Language and Literacy Are Central to Working With Children Following a Catastrophic Event

When I work as an ethnographer, the research imperative is to heighten awareness of how language and literacy are used during times of social and natural disasters and how language and literacy are used to position children and their families in times of local, national, and global struggles. But what takes most of my time is the pedagogical necessity to find ways to support teachers who are working with children during and after catastrophic events. I am interested in the ways in which language and literacy are central to recovery. This work has significance not only in supporting teachers who are working with children during present and future catastrophic events, but also in the here and now of teaching children in less stressful times.

"More than during peacetime, education during and soon after emergencies centers on teachers," Marc Sommers (2002) states. "If teachers are present and able to respond, educating children can continue." Sommers writes of education as a protective measure and argues for the investment in creative, participatory work. The idea that teachers can make a difference makes me hopeful, which surprises many who ask me about my work. I *am* hopeful. I am hopeful because of the teachers I know, because of the imaginative ways in which they, *you,* teach, and because there is no limit to the imagination of the children that *we* teach.

THERE ARE NO LIMITS TO HUMAN IMAGINATION

We live in a world of endless possibilities, tragic, brutal, life-ending, life-sustaining, magical, courageous, compassionate, and kind. I am also hopeful because of the company I keep-the teachers who share their lives with me, and the writers, scholars, the authors of chapters in this book, and the philosophers, historians, novelists, and poets whose writings I read.

First among these, at the present time, is Hannah Arendt (1998), whose writings are teaching me about humanity. At the moment I am reading *The Human Condition,* in which Hannah reminds us of the miracle of beginnings. I use miracle in a secular sense because I have no formal religion—although being Welsh sometimes feels like a religion. In the introduction to *The Human Condition,* Margaret Canovan argues that Arendt's faith and hope in human affairs comes from the fact that new people are continually coming into the world, each of them unique, each capable of new initiatives that may interrupt or divert the chains of events set in motion by previous motions. Canovan goes on to state of Arendt: "She speaks of action pointing out that in human affairs it is actually quite reasonable to expect the unexpected, and that new beginnings cannot be ruled out even when society seems locked in stagnation or set on an inexorable course."

TEACHING, AGENCY, AND THE THREE "IF'S"

I am hopeful because for teachers there is always the possibility of new beginnings, and we are not locked into stagnation or set on an inexorable course. We do have agency and we can participate in the education of children in very powerful ways. "Agency" is a very complex idea, but here are three "if's" that can help establish agency in our classrooms:

1. *If* we position ourselves alongside the children we teach, rather than in front of them as we are told we must do, then our pedagogical practices are supportive of children's learning.
2. *If* we support their learning and think of language and literacy in the larger contexts of their everyday lives, rather than as a set of skills that they must master to pass a series of test which are irrelevant to their being in the world, then language and literacy can become deeply embedded in our students' personal and shared identities and their ways of being in the world.
3. *If* we consider literacy to be a human right and try to use literacy for the common good and literacy for mutual aid in our classroom practices, then we can provide children with the opportunities to create communities in which they can support one another in troubled times in imaginative as well as practical ways.

These three "if's" are among the central tenets of pedagogical practices for many teachers of literacy. But for beginning teachers these "if's" represent ideas that they know about but have not been able to explore because of the restrictive curricular controls imposed by federal laws and state mandates. To take such a stance requires that we reflect on the ways in which our personal and intellectual histories influence us as teachers and scholars, and how our life experiences influence our understandings of science, our theories about language and literacy, and our pedagogical practices.

PERSONAL AND INTELLECTUAL HISTORIES OF TEACHERS

At the International Scholars Forum in September 2001, Louise Rosenblatt shared her personal and intellectual life history. "I went to college in nineteen twenty-one. Women got the vote in nineteen twenty." The audience continues to clap. Louise talks about her father and mother and her childhood. "My father-Jewish, working-class, self-educated-came from Russia young enough to acquire English. English has always been my language. My father was very much concerned about socioeconomic and political affairs and the plight of poor people. That was the atmosphere I grew up in" (Rosenblatt, 2001).

"We didn't have many books, but there were books, books that were important to me because my father talked to me about them." Louise is not at the podium. She is standing in the midst of the master's students who sit at tables at the front of the room. "In those days, the Darwinian idea of 'survival of the fittest' was being used to justify unbridled economic competition. The government accepted no responsibility for the inequality of opportunities for the individual. When workers joined in unions, employers could hire thugs to attack them. I can remember hearing about such events. Kropotkin's (1976) *Mutual Aid* presented a different view of evolution. There was also cooperation. For me to make meaningful an idea such as mutual aid was very important. I acquired the belief that, no matter what your gender, your 'race,' your religion, everyone is entitled to life, liberty, and the pursuit of happiness that did not harm others."

"Those who sit back and wait are, I believe, ignoring the children whose lives will be affected," Louise writes. "To minimize the bad effects on good schools as well as the poor ones, we must try to influence what is happening. If we fail, as well we may, we shall at least have spread the ideas, have educated some who will continue the resistance."

Louise was 100 years old when she died in 2005 and we miss her. What she learned as a child framed her life, her work, and her identity. Who she was will endure and stay with us through her writings.

I encourage you to write your own histories. To teach, we must know ourselves, reflect on the ways in which our personal and intellectual histories influence us as teachers and scholars. We understand the importance of cultural heritage for ourselves and the students we teach. We know it is essential that we take into account the sociological and the psychological as well as the political. It is clear to us that we cannot teach children to read without understanding socio- and psycholinguistics and that children's language processes are deeply imbedded in their personal and family life histories. We know language and literacy are central to identity, theirs and ours. Who they are as students depends on who we are as teachers, and we are anthropologists, sociologists, psychologists, linguists and pedagogists. Our understandings of science, our theories about language and literacy, and our pedagogical practices are as complex as the present approaches to government-promoted reading programs are simplistic, fragmented, and formulaic.

SCIENTIFIC BASIS FOR TEACHING LITERACY AS A HUMAN RIGHT

In recent years "science" has been complicated by governmental laws that define science as "reliable replicable research." It is somewhat inexplicable to me that at the beginning of the 21st century we have allowed the federal government to take control of the way science is conducted and, by doing so, to control how reading and writing are taught.

"In other words," Hannah Arendt, writes (1998, p. 288), as if joining us in this conversation, "the world of the experiment seems always capable of becoming a man-made reality, and this, while it may increase man's power of making and acting, even of creating a world, far beyond what any previous age dared to imagine in dream and fantasy, unfortunately puts man back once more—and now even more forcefully—into the prison of his own mind, into the limitations of patterns he himself created."

"The structure of one man's mind is supposed to differ no more from that of another than the shape of his body," Hannah continues (p. 288) "Whatever difference there may be is a difference of mental power, which can be tested and measured like horsepower."

In good company, I would argue, like Hannah, that as teachers, our personal understandings of science and our experience of teaching young children to read and write leave us no option other than the rejection of the reliable, replicable but not so reputable research that is the basis of government-controlled reading and writing instruction in American schools.

Let's eavesdrop for a moment on this conversation between Oliver Sacks and Wim Kayzer about science, which took place in New York in 1992.

"One of the reasons I'm against mechanical models is that they are too physicalistic," Oliver Sacks says, "and too reductive and too impoverished and too boring and I think they breakdown hopelessly finally before the sheer creativity of the brain."

"Where is memory stored? "Wim Kayzer asks.

"First I don't think anything is stored in this sort of way," Oliver responds, "and I'm not sure that the notion of a store is the right one."

"The brain is not a library?" Wim questions..

"No. I think it's not a library. It's not a granary. It's not a computer," Oliver states. "And I think that what happens comes into the mind again always with a different context and a different construction so I think memory is close to imagination and I think remembering, memories are constructions and not Xeroxes, not facsimiles, not reproductions."

"Every memory is in a context," Oliver explains after a pause. "There is no snapshot of how things are. Whatever comes into the mind always comes in a new context and in some sense colored by the present. This doesn't mean that it is distorted but it is against any mechanical reproduction." And then, most importantly, Oliver states, " We have no way of saying what objective reality is. Everything is related to ourselves. This is our impression."

Our understandings of science are related to ourselves, to our personal histories, who we are as teachers and scholars and moms and dads and granddaughter and grandmothers. Remember the pink umbrella?

But however complex our understandings are, we cannot just dismiss the dominant view of science; we must refute it and state clearly our own view of science. Here are some of my understandings first of science and then of science as it relates to language and literacy:

1. *Science* is both mindful and social. The researcher and the researched, the observer and the observed are inextricably linked, connected, constitutive of each other (Frattaroli, 2001; Rose, 2005).
2. *Science is based on observation,* whether of molecules or miscues every scientific observation is really a participant–observation interaction. The interaction between the observer and the observed changes the state of the observed in the very act of observing it. What we see depends on how we look at it (Rose, 2005).
3. *Reductive science,* which attempts to control factors of causality, works on some level—for example, at the periodic table of elements. But not for dynamic, irreducibly complex phenomena, such as quantum physics, human behavior, or young children learning to read and write (Gould, 1994; Rose, 2005; Taylor, 1990, 1998).
4. *Human experience* cannot be omitted from scientific explanations of how literacy works (Taylor, 2000, 2005).
5. *Science, language, literacy, and learning* are both mindful and social and highly dependent on experiential interpretations of mind–world relationships (Taylor, 2000).
6. *Scientific explanations* of language, literacy, and learning can only be reached through nonlinear dynamic explanations that take into consideration the selective experiential interpretations of mind–world relationships (Modell, 2003; Taylor, 1990, 1993a, 1993b).
7. *The construction of meaning* is not the same as the processing of information (Modell, 2003; Taylor, 1990).
8. *Meaning,* which is irreducibly complex, cannot be directly represented by a formal symbolic code, which is inevitably reductive and oversimplified (Modell, 2003; Taylor, 1998).

Much more could be written about science and language, literacy and learning, but from the perspective I have presented it is clear that the dominant received theories, commercially promoted and legally imposed by the federal government, are based on computational, mechanistic symbolic logic and on linear algorithms that cannot accommodate the complexities of human behavior or language literacy and learning. Meaning cannot be constructed with a disembodied view of language and independent of mind and metaphor, creativity and imagination. *Disembodied language dehumanizes children.*

The lives of children, language and literacy, teaching and learning can be reimagined and redescribed in the course of an endless conversation. But we are stuck with textual fixity, authorized texts that come with the government's seal of approval based on scientific research that is primitive and prescriptive. Federal funding that is tied to specific commercial reading programs denies teachers the right to teach and children the right to learn. When programs focus on phonemic awareness, phonics, and reading words, instruction is synthetic, didactic, and rote. In some programs teachers are told when to take a breath; the skill of the day has to be posted on the classroom door, and classrooms are patrolled to make sure that the correct phonics skill is taught by every teacher and "learned" by every child.

Based on primitive views of science, reading instruction is dependent on tests. DIBELS—Dynamic Indicators of Basic Early Literacy Skills, produced by the University of Oregon—is the test of choice right now. Kindergarteners, irrespective of their life experience, culture, or history, or whether they can already read and write, are taught initial sound fluency, letter naming fluency, phoneme segmentation fluency, nonsense word fluency. These skills are then tested. Word use fluency is optional; reading words doesn't count, but sounding out nonsense word fluency does.

"Hoj vab lak bol em, zep vum zus wob dac jom tuc vab."

These are make believe words that you can read. Try reading them. On this test, reading is "sounding out" and devoid of meaning. Scripts that are reliable and replicable can be harmful to children. The damage to children's minds and to their health and well-being can be immeasurable.

In schools, at conferences, and in graduate classes, teachers make it clear that they know that pedagogical practices that support children's literacy learning cannot be derived from scientific experimentation that reduces children to data points on scatter plots or language and literacy to reading pseudo-words. Troubled by the ways in which they are expected to teach, they search for explanations. Perhaps one reason is that teaching reading as informational processing increases the possibilities for orderliness. Stephen Toulmin (1992) points out that the quest for certainty often occurs in times of social disorder, and these chaotic times certainly could be described as that. Toulmin contrasts Descartes's "quest for certainty" with Montaigne, the late Renaissance philosopher, who accepted pluralism and uncertainty. Descartes attempted to mathematize the human mind and it is this idea that has framed the 20th-century myth that everything can be quantified and any research that does not quantify is not science. At the beginning of the 21st century the teaching of reading and writing is still framed by Descartes's mythology, the computational metaphor that perfection can be realized through measurement.

Again, the construction of meaning is very different from the processing of information. Such theories cannot account for thinking in images or for fantasy or imagination. The cultural and historical heritages of children are not recognized and their everyday lives are discounted.

Next, Bobbie Kabuto provides us with ethnographic documentation which serves to emphasize how problematic such a narrow approach to the teaching of language and literacy can be. By focusing on Emma's languages and emergent language ideologies Bobbie grounds our understandings of complexity.

Bobbie Kabuto: "Daddy, I don't want to be Japanese anymore," said Emma when she was 5 years, 3 months old and 3 months into her kindergarten year. Emma's statement was almost made in passing between her pleas with her father to play like sumo wrestlers. Listening to their conversation from the next room, I heard Jay reply, "Soo. Zyaa, sumo shiyo." ["Really. Then let's play like sumo wrestlers."] Emma and Jay took their opposing positions and charged one another to see who would get knocked down first. In this section I focus on the ways in which Emma began to organize the symbolic space in which she lives and how, through her writing in multiple languages using multiple writing systems, she began to situate and negotiate her social and language identities within multiple social and cultural worlds.

LEARNING FROM EMMA ABOUT EARLY BILINGUALISM AND BILITERACY

Emma was born in Tokyo, Japan, in August 1998. She is a bilingual and biliterate child who participates in a variety of literacy practices and events in Japanese and English in family and social activities inside and outside the home. In order to keep childhood memories, I began collecting writing samples, which start with a drawing done at her friend's birthday party when Emma was 2 years, 1 month. After moving to New York, I enrolled in graduate school and Emma (2 years, 5 months) began a local preschool and Japanese Saturday school. The more I learned about the complexities of young children learning to read and write in my graduate classes, the more I became fascinated with the ways she used reading and writing at home and in her surrounding environment. Seeing new possibilities of understanding how young children become biliterate individuals, I returned to my collected writing samples and started to see them as "data."

My initial analyses focused on Emma's learning to read and write in two languages and her growing repertoire of linguistic knowledge of

English and Japanese, which uses three orthographic systems of writing (*hiragana*, *katakana*, and *kanji*) (Kabuto, 2005). However, these relationships did not fascinate me as much as the question of why would an early proficient bilingual/biliterate child who has a wealth of working linguistic knowledge in multiple languages want to lose her language identities? What I had been observing, which I did not realize until Emma's comment cited earlier, is language being more than words, sentences, and phonemes. Language is a semiotic system of signs and symbols created through co-constructing social and cultural processes. Language is a lived experience and paradoxical; it can unify and divide; it can "self" and "other"; it can index particular identities; it can exert power in social, cultural, political, and historical contexts (Wei, 2000). What young children learn when they learn to read and write in multiple languages cannot be separated from the social, cultural, historical and political factors within which language is embedded.

Book Making

Emma (4 years, 9 months) is making shapes with origami paper on the home office floor. She is folding cats, dogs, flowers, frogs, and boats. The origamis that Emma has been making and collecting over the months are spread all over. Overwhelmed, I say to Emma, "Please do something with your origamis."

"Okay," Emma answers. "I'll make a book."

Emma proceeded to make her origami book by taking each origami and gluing it on a sheet of white paper. After she collected enough pages, she divided the papers into four piles and, with my help, stapled the pages together on the right hand side, making a total of four books. Once the pages were bound together, she wrote the title of her book, *Emma's Origami* (written in *hiragana*) on the cover (see Figure 19.1).

Emma then drew pictures of the folded origami on the top of each page.

"Ganbare Matsui!"

Three months later, Emma (5 years) and her father were watching the Yankees game on TV. Emma became enthralled in the game as her father began making comments and cheering on players. After Jay expressed disappointment over another one of Hideki Matsui's outs at bat, Emma began asking her father a series of questions as to why he was upset. Emma decided to make a sign to cheer Matsui. Emma wrote "Matsui" in *kanji* in the middle from top to bottom and "Let's go" in *hiragana* on the bottom from left to right (see Figure 19.2).

Language and ways of representing come out of emotional, social, cultural, and historical influences. Emma's developing linguistic competence is not isolated from the complex social and cultural factors playing a role in Emma learning to write. For instance, Emma received the origamis from

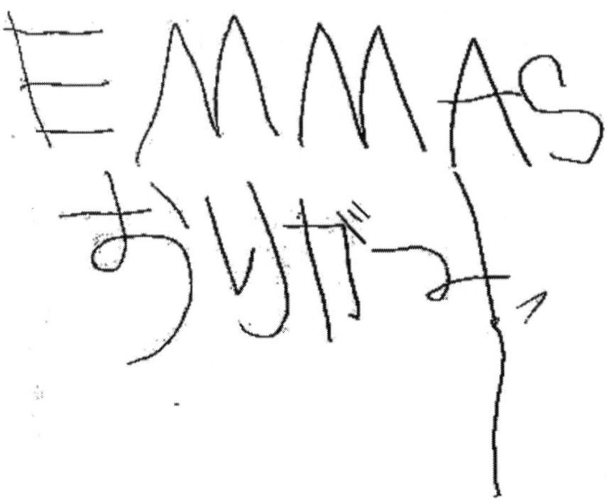

Figure 19.1. Emma makes an origami book and writes *Emma's Origami* on the front cover.

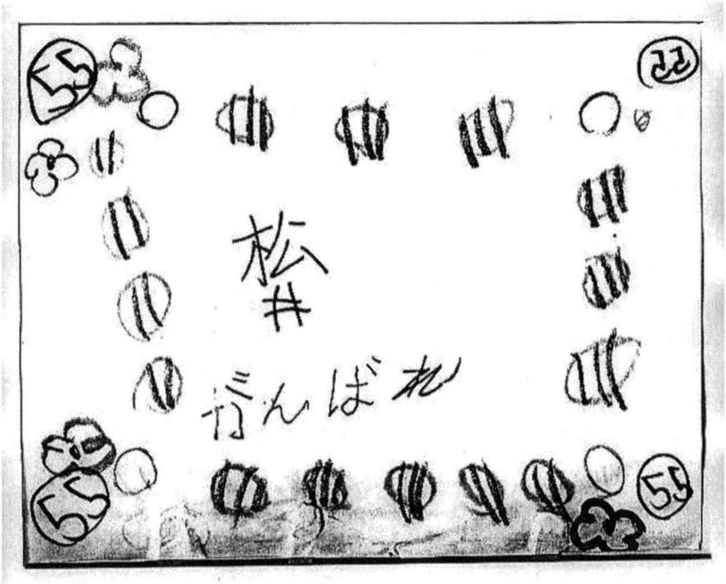

Figure 19.2. Emma makes a sign to cheer on the Yankees baseball player Hideki Matsui. She writes his name in the middle, top to bottom, and writes, "Let's go" in *hiragana* on the bottom, left to right.

her grandmother, who lives in Japan, along with Japanese books. Emma made origami cards for her grandparents and sent them with pictures and other little gifts. While making her baseball sign, she is supported by her father, who helps Emma to write the first *kanji* for *matsu* (the top *kanji*) by placing his hand over hers and gently guiding the stroke directionality. However, he writes the *kanji* for *i* on a separate piece of paper for Emma to copy and encourages her independently to write *ganbare* in *hiragana*. Emma's language learning allows her to align herself with family as she acts on her perceptions of her experiences to imagine new possibilities in her writing as well as who she is in her figured worlds.

Research on early bilingualism and biliteracy from the perspective of cognitive psychology has provided insights into the relationships between multiple language systems (e.g., unitary language systems, differentiated systems, simultaneous bilingualism, and sequential bilingualism), the notion of language transfer, and the chronological acquisition of grammatical structures (Bialystok & Hakuta, 1994; Genesee, 2000; Hakuta, 1986; McLaughlin, 1984). Although this perspective has raised interesting questions and provided insights about the linguistic and cognitive aspects of learning multiple languages, it has focused on the acquisition and learning of formal symbolic codes representing "language" with little attention to the social practices and contexts in which young children engage. To explain Emma's multiple use of language only through relationships between linguistic codes as unitary, differentiated, simultaneous, or as transfer between languages can oversimplify and reduce a complex, multidimensional act situated in human and social experiences. Emma's uses of Japanese and English are first and foremost a demonstration of her sociocultural knowledge in which contesting ideologies influence her choices of linguistic and semiotic cues to represent her identity.

Today's Homework: Phonics Worksheet

For homework, Emma (5 years, 6 months) has a phonics worksheet to complete. I explained the directions to Emma, that on the lines she is to write the letter representing the initial sound of the object in the picture, and leave her to her work. I happened to glance at her as she was writing the letter *p* in front of the picture of the pig. Without using both the baseline and midline to write the *p*, Emma wrote the entire *p* in between the pair of lines. I stopped her and suggested that I show her how to use the lines. With a ruler, I drew similar lines and demonstrated: When writing *p*, you start at the midline and draw a line down past the baseline, go back up to the midline and curve around to the baseline. Then I modeled the other letters. When she showed me her finished work, I asked, "Emma, why did you write your name in Japanese next to your name in English?" (see Figure 19.3).

Figure 19.3 Emma writes her name in Japanese and English on her phonics worksheet.

Emma answered, "Because I'm the only one in my class who can speak Japanese so nobody will know what I'm writing but me."

Emma started bringing home homework after the winter break in her kindergarten year. Worksheets such as this phonics worksheet are typical of the types of homework Emma completed two to three times a week. If, as Kress (1997) suggests, "signs therefore have a double social motivation: once because of who the sign-maker is, and what her or his history has been" (p. 93), then these signs tell very little of who Emma is and what her history has been. At most, these types of literacy events masquerade reduced, mechanistic writing skills as meaningful educational content. Worksheets such as these are disembodied skills of language that are isolated from the social, cultural, and language identities of the children with whom we all teach. At worst, they realign the values, beliefs, power relationships, and social roles of the students and their families by redescribing what counts as language and what counts as literacy.

When Emma entered kindergarten, she became socialized into a particular way of using language and as she transacted with these types of dominant school related literacy practices and events, they began to re-align her values, beliefs, social roles and relationships, and power relationships associated with English and Japanese.

Denny Taylor and Bobbie Kabuto: If we position ourselves along side Emma and consider her experiences at home and at school, we are reminded that children are socialized through and by the languages of their families and communities. Their language ideologies are socially constructed and central to their individual and shared social identities. Irrespective of their ethnicity, race, or religion, children have multiple, competing, negotiated, and situated identities (Taylor, 2005); they belong to multiple social and cultural groups (Gumperz, 1982; Ivanic, 1988; Wei, 2000), and to many language and discourse communities (Gee, 1996; Rogers, Purcell-Gates, Mahiri, & Bloome, 2000). We also learn from Emma that problems can occur *if* the complexities of a child's languages and language ideologies are not taken into consideration in classroom settings. When language is artificially invented to meet current governmental curricular requirements, the cultural, psychological, and sociological aspects of children's identities are denied (Taylor, 1990).

There is clear evidence through ethnographic documentation that children's emotional well-being and their sense of family and community are placed in jeopardy if their lives, languages, and literacies are not recognized and used as the foundation of school-based teaching and learning (Jiang, 1997; Taylor, 1990). The capacity of children to participate in the many social and cultural groups that are a part of their everyday lives is critically effected by the ways in which they are taught to read and write in school. In narrowing our perspective on how children learn language, we distance ourselves from the child. Language, learning and literacy can be described as a set of skills and developmental processes, but a child can get lost when separated from evolving social and cultural identities (Taylor, 2005). Language learning, whether in one language or multiple languages, is not an orderly, predictable process, and cannot be separated from the complex relationships between language and literacy deeply embedded in children's personal and shared identities and their ways of being in the world.

We know that the breaks between home and school can negatively impact the lives of children who have experienced individual trauma (Taylor, 1990), or mass trauma that is the result of catastrophic events, whether armed conflict or natural disasters. In each of these situations, teachers are often first responders. When children's lives fall apart, teachers are there. It is important to remember that we are not clinical psychologists or psychotherapists but there is much that we can do as teachers because of our knowledge and understandings and the ways in which we position ourselves in the world (Taylor & Yamasaki, 2005). We have agency and can make a lasting difference in the lives of children we teach.

At the present time, when science is defined for us we must also clearly articulate what we mean by *science* and especially *neuroscience* if we are going to support the language and literacy learning of children. This is a daunting task for many of us, but we are not alone in our criticisms of the current misuse of science. Here is the renowned biologist Steven Rose, who writes on science, to help us.

"Because we have minds that are constituted through the evolutionary, developmental and historical interaction of our bodies and brains," Rose (2005) writes, "with the social and natural worlds that surround us, that we retain responsibility for our actions, that we, as humans, possess the agency to create and recreate our worlds. Our ethical understandings may be enriched by neuro-scientific knowledge, but cannot be replaced, and it will be through agency, socially expressed, that we will be able, if at all, to manage the ethical, legal and social aspects of the emerging neurotechnologies" (p. 305).

We have agency and we have the knowledge but we often don't realize the importance of the work that we do. At another International Scholars' Forum three years after Louise Rosenblatt spoke, Adam Shapiro (2005), a human rights activist who has made a film about Darfur and another in Bagdad at the beginning of the war with Iraq, spoke. "The leaders I have known are nearly always teachers," he said. Adam, who has most recently been living and working in Kabul, Afghanistan, then said this: "Education is more than about learning. Education is first a form of resistance. It is part of a struggle. Education is a struggle for identity, 'this is who I am,' 'this is who I want to be.' Education is also about survival. Whatever we can do, we should do." As teachers of literacy we are part of the struggle, and we must do what we can do if our students are to live healthy, meaningful lives.

REFERENCES

Arendt, H. (1998). *The human condition (2nd edition)*. Chicago,: University of Chicago Press. (Original work published)

Bialystok, E., & Hakuta, K. (1994). *In other words: The science and psychology of second-language acquisition*. New York: Basic Books.

Frattaroli, E. (2001). *Healing the soul in the age of the brain: Becoming conscious in an unconscious world*. New York: Penguin Books.

Gee, J. (1996). *Social linguistics and literacies: Ideology in discourse*. Philadelphia, PA: Routledge Falmer.

Genesee, F. (2000). Early bilingual language development: One language or two? In L. Wei (Ed.), *The bilingualism reader* (pp. 327–343). New York: Routledge.

Gould, S. (1994). *A glorious accident: Understanding our place in the cosmic puzzle*. Videoed interview by W. Kayzer, Films for the Humanities, New York.

Gumperz, J. (1982). *Language and social identity*. Cambridge, UK: Cambridge University Press.

Hakuta, K. (1986). *Mirror of language: The debate on bilingualism*. New York: Basic Books.

Ivanic, R. (1988). *Writing and identity: The discoursal construction of identity in academic writing*. Philadelphia, PA: John Benjamins.

Jiang, N. (1997). Early biliteracy: Ty's story. In D. Taylor, D. Coughlin, & J. Marasco (eds.), *Teaching and advocacy* (pp. 143–154). York, MA: Stenhouse.

Kabuto, B. (2005). Understanding early biliteracy development through book-handling behaviors. *Talking Points, 16*(2), 10–15.

Kress, G. (1997). *Before writing: Rethinking the paths to literacy*. New York: Routledge.

Kropotkin, P. (1976). *Mutual aid: A factor of evolution*. Manchester, NH: Porter Sargent.

McLaughlin, B. (1984). *Second-language acquisition in childhood: Preschool children* (2nd ed., Vol. 1). Hillsdale, NJ: Lawrence Erlbaum Associates.

Modell, A. H. (2003). *Imagination and the meaningful brain*. Cambridge, MA: MIT Press.

Rogers, T., Purcell-Gates, V., Mahiri, J., & Bloome, D. (2000). RRQ snippet: What will be the social implications and interactions of schooling in the next millennium? *Reading Research Quarterly, 35*(3), 420–424.

Rose, S. (2005). *The 21st century brain: Explaining, mending, and manipulating the mind*. London: Jonathan Cape.

Rosenblatt, L. (2001) *Remarks made at International Scholar's Forum: Language, Literacy, Politics and Public Education*. Hempstead, NY: Hofstra University.

Sacks, O. (1994). *A glorious accident: Understanding our place in the cosmic puzzle.* Video interview by W. Kayzer, Films for the Humanitus, New York.
Shapiro, A. (2005). *Remarks made at International Scholar's Forum: Teachers Helping Teachers.* Hempstead, NY: Hofstra University.
Sommers, M. (2002). *Children, education, and war: Reaching education for all (EFA) objectives in countries affected by conflict.* CPR Working Papers. Retrieved on July 2003, from http://www.worldbank.org/conflict.
Taylor, D. (1990). *Learning denied.* Portsmouth, NH: Heinemann.
Taylor, D. (1993a). *From the child's point of view.* Portsmouth, NH: Heinemann.
Taylor, D. (1993b). The trivial pursuit of reading psychology in the real world. *Reading Research Quarterly, 28*(3), 276–288.
Taylor, D. (1998). *Beginning to read and the spin doctors of science: The political campaign to change American's mind about how children learn to read.* Urbana, IL: National Council of Teachers of English.
Taylor, D. (2000). Teaching in the cracks for a more just and caring world. In N. Padak, K. Roskos, T. Rasinski, & J. Peck (Eds.), *Distinguished educators on reading: Contributions that have shaped effective literacy instruction* (pp.). Newark, DE: International Reading Association.
Taylor, D. (2005). Resisting the new word order: Conceptualizing freedom in contradictory symbolic spaces. *Anthropology in Education Quarterly, 36*(4), 341–353.
Taylor, D., & Yamasaki, T. (2005). *The Kate Middleton Elementary School: Portraits of hope & courage after Katrina.* New York: Scholastic.
Taylor, D & Yamasaki, T. (2006). Children, literacy, and mass trauma: Teaching in times of catastrophic events and ongoing emergency situations. *GSE Perspectives on Urban Education, 4*(2). Website: www.ubranedjournal.org
Toulmin, (1994). *A glorious accident: Understanding our place in the cosmic puzzle.* Video interview by W. Kayzer, Films for the Humanities, New York.
Wei, L. (2000). Dimensions of bilingualism. In L. Wei (Ed.), *The bilingualism reader* (pp. 3–25). New York: Routledge.

Author Index

A

B

Subject Index

A

B

C

Z